Expert Scripting and Automation for SQL Server DBAs

Peter A. Carter

Apress®

Expert Scripting and Automation for SQL Server DBAs

Peter A. Carter
Botley
United Kingdom

ISBN-13 (pbk): 978-1-4842-1942-3   ISBN-13 (electronic): 978-1-4842-1943-0
DOI 10.1007/978-1-4842-1943-0

Library of Congress Control Number: 2016948124

Managing Director: Welmoed Spahr
Lead Editor: Jonathan Gennick
Technical Reviewer: Philip Browne
Editorial Board: Steve Anglin, Pramila Balen, Laura Berendson, Aaron Black, Louise Corrigan, Jim DeWolf,
    Jonathan Gennick, Robert Hutchinson, Celestin Suresh John, James Markham, Susan McDermott,
    Matthew Moodie, Natalie Pao, Ben Renow-Clarke, Gwenan Spearing
Coordinating Editor: Jill Balzano
Copy Editor: Michael G. Laraque
Compositor: SPi Global
Indexer: SPi Global
Artist: SPi Global

Distributed to the book trade worldwide by Springer Science+Business Media New York, 233 Spring Street, 6th Floor, New York, NY 10013. Phone 1-800-SPRINGER, fax (201) 348-4505, e-mail orders-ny@springer-sbm.com, or visit www.springer.com. Apress Media, LLC is a California LLC and the sole member (owner) is Springer Science+Business Media Finance Inc (SSBM Finance Inc). SSBM Finance Inc is a Delaware corporation.

For information on translations, please e-mail rights@apress.com, or visit www.apress.com.

Apress and friends of ED books may be purchased in bulk for academic, corporate, or promotional use. eBook versions and licenses are also available for most titles. For more information, reference our Special Bulk Sales–eBook Licensing web page at www.apress.com/bulk-sales.

Any source code or other supplementary material referenced by the author in this text is available to readers at www.apress.com. For detailed information about how to locate your book's source code, go to www.apress.com/source-code/.

Printed on acid-free paper

This book is dedicated to my wonderful children: Finola, Iris, and Reuben.

Contents at a Glance

Contents

About the Author

Peter A. Carter is an SQL Server expert with more than a decade of experience in developing, administering, and architecting SQL Server platforms, data-tier applications, and ETL solutions. Peter has a passion for SQL Server and hopes that his enthusiasm for this technology helps or inspires others.

About the Technical Reviewer

Philip Browne has been in the IT industry for nearly 20 years, starting with client and infrastructure solutions for business, with his main areas of expertise being application development (VB, VB.NET), web technologies and Microsoft SQL products, and developing and releasing various software applications, front ends, and custom tools. Philip also has a real passion for hardware and systems security. He currently holds various Microsoft certifications and works as an applications developer with Microsoft's latest technologies, SQL products, T-SQL, SSIS, and SSRS for Millbrook Industries HQ in Totton, Southampton, England, with a great team. Philip can be reached at philip.browne@ntlworld.com.

Introduction

As the ratio of DBAs to supported instances and supported databases continues to drop, DBAs must look to automation, to allow them to continue to improve or, in some cases, even offer the same level of service to the business as they have historically. This book attempts to give DBAs the tools they need to implement strategic automation solutions, using the Microsoft standard suite of tools, specifically, PowerShell, T-SQL, and SQL Server Agent.

Some large enterprises will be lucky enough to have enterprise class monitoring and orchestration toolsets at their disposal. Even if this is the case, DBAs should find the scripts and the ideas for automated scenarios contained within this book useful, as they can be plugged into enterprise class toolsets, despite this book focusing on DBA written orchestrations.

The majority of examples in this book, use the topology laid out in Figure 1.

ESASSMGMT1

ESPROD1

ESPROD2

ESPROD3

Figure 1. *Topology*

ESASSMGMT1 is a management server, while ESPROD1, ESPROD2, and ESPROD3 represent servers used by the business. Each server has a default instance of SQL Server 2016 installed, both the instances host a copy of the AdventureWorks2016 database. The AdventureWorks2016 database can be downloaded from www.microsoft.com/en-us/download/details.aspx?id=49502.

If you wish to follow the examples and demonstrations in this book, you may choose to configure a similar topology, or you can simply change the server\instance and database names in the script.

As you move through the book, you will create further instances, in order to learn the skills required for automating instance builds. In Chapter 9, you will also learn how to automate patching routines. For this demonstration, I use two SQL Server 2014 instances called ESPRODSQL14_001\SQL14INSTANCE1 and ESPRODSQL14_001\SQL14INSTANCE2. SQL Server 2014 instances were used for this demonstration, due to no SQL Server 2016 patches being available at the time of writing. When following the demonstrations, however, you may choose to use either SQL Server 2014 or existing SQL Server 2016 instances that you have used in other chapters of the book (subject to availability of patches).

CHAPTER 1

■ ■ ■

T-SQL Techniques for DBAs

As a DBA, you will almost certainly understand the basics of the T-SQL language and use it for querying metadata views, such as sys.databases or sys.tables. Often, DBAs do not have advanced T-SQL skills, however, as they do not need them in day-to-day operations. In order to implement sophisticated automation and, in turn, reduce operational costs and overheads, DBAs should gain an understanding of some more advanced scripting techniques. Therefore, this chapter will focus on exploring some of the T-SQL techniques that we will use in this book. I will make the assumption that if you are reading this book, you are familiar with rudimentary T-SQL, such as the SELECT statement, including FROM, JOIN, WHERE, GROUP BY, HAVING, and ORDER BY clauses. If you do need a refresher, however, full details of the SELECT statement can be found at https://msdn.microsoft.com/en-us/library/ms189499.aspx#.

We will start by looking at the APPLY operator to call a function against rows within a result set. We will then look at how XML (eXtensible Markup Language) and how the native XML data type can be harnessed by SQL Server DBAs. It is critical for DBAs to have a handle on the use of XML, due to the volume of metrics and information that are exposed via this data type. We will then explore how to efficiently iterate through multiple objects.

Using the APPLY Operator

The T-SQL APPLY operator allows you to call a table valued function against every row in a result set returned by a query. There are two variations of the APPLY operator: CROSS APPLY and OUTER APPLY. When CROSS APPLY is used, the query will only return rows in which a result set has been produced by the table valued function. When OUTER APPLY is used, no filter will be applied to the result set, and where no result is returned by the table valued function, NULL will be returned, in each column of the table valued function.

The APPLY operator can be very useful to DBAs when they are retrieving metadata from dynamic management views (DMV) and functions (DMF). For example, the query in Listing 1-1 will return a list of all sessions, detailing the session ID, the login time, the login name, and whether the process is a user or system process. It will then use OUTER APPLY to run the sys.dm_exec_sql_text dynamic management function against each row. This function returns a column called text, which is the SQL statement associated with the SQL handle in the sql_handle column in the sys.dm_exec_requests dynamic management view.

■ **Note**   The text column that is referenced in the SELECT list is the column returned by the sys.dm_exec_sql_text DMF.

Electronic supplementary material   The online version of this chapter (doi:10.1007/978-1-4842-1943-0_1) contains supplementary material, which is available to authorized users.

Listing 1-1. Using OUTER APPLY

```
SELECT s.session_id
      ,s.login_time
      ,s.login_name
      ,s.is_user_process
      ,[text]
FROM sys.dm_exec_sessions s
INNER JOIN sys.dm_exec_requests r
    ON r.session_id = s.session_id
OUTER APPLY sys.dm_exec_sql_text(sql_handle) ;
```

You will notice that this query returns many rows in this result set with NULL values for the text column. This is because they are system processes, running background tasks for SQL Server, such as the Lazy Writer and the Ghost Cleanup Task.

■ **Tip**   We can be sure that they are system processes because of the is_user_process flag. We will not rely on the session ID being less than 50. The assertion that all system processes have a session ID of less than 50 is widely believed, but also a fallacy, because there can potentially be more than 50 system sessions running in parallel.

If we use the CROSS APPLY operator for the same query, as shown in Listing 1-2, the only rows that will be returned will be rows where the result of applying the tabled valued function is not NULL.

Listing 1-2. Using APPLY

```
SELECT s.session_id
      ,s.login_time
      ,s.login_name
      ,[text]
      ,s.is_user_process
FROM sys.dm_exec_sessions s
INNER JOIN sys.dm_exec_requests r
    ON r.session_id = s.session_id
CROSS APPLY sys.dm_exec_sql_text(sql_handle) ;
```

Understanding XML

XML is a markup language, similar to HTML, that was designed for the purpose of storing and transporting data. Like HTML, XML consists of tags. Unlike HTML, however, these tags are not predefined. Instead, they are defined by the document author. An XML document has a tree structure, beginning with a root node and containing child nodes (also known as child elements). Each element can contain data but also attributes. Each attribute can contain data that describes the element. For example, imagine that you require details of sales orders to be stored in XML format. It would be sensible to assume that each sales order would be stored in a separate element within the document. But what about sales order properties, such as order date, customer ID, product IDs, quantities, and prices? These pieces of information could either be stored as child elements of the sales order element, or they could be stored as attributes of the sales order element. There are no set rules for when you should use child elements or attributes to describe properties of an element. This choice is at the discretion of the document author. The XML document in Listing 1-3 provides a sample XML document, which holds the details of sales orders for a fictional organization.

Listing 1-3. Sales Orders Stored in an XML Document

```xml
<SalesOrders>
  <SalesOrder CustomerID="29825" OrderDate="2011-05-31T00:00:00" SalesOrderID="43659">
    <LineItem UnitPrice="2024.9940" OrderQty="1" />
    <LineItem UnitPrice="2024.9940" OrderQty="3" />
    <LineItem UnitPrice="2024.9940" OrderQty="1" />
    <LineItem UnitPrice="2039.9940" OrderQty="1" />
    <LineItem UnitPrice="2039.9940" OrderQty="1" />
    <LineItem UnitPrice="2039.9940" OrderQty="2" />
    <LineItem UnitPrice="2039.9940" OrderQty="1" />
    <LineItem UnitPrice="28.8404" OrderQty="3" />
    <LineItem UnitPrice="28.8404" OrderQty="1" />
    <LineItem UnitPrice="5.7000" OrderQty="6" />
    <LineItem UnitPrice="5.1865" OrderQty="2" />
    <LineItem UnitPrice="20.1865" OrderQty="4" />
  </SalesOrder>
  <SalesOrder CustomerID="29825" OrderDate="2011-08-31T00:00:00" SalesOrderID="44305">
    <LineItem UnitPrice="2024.9940" OrderQty="2" />
    <LineItem UnitPrice="2039.9940" OrderQty="2" />
    <LineItem UnitPrice="2039.9940" OrderQty="2" />
    <LineItem UnitPrice="2039.9940" OrderQty="2" />
    <LineItem UnitPrice="714.7043" OrderQty="2" />
    <LineItem UnitPrice="818.7000" OrderQty="1" />
    <LineItem UnitPrice="28.8404" OrderQty="2" />
    <LineItem UnitPrice="28.8404" OrderQty="1" />
    <LineItem UnitPrice="28.8404" OrderQty="2" />
    <LineItem UnitPrice="5.5100" OrderQty="12" />
    <LineItem UnitPrice="5.7000" OrderQty="3" />
    <LineItem UnitPrice="5.1865" OrderQty="3" />
    <LineItem UnitPrice="20.1865" OrderQty="2" />
    <LineItem UnitPrice="20.1865" OrderQty="2" />
    <LineItem UnitPrice="20.1865" OrderQty="1" />
  </SalesOrder>
  <SalesOrder CustomerID="29825" OrderDate="2011-12-01T00:00:00" SalesOrderID="45061">
    <LineItem UnitPrice="2024.9940" OrderQty="3" />
    <LineItem UnitPrice="2024.9940" OrderQty="2" />
    <LineItem UnitPrice="2024.9940" OrderQty="5" />
    <LineItem UnitPrice="2024.9940" OrderQty="8" />
    <LineItem UnitPrice="2039.9940" OrderQty="6" />
    <LineItem UnitPrice="2039.9940" OrderQty="2" />
    <LineItem UnitPrice="2039.9940" OrderQty="5" />
    <LineItem UnitPrice="2039.9940" OrderQty="5" />
    <LineItem UnitPrice="28.8404" OrderQty="2" />
    <LineItem UnitPrice="5.7000" OrderQty="5" />
    <LineItem UnitPrice="5.1865" OrderQty="1" />
  </SalesOrder>
</SalesOrders>
```

There are several things to note when looking at this XML document. First, elements begin with the element name, encapsulated within angle brackets. They end with the element name, preceded by a backslash and enclosed in angle brackets. Any elements that fall between these two tags are child elements of the tag.

Attributes are enclosed in double quotation marks and reside within the beginning tag of an element. For example, OrderID is an attribute of the <SalesOrder> element.

It is acceptable to have repeating elements. You can see that <SalesOrder> is a repeating element, as two separate sales orders are stored in this XML document. The <SalesOrders> element is the document's root element and is the only element that is not allowed to be complex. This means that it cannot have attributes and cannot be repeating. Attributes can never repeat within an element. Therefore, if you require a node to repeat, you should use a nested element as opposed to an attribute.

The format of an XML document can be defined by an XSD schema. An XSD schema will define the document's structure, including data types, if complex types (complex elements) are allowed, and how many times an element must occur (or is limited to occurring) within a document. It also defines the sequence of elements. A full description of XSD schemas can be found at en.wikipedia.org/wiki/XML_Schema_(W3C).

■ **Tip** An XML document requires a root element in order to be "well-formed." An XML document without a root element is known as an XML fragment. This is important, because it is not possible to bind an XML fragment to an XSD schema. This means that the structure of the document, including data types, cannot be enforced.

Converting Results Sets to XML

T-SQL allows you to convert relational results sets into XML, by using the FOR XML clause in your SELECT statement. There are four modes that can be used with the FOR XML clause: FOR XML RAW, FOR XML AUTO, FOR XML PATH, and FOR XML EXPLICIT. The following sections will demonstrate how the FOR XML clause works in RAW mode, AUTO mode, and PATH mode. EXPLICIT mode is beyond the scope of this book, as its functionality is very similar to PATH mode but is far more complex and does not often prove useful for DBAs.

■ **Note** The value of a DBA understanding FOR XML will become evident in Chapter 8.

Using FOR XML RAW

The simplest and easiest to understand of the FOR XML modes is FOR XML RAW. This mode will transform each row in a relational result set into an element within a flat XML document. Consider the query in Listing 1-4, which extracts details of a sales order from the AdventureWorks2016 database.

Listing 1-4. AdventureWorks Sales Order Query

```
SELECT
      SalesOrder.CustomerID
     ,SalesOrder.OrderDate
     ,SalesOrder.SalesOrderID
     ,LineItem.UnitPrice
     ,LineItem.OrderQty
     ,p.Name
```

```
FROM Sales.SalesOrderHeader SalesOrder
INNER JOIN Sales.SalesOrderDetail LineItem
    ON SalesOrder.SalesOrderID = LineItem.SalesOrderID
    INNER JOIN Production.Product P
        ON LineItem.ProductID = p.ProductID
WHERE SalesOrder.CustomerID = 29825
    AND SalesOrder.OrderDate < '2012-01-01' ;
```

This query extracts the details of orders placed by customer 29825, before January 1, 2012. A partial output of the query can be found in Figure 1-1.

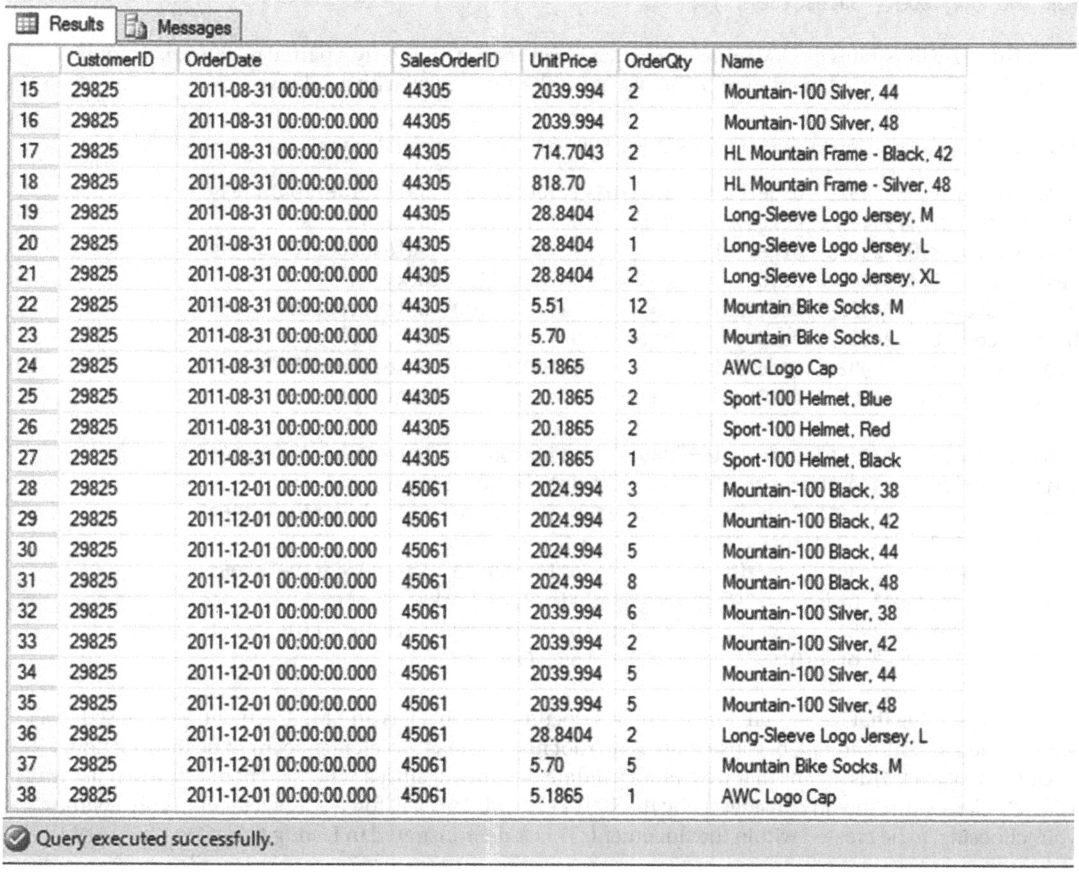

	CustomerID	OrderDate	SalesOrderID	UnitPrice	OrderQty	Name
15	29825	2011-08-31 00:00:00.000	44305	2039.994	2	Mountain-100 Silver, 44
16	29825	2011-08-31 00:00:00.000	44305	2039.994	2	Mountain-100 Silver, 48
17	29825	2011-08-31 00:00:00.000	44305	714.7043	2	HL Mountain Frame - Black, 42
18	29825	2011-08-31 00:00:00.000	44305	818.70	1	HL Mountain Frame - Silver, 48
19	29825	2011-08-31 00:00:00.000	44305	28.8404	2	Long-Sleeve Logo Jersey, M
20	29825	2011-08-31 00:00:00.000	44305	28.8404	1	Long-Sleeve Logo Jersey, L
21	29825	2011-08-31 00:00:00.000	44305	28.8404	2	Long-Sleeve Logo Jersey, XL
22	29825	2011-08-31 00:00:00.000	44305	5.51	12	Mountain Bike Socks, M
23	29825	2011-08-31 00:00:00.000	44305	5.70	3	Mountain Bike Socks, L
24	29825	2011-08-31 00:00:00.000	44305	5.1865	3	AWC Logo Cap
25	29825	2011-08-31 00:00:00.000	44305	20.1865	2	Sport-100 Helmet, Blue
26	29825	2011-08-31 00:00:00.000	44305	20.1865	2	Sport-100 Helmet, Red
27	29825	2011-08-31 00:00:00.000	44305	20.1865	1	Sport-100 Helmet, Black
28	29825	2011-12-01 00:00:00.000	45061	2024.994	3	Mountain-100 Black, 38
29	29825	2011-12-01 00:00:00.000	45061	2024.994	2	Mountain-100 Black, 42
30	29825	2011-12-01 00:00:00.000	45061	2024.994	5	Mountain-100 Black, 44
31	29825	2011-12-01 00:00:00.000	45061	2024.994	8	Mountain-100 Black, 48
32	29825	2011-12-01 00:00:00.000	45061	2039.994	6	Mountain-100 Silver, 38
33	29825	2011-12-01 00:00:00.000	45061	2039.994	2	Mountain-100 Silver, 42
34	29825	2011-12-01 00:00:00.000	45061	2039.994	5	Mountain-100 Silver, 44
35	29825	2011-12-01 00:00:00.000	45061	2039.994	5	Mountain-100 Silver, 48
36	29825	2011-12-01 00:00:00.000	45061	28.8404	2	Long-Sleeve Logo Jersey, L
37	29825	2011-12-01 00:00:00.000	45061	5.70	5	Mountain Bike Socks, M
38	29825	2011-12-01 00:00:00.000	45061	5.1865	1	AWC Logo Cap

Query executed successfully.

Figure 1-1. AdventureWorks sales order output

If we were to add a FOR XML clause using RAW mode, the results would be returned in the form of an XML fragment. The amended query in Listing 1-5 will return the XML document instead of a relational result set.

Listing 1-5. AdventurWorks Sales Orders Using FOR XML RAW

```
SELECT
    SalesOrder.CustomerID
    ,SalesOrder.OrderDate
```

```
    ,SalesOrder.SalesOrderID
    ,LineItem.UnitPrice
    ,LineItem.OrderQty
    ,p.Name
FROM Sales.SalesOrderHeader SalesOrder
INNER JOIN Sales.SalesOrderDetail LineItem
    ON SalesOrder.SalesOrderID = LineItem.SalesOrderID
    INNER JOIN Production.Product P
        ON LineItem.ProductID = p.ProductID
WHERE SalesOrder.CustomerID = 29825
    AND SalesOrder.OrderDate < '2012-01-01'
FOR XML RAW, ROOT('SalesOrders') ;
```

Listing 1-6 illustrates the XML document that is returned. This is only a partial results set, as some results have been omitted to save space. Breaks in results are marked with an ellipsis.

Listing 1-6. AdventurWorks Sales Orders Using FOR XML RAW—Partial Results

```
<row CustomerID="29825" OrderDate="2011-05-31T00:00:00" SalesOrderID="43659"
UnitPrice="2024.9940" OrderQty="1" Name="Mountain-100 Black, 42" />
<row CustomerID="29825" OrderDate="2011-05-31T00:00:00" SalesOrderID="43659"
UnitPrice="2024.9940" OrderQty="3" Name="Mountain-100 Black, 44" />
<row CustomerID="29825" OrderDate="2011-05-31T00:00:00" SalesOrderID="43659"
UnitPrice="2024.9940" OrderQty="1" Name="Mountain-100 Black, 48" />
<row CustomerID="29825" OrderDate="2011-05-31T00:00:00" SalesOrderID="43659"
UnitPrice="2039.9940" OrderQty="1" Name="Mountain-100 Silver, 38" />
...
<row CustomerID="29825" OrderDate="2011-12-01T00:00:00" SalesOrderID="45061"
UnitPrice="2039.9940" OrderQty="5" Name="Mountain-100 Silver, 48" />
<row CustomerID="29825" OrderDate="2011-12-01T00:00:00" SalesOrderID="45061"
UnitPrice="28.8404" OrderQty="2" Name="Long-Sleeve Logo Jersey, L" />
<row CustomerID="29825" OrderDate="2011-12-01T00:00:00" SalesOrderID="45061"
UnitPrice="5.7000" OrderQty="5" Name="Mountain Bike Socks, M" />
<row CustomerID="29825" OrderDate="2011-12-01T00:00:00" SalesOrderID="45061"
UnitPrice="5.1865" OrderQty="1" Name="AWC Logo Cap" />
```

The first thing that we should note about this document is that it is an XML fragment, as opposed to a well-formed XML document, because there is no root node. The `<row>` element cannot be the root node, because it repeats. This means that we cannot validate the XML against a schema. Therefore, when using the FOR XML clause, you should consider using the ROOT keyword. This will force a root element, with a name of your choosing, to be created within the document. This is demonstrated in Listing 1-7.

Listing 1-7. Adding a Root Node

```
SELECT
    SalesOrder.CustomerID
    ,SalesOrder.OrderDate
    ,SalesOrder.SalesOrderID
    ,LineItem.UnitPrice
    ,LineItem.OrderQty
    ,p.Name
FROM Sales.SalesOrderHeader SalesOrder
```

```
INNER JOIN Sales.SalesOrderDetail LineItem
    ON SalesOrder.SalesOrderID = LineItem.SalesOrderID
    INNER JOIN Production.Product P
        ON LineItem.ProductID = p.ProductID
WHERE SalesOrder.CustomerID = 29825
    AND SalesOrder.OrderDate < '2012-01-01'
FOR XML RAW, ROOT('SalesOrders') ;
```

Partial output of the resulting well-formed XML document can be found in Listing 1-8.

Listing 1-8. Partial Output of XML Document with Root Node

```
<SalesOrders>
  <row CustomerID="29825" OrderDate="2011-05-31T00:00:00" SalesOrderID="43659"
UnitPrice="2024.9940" OrderQty="1" Name="Mountain-100 Black, 42" />
  <row CustomerID="29825" OrderDate="2011-05-31T00:00:00" SalesOrderID="43659"
UnitPrice="2024.9940" OrderQty="3" Name="Mountain-100 Black, 44" />
  <row CustomerID="29825" OrderDate="2011-05-31T00:00:00" SalesOrderID="43659"
UnitPrice="2024.9940" OrderQty="1" Name="Mountain-100 Black, 48" />
  <row CustomerID="29825" OrderDate="2011-05-31T00:00:00" SalesOrderID="43659"
UnitPrice="2039.9940" OrderQty="1" Name="Mountain-100 Silver, 38" />
...
  <row CustomerID="29825" OrderDate="2011-12-01T00:00:00" SalesOrderID="45061"
UnitPrice="2039.9940" OrderQty="5" Name="Mountain-100 Silver, 48" />
  <row CustomerID="29825" OrderDate="2011-12-01T00:00:00" SalesOrderID="45061"
UnitPrice="28.8404" OrderQty="2" Name="Long-Sleeve Logo Jersey, L" />
  <row CustomerID="29825" OrderDate="2011-12-01T00:00:00" SalesOrderID="45061"
UnitPrice="5.7000" OrderQty="5" Name="Mountain Bike Socks, M" />
  <row CustomerID="29825" OrderDate="2011-12-01T00:00:00" SalesOrderID="45061"
UnitPrice="5.1865" OrderQty="1" Name="AWC Logo Cap" />
</SalesOrders>
```

The other important thing to notice about the document is that it is completely flat. There is no nesting. This means that the document's granularity is at the level of line item, which does not make a lot of sense.

It is also worth noting that all data is contained in attributes, as opposed to elements. We can alter this behavior by using the ELEMENTS keyword in the FOR XML clause. The ELEMENTS keyword will cause all data to be contained within child elements, as opposed to attributes. This is demonstrated in the modified query that can be found in Listing 1-9.

Listing 1-9. Using the ELEMENTS Keyword

```
SELECT
    SalesOrder.CustomerID
    ,SalesOrder.OrderDate
    ,SalesOrder.SalesOrderID
    ,LineItem.UnitPrice
    ,LineItem.OrderQty
    ,p.Name
FROM Sales.SalesOrderHeader SalesOrder
INNER JOIN Sales.SalesOrderDetail LineItem
    ON SalesOrder.SalesOrderID = LineItem.SalesOrderID
    INNER JOIN Production.Product P
        ON LineItem.ProductID = p.ProductID
```

```
WHERE SalesOrder.CustomerID = 29825
    AND SalesOrder.OrderDate < '2012-01-01'
FOR XML RAW, ELEMENTS, ROOT('SalesOrders') ;
```

The well-formed XML document that is returned can be partially seen in Listing 1-10.

Listing 1-10. Using the ELEMENTS Keyword—Partial Results

```
<SalesOrders>
  <row>
    <CustomerID>29825</CustomerID>
    <OrderDate>2011-05-31T00:00:00</OrderDate>
    <SalesOrderID>43659</SalesOrderID>
    <UnitPrice>2024.9940</UnitPrice>
    <OrderQty>1</OrderQty>
    <Name>Mountain-100 Black, 42</Name>
  </row>
  <row>
    <CustomerID>29825</CustomerID>
    <OrderDate>2011-05-31T00:00:00</OrderDate>
    <SalesOrderID>43659</SalesOrderID>
    <UnitPrice>2024.9940</UnitPrice>
    <OrderQty>3</OrderQty>
    <Name>Mountain-100 Black, 44</Name>
  </row>
  <row>
    <CustomerID>29825</CustomerID>
    <OrderDate>2011-05-31T00:00:00</OrderDate>
    <SalesOrderID>43659</SalesOrderID>
    <UnitPrice>2024.9940</UnitPrice>
    <OrderQty>1</OrderQty>
    <Name>Mountain-100 Black, 48</Name>
  </row>
  <row>
    <CustomerID>29825</CustomerID>
    <OrderDate>2011-05-31T00:00:00</OrderDate>
    <SalesOrderID>43659</SalesOrderID>
    <UnitPrice>2039.9940</UnitPrice>
    <OrderQty>1</OrderQty>
    <Name>Mountain-100 Silver, 38</Name>
  </row>
...
  <row>
    <CustomerID>29825</CustomerID>
    <OrderDate>2011-12-01T00:00:00</OrderDate>
    <SalesOrderID>45061</SalesOrderID>
    <UnitPrice>2039.9940</UnitPrice>
    <OrderQty>5</OrderQty>
    <Name>Mountain-100 Silver, 48</Name>
  </row>
```

```
<row>
  <CustomerID>29825</CustomerID>
  <OrderDate>2011-12-01T00:00:00</OrderDate>
  <SalesOrderID>45061</SalesOrderID>
  <UnitPrice>28.8404</UnitPrice>
  <OrderQty>2</OrderQty>
  <Name>Long-Sleeve Logo Jersey, L</Name>
</row>
<row>
  <CustomerID>29825</CustomerID>
  <OrderDate>2011-12-01T00:00:00</OrderDate>
  <SalesOrderID>45061</SalesOrderID>
  <UnitPrice>5.7000</UnitPrice>
  <OrderQty>5</OrderQty>
  <Name>Mountain Bike Socks, M</Name>
</row>
<row>
  <CustomerID>29825</CustomerID>
  <OrderDate>2011-12-01T00:00:00</OrderDate>
  <SalesOrderID>45061</SalesOrderID>
  <UnitPrice>5.1865</UnitPrice>
  <OrderQty>1</OrderQty>
  <Name>AWC Logo Cap</Name>
</row>
</SalesOrders>
```

You can see that the element-centric document still returns one element, called <row>, per row in the relational result set. Instead of the data being contained in attributes, however, it is stored in the form of child elements. Each child element has been given the name of the column, from which the data has been returned. The data is still flat, however. There is no hierarchy based on logic or physical table structure.

It is possible to give the <row> element a more meaningful name. In our example, the most meaningful name would be <LineItem>. Listing 1-11 demonstrates how we can use an optional argument in our FOR XML clause to generate this name for the element.

Listing 1-11. Generate a Name for the <row> Element

```sql
SELECT
    SalesOrder.CustomerID
    ,SalesOrder.OrderDate
    ,SalesOrder.SalesOrderID
    ,LineItem.UnitPrice
    ,LineItem.OrderQty
    ,p.Name
FROM Sales.SalesOrderHeader SalesOrder
INNER JOIN Sales.SalesOrderDetail LineItem
    ON SalesOrder.SalesOrderID = LineItem.SalesOrderID
    INNER JOIN Production.Product P
        ON LineItem.ProductID = p.ProductID
WHERE SalesOrder.CustomerID = 29825
    AND SalesOrder.OrderDate < '2012-01-01'
FOR XML RAW ('LineItem'), ELEMENTS, ROOT('SalesOrders') ;
```

The partial resulting XML document can be found in Listing 1-12.

Listing 1-12. Generating a Name for the `<row>` Element—Partial Results

```
<SalesOrders>
  <LineItem>
    <CustomerID>29825</CustomerID>
    <OrderDate>2011-05-31T00:00:00</OrderDate>
    <SalesOrderID>43659</SalesOrderID>
    <UnitPrice>2024.9940</UnitPrice>
    <OrderQty>1</OrderQty>
    <Name>Mountain-100 Black, 42</Name>
  </LineItem>
  <LineItem>
    <CustomerID>29825</CustomerID>
    <OrderDate>2011-05-31T00:00:00</OrderDate>
    <SalesOrderID>43659</SalesOrderID>
    <UnitPrice>2024.9940</UnitPrice>
    <OrderQty>3</OrderQty>
    <Name>Mountain-100 Black, 44</Name>
  </LineItem>
  <LineItem>
    <CustomerID>29825</CustomerID>
    <OrderDate>2011-05-31T00:00:00</OrderDate>
    <SalesOrderID>43659</SalesOrderID>
    <UnitPrice>2024.9940</UnitPrice>
    <OrderQty>1</OrderQty>
    <Name>Mountain-100 Black, 48</Name>
  </LineItem>
  <LineItem>
    <CustomerID>29825</CustomerID>
    <OrderDate>2011-05-31T00:00:00</OrderDate>
    <SalesOrderID>43659</SalesOrderID>
    <UnitPrice>2039.9940</UnitPrice>
    <OrderQty>1</OrderQty>
    <Name>Mountain-100 Silver, 38</Name>
  </LineItem>
  <LineItem>
    <CustomerID>29825</CustomerID>
    <OrderDate>2011-12-01T00:00:00</OrderDate>
    <SalesOrderID>45061</SalesOrderID>
    <UnitPrice>2039.9940</UnitPrice>
    <OrderQty>5</OrderQty>
    <Name>Mountain-100 Silver, 48</Name>
  </LineItem>
  <LineItem>
    <CustomerID>29825</CustomerID>
    <OrderDate>2011-12-01T00:00:00</OrderDate>
    <SalesOrderID>45061</SalesOrderID>
    <UnitPrice>28.8404</UnitPrice>
    <OrderQty>2</OrderQty>
    <Name>Long-Sleeve Logo Jersey, L</Name>
  </LineItem>
```

```
  <LineItem>
    <CustomerID>29825</CustomerID>
    <OrderDate>2011-12-01T00:00:00</OrderDate>
    <SalesOrderID>45061</SalesOrderID>
    <UnitPrice>5.7000</UnitPrice>
    <OrderQty>5</OrderQty>
    <Name>Mountain Bike Socks, M</Name>
  </LineItem>
  <LineItem>
    <CustomerID>29825</CustomerID>
    <OrderDate>2011-12-01T00:00:00</OrderDate>
    <SalesOrderID>45061</SalesOrderID>
    <UnitPrice>5.1865</UnitPrice>
    <OrderQty>1</OrderQty>
    <Name>AWC Logo Cap</Name>
  </LineItem>
</SalesOrders>
```

Using FOR XML AUTO

Unlike FOR XML RAW, FOR XML AUTO is able to return nested results. It is also refreshingly simple to use, because it will automatically nest the data, based on the joins within your query. The modified query in Listing 1-13 uses AUTO mode to return a hierarchical XML document.

Listing 1-13. Using FOR XML AUTO

```
SELECT
    SalesOrder.CustomerID
    ,SalesOrder.OrderDate
    ,SalesOrder.SalesOrderID
    ,LineItem.UnitPrice
    ,LineItem.OrderQty
    ,Product.Name
FROM Sales.SalesOrderHeader SalesOrder
INNER JOIN Sales.SalesOrderDetail LineItem
    ON SalesOrder.SalesOrderID = LineItem.SalesOrderID
    INNER JOIN Production.Product Product
        ON LineItem.ProductID = Product.ProductID
WHERE SalesOrder.CustomerID = 29825
    AND SalesOrder.OrderDate < '2012-01-01'
FOR XML AUTO ;
```

The XML fragment that is returned by this query can be partially seen in Listing 1-14.

Listing 1-14. Using FOR XML AUTO—Results

```
<SalesOrder CustomerID="29825" OrderDate="2011-05-31T00:00:00" SalesOrderID="43659">
  <LineItem UnitPrice="2024.9940" OrderQty="1">
    <Product Name="Mountain-100 Black, 42" />
  </LineItem>
  <LineItem UnitPrice="2024.9940" OrderQty="3">
```

```
  <Product Name="Mountain-100 Black, 44" />
 </LineItem>
 <LineItem UnitPrice="2024.9940" OrderQty="1">
  <Product Name="Mountain-100 Black, 48" />
 </LineItem>
 <LineItem UnitPrice="2039.9940" OrderQty="1">
  <Product Name="Mountain-100 Silver, 38" />
  <Product Name="Mountain-100 Silver, 42" />
 </LineItem>
 •••
</SalesOrder>
<SalesOrder CustomerID="29825" OrderDate="2011-08-31T00:00:00" SalesOrderID="44305">
 <LineItem UnitPrice="2024.9940" OrderQty="2">
  <Product Name="Mountain-100 Black, 48" />
 </LineItem>
 <LineItem UnitPrice="2039.9940" OrderQty="2">
  <Product Name="Mountain-100 Silver, 38" />
  <Product Name="Mountain-100 Silver, 44" />
  <Product Name="Mountain-100 Silver, 48" />
 </LineItem>
 <LineItem UnitPrice="714.7043" OrderQty="2">
  <Product Name="HL Mountain Frame - Black, 42" />
 </LineItem>
 <LineItem UnitPrice="818.7000" OrderQty="1">
  <Product Name="HL Mountain Frame - Silver, 48" />
 </LineItem>
</SalesOrder>
```

You can see that when AUTO mode is used, the FOR XML clause has automatically nested the data based on the JOIN clauses within the query. Each element has been assigned a name based on the table alias of the table from which it was retrieved. Just as with RAW mode, we are able to use the ROOT keyword to add a root node, to make the document well-formed or the document element centric with the ELEMENTS keyword.

Nesting based on table joins is not always sufficient. If you look closely at Listing 1-14, you will notice that there are some <LineItem> elements that contain multiple <Product> elements, which is obviously not correct. There cannot be more than one product per line on a sales order. This is because the primary key of the Sales.SalesOrderDetail table has not been included in the query, meaning that not every set of tuples returned from the Sales.SalesOrderDetail table is unique. Some have the same values for UnitPrice and OrderQty. Where this has occurred, FOR XML AUTO has grouped them. If the primary key had been included, the resulting document would appear as in Listing 1-15.

Listing 1-15. FOR XML AUTO Results When SalesOrderDetail Primary Key Is Included

```
<SalesOrder CustomerID="29825" OrderDate="2011-05-31T00:00:00" SalesOrderID="43659">
 <LineItem UnitPrice="2039.9940" OrderQty="1" SalesOrderDetailID="4">
  <Product Name="Mountain-100 Silver, 38" ProductID="771" />
 </LineItem>
 <LineItem UnitPrice="2039.9940" OrderQty="2" SalesOrderDetailID="6">
  <Product Name="Mountain-100 Silver, 44" ProductID="773" />
 </LineItem>
 <LineItem UnitPrice="2039.9940" OrderQty="1" SalesOrderDetailID="7">
  <Product Name="Mountain-100 Silver, 48" ProductID="774" />
 </LineItem>
```

```
</SalesOrder>
<SalesOrder CustomerID="29825" OrderDate="2011-08-31T00:00:00" SalesOrderID="44305">
  <LineItem UnitPrice="2039.9940" OrderQty="2" SalesOrderDetailID="2492">
    <Product Name="Mountain-100 Silver, 38" ProductID="771" />
  </LineItem>
  <LineItem UnitPrice="2039.9940" OrderQty="2" SalesOrderDetailID="2493">
    <Product Name="Mountain-100 Silver, 44" ProductID="773" />
  </LineItem>
  <LineItem UnitPrice="2039.9940" OrderQty="2" SalesOrderDetailID="2494">
    <Product Name="Mountain-100 Silver, 48" ProductID="774" />
  </LineItem>
</SalesOrder>
<SalesOrder CustomerID="29825" OrderDate="2011-12-01T00:00:00" SalesOrderID="45061">
  <LineItem UnitPrice="2039.9940" OrderQty="6" SalesOrderDetailID="5378">
    <Product Name="Mountain-100 Silver, 38" ProductID="771" />
  </LineItem>
  <LineItem UnitPrice="2039.9940" OrderQty="5" SalesOrderDetailID="5380">
    <Product Name="Mountain-100 Silver, 44" ProductID="773" />
  </LineItem>
  <LineItem UnitPrice="2039.9940" OrderQty="5" SalesOrderDetailID="5381">
    <Product Name="Mountain-100 Silver, 48" ProductID="774" />
  </LineItem>
</SalesOrder>
```

Using FOR XML PATH

Sometimes you need more control over the shape of the resultant XML document than can be provided by either RAW mode or AUTO mode. When you have a requirement to define custom heuristics, PATH mode can be used. PATH mode offers great flexibility, as it allows you to define the location of each node within the resultant XML. This is achieved by specifying how each column in the query maps to the XML, with the use of column names or aliases.

If a column alias begins with the @ symbol, an attribute will be created. If no @ symbol is used, the column will map to an element. Columns that will become attributes must be specified before columns that will be sibling nodes but defined as elements.

If you wish to define a node's location in the hierarchy, you can use the / symbol. For example, if you require the order date to appear nested under an element called <OrderHeader>, you can specify that column alias as '/OrderHeader/OrderDate' for the OrderDate column.

PATH mode allows you to create highly customized and complex structures. For example, imagine that you have a requirement to create an XML document in the format displayed in Listing 1-16. Here, you will notice that there is a root node called <SalesOrders>, the next node in the hierarchy is <Orders>. This is a repeating element, with a new occurrence for every order raised by the customer, which is the same as when we explored AUTO mode. The difference is that each sales order has its own hierarchy. First, there is a section for generic order information, stored within a node called <OrderHeader>. This element is the parent element for <CustID>, <OrderDate>, and <SalesID>. These values are to be stored as simple elements.

There is also a section for the line details of the order, which are stored in a node called <OrderDetails>. This element contains a repeating child element named <Product>. This repeating element is the parent node for each <ProductID> and <Name> (product name) within the order, as well as the <Price> (unit price) and <Qty> of each item. These values are all stored as attributes of the <Product> element.

Listing 1-16. Required Format of XML Output

```xml
<SalesOrders>
  <Order>
    <OrderHeader>
      <CustID>29825</CustID>
      <OrderDate>2011-05-31T00:00:00</OrderDate>
      <SalesID>43659</SalesID>
    </OrderHeader>
    <OrderDetails>
      <Product ProductID="776" Name="Mountain-100 Black, 42" Price="2024.9940" Qty="1" />
      <Product ProductID="777" Name="Mountain-100 Black, 44" Price="2024.9940" Qty="3" />
      <Product ProductID="778" Name="Mountain-100 Black, 48" Price="2024.9940" Qty="1" />
      <Product ProductID="771" Name="Mountain-100 Silver, 38" Price="2039.9940" Qty="1" />
      <Product ProductID="772" Name="Mountain-100 Silver, 42" Price="2039.9940" Qty="1" />
      <Product ProductID="773" Name="Mountain-100 Silver, 44" Price="2039.9940" Qty="2" />
      <Product ProductID="774" Name="Mountain-100 Silver, 48" Price="2039.9940" Qty="1" />
      <Product ProductID="714" Name="Long-Sleeve Logo Jersey, M" Price="28.8404" Qty="3" />
      <Product ProductID="716" Name="Long-Sleeve Logo Jersey, XL" Price="28.8404" Qty="1" />
      <Product ProductID="709" Name="Mountain Bike Socks, M" Price="5.7000" Qty="6" />
      <Product ProductID="712" Name="AWC Logo Cap" Price="5.1865" Qty="2" />
      <Product ProductID="711" Name="Sport-100 Helmet, Blue" Price="20.1865" Qty="4" />
    </OrderDetails>
  </Order>
  <Order>
    <OrderHeader>
      <CustID>29825</CustID>
      <OrderDate>2011-08-31T00:00:00</OrderDate>
      <SalesID>44305</SalesID>
    </OrderHeader>
    <OrderDetails>
      <Product ProductID="778" Name="Mountain-100 Black, 48" Price="2024.9940" Qty="2" />
      <Product ProductID="771" Name="Mountain-100 Silver, 38" Price="2039.9940" Qty="2" />
      <Product ProductID="773" Name="Mountain-100 Silver, 44" Price="2039.9940" Qty="2" />
      <Product ProductID="774" Name="Mountain-100 Silver, 48" Price="2039.9940" Qty="2" />
      <Product ProductID="743" Name="HL Mountain Frame - Black, 42" Price="714.7043" Qty="2" />
      <Product ProductID="741" Name="HL Mountain Frame - Silver, 48" Price="818.7000" Qty="1" />
      <Product ProductID="714" Name="Long-Sleeve Logo Jersey, M" Price="28.8404" Qty="2" />
      <Product ProductID="715" Name="Long-Sleeve Logo Jersey, L" Price="28.8404" Qty="1" />
      <Product ProductID="716" Name="Long-Sleeve Logo Jersey, XL" Price="28.8404" Qty="2" />
      <Product ProductID="709" Name="Mountain Bike Socks, M" Price="5.5100" Qty="12" />
      <Product ProductID="710" Name="Mountain Bike Socks, L" Price="5.7000" Qty="3" />
      <Product ProductID="712" Name="AWC Logo Cap" Price="5.1865" Qty="3" />
      <Product ProductID="711" Name="Sport-100 Helmet, Blue" Price="20.1865" Qty="2" />
      <Product ProductID="707" Name="Sport-100 Helmet, Red" Price="20.1865" Qty="2" />
      <Product ProductID="708" Name="Sport-100 Helmet, Black" Price="20.1865" Qty="1" />
    </OrderDetails>
  </Order>
  <Order>
    <OrderHeader>
      <CustID>29825</CustID>
```

```
      <OrderDate>2011-12-01T00:00:00</OrderDate>
      <SalesID>45061</SalesID>
    </OrderHeader>
    <OrderDetails>
      <Product ProductID="775" Name="Mountain-100 Black, 38" Price="2024.9940" Qty="3" />
      <Product ProductID="776" Name="Mountain-100 Black, 42" Price="2024.9940" Qty="2" />
      <Product ProductID="777" Name="Mountain-100 Black, 44" Price="2024.9940" Qty="5" />
      <Product ProductID="778" Name="Mountain-100 Black, 48" Price="2024.9940" Qty="8" />
      <Product ProductID="771" Name="Mountain-100 Silver, 38" Price="2039.9940" Qty="6" />
      <Product ProductID="772" Name="Mountain-100 Silver, 42" Price="2039.9940" Qty="2" />
      <Product ProductID="773" Name="Mountain-100 Silver, 44" Price="2039.9940" Qty="5" />
      <Product ProductID="774" Name="Mountain-100 Silver, 48" Price="2039.9940" Qty="5" />
      <Product ProductID="715" Name="Long-Sleeve Logo Jersey, L" Price="28.8404" Qty="2" />
      <Product ProductID="709" Name="Mountain Bike Socks, M" Price="5.7000" Qty="5" />
      <Product ProductID="712" Name="AWC Logo Cap" Price="5.1865" Qty="1" />
    </OrderDetails>
  </Order>
</SalesOrders>
```

Queries to build XML documents using FOR XML PATH can seem a little complicated at first, but once you understand the principles, they become fairly straightforward. Let's examine each requirement and how we can achieve the required shape.

First, we will need a root node called <SalesOrders>, and we will also have to rename the <row> element <Orders>. This can be achieved in the same way as when we were exploring RAW mode, using the optional argument for the <row> element and the ROOT keyword in the FOR XML clause and the root node, as shown in Listing 1-17.

Listing 1-17. Creating a Root and Naming the <row> Element with FOR XML PATH

```
FOR XML PATH('Order'), ROOT ('SalesOrders') ;
```

The next requirement is to create a complex element called <OrderHeader>, which will contain the <CustID>, <OrderDate>, and <SalesID> elements. This can be achieved by specifying a path to the element as well as the element name. As demonstrated in Listing 1-18, when using this technique, the / character denotes a step down the hierarchy.

Listing 1-18. Creating Hierarchy Levels

```
SELECT CustomerID 'OrderHeader/CustID'
    ,OrderDate 'OrderHeader/OrderDate'
    ,SalesOrderID 'OrderHeader/SalesID'
```

In order to create the nested line items, we will have to use a subquery, which returns the XML data type. For the process to work properly, we will have to use the TYPE keyword in the FOR XML clause of the subquery. This will cause the results to be returned to the outer query in native XML, as it can be processed server-side. Failure to use this keyword will result in some characters being replaced by control character sequences.

Because we want the values to be stored as attributes of an element called <Product>, we will have to rename the <row> element and prefix our column aliases with the @ symbol. Finally, to ensure that the <Product> elements are nested under an element named <OrderDetails>, we will use OrderDetails as the alias for the column returned by the subquery, as demonstrated in Listing 1-19.

Listing 1-19. OrderDetails CROSS Subquery

```
(
        SELECT
            SOD2.ProductID '@ProductID'
            ,P.Name '@Name'
            ,UnitPrice '@Price'
            ,OrderQty '@Qty'
        FROM Sales.SalesOrderDetail SOD2
        INNER JOIN Production.Product P
            ON SOD2.ProductID = P.ProductID
        WHERE SOD2.SalesOrderID = Base.SalesOrderID
        FOR XML PATH('Product'), TYPE
) 'OrderDetails'
```

Listing 1-20 pulls together the aspects that I have discussed and returns an XML document in the required format.

Listing 1-20. Putting It All Together

```
SELECT
    CustomerID 'OrderHeader/CustID'
    ,OrderDate 'OrderHeader/OrderDate'
    ,SalesOrderID 'OrderHeader/SalesID'
    ,(
        SELECT
            SOD2.ProductID '@ProductID'
            ,P.Name '@Name'
            ,UnitPrice '@Price'
            ,OrderQty '@Qty'
        FROM Sales.SalesOrderDetail SOD2
        INNER JOIN Production.Product P
            ON SOD2.ProductID = P.ProductID
        WHERE SOD2.SalesOrderID = Base.SalesOrderID
        FOR XML PATH('Product'), TYPE
    ) 'OrderDetails'
FROM
    (
        SELECT DISTINCT
            SalesOrder.CustomerID
            ,SalesOrder.OrderDate
            ,SalesOrder.SalesOrderID
        FROM Sales.SalesOrderHeader SalesOrder
        INNER JOIN Sales.SalesOrderDetail LineItem
            ON SalesOrder.SalesOrderID = LineItem.SalesOrderID
        WHERE SalesOrder.CustomerID = 29825
            AND SalesOrder.OrderDate < '2012-01-01'
    ) Base
FOR XML PATH('Order'), ROOT ('SalesOrders') ;
```

Extracting Values from XML Documents

When scripting, or even performance tuning, DBAs will often have to extract values from native XML. In order to demonstrate this, we will use the new Query Store feature of SQL Server 2016. The Query Store captures a history of query plans and their statistics, so that DBAs can easily compare the performance difference between different plans. As well as a graphical dashboard style tool, the Query Store also exposes plans and their metadata through a series of catalog views.

Let's imagine that we want to examine the most expensive query plans, which use a scan operation. This information can be retrieved by joining the sys.query_store_runtime_statistics catalog view with the sys.query_store plan catalog view. In order to retrieve the results that we require, however, we will have to interrogate the XML execution plan. This means that we will have to introduce the concepts of XQuery.

XQuery is a language for querying XML, in the same way that SQL is a language for querying relational data. The language is built on XPath and consists of XPath expressions to address a specific area of the document and FLOWR (pronounced *flower*) statements. FLOWR is an abbreviation of "For, Let, Where, Order by, and Return."

For statements allow you to iterate through a sequence of nodes. Let statements bind a sequence to a variable. Where statements filter nodes based on a Boolean expression. Order by statements order nodes before they are returned. Return statements specify what should be returned.

The majority of DBAs (even those concerned with automation) rarely need to concern themselves with FLOWR statements. Therefore, a complete discussion of the topic is beyond the scope of this book. Instead, I will focus on the core methods that are of use for automation and scripting in SQL Server. These methods are query, value, exist, and nodes.

■ **Note**   The examples in the following sections use the showplan schema. Full details of this XSD can be found at http://schemas.microsoft.com/sqlserver/2004/07/showplan.

---

query Method

The XQuery query method can be used against columns or variables with the XML data type. It extracts part of the document. The extracted parts of the document will form an untyped XML document, even if the original document conforms to a schema (typed XML).

Calling the method uses the syntax XMLDoc.query('/Path/To/Node'). If the document is bound to an XSD, you can declare the namespace, prior to specifying the node path, with the syntax XMLDoc.query(declare namespace alias="//domain.com/schemalocation"; //alias:node').

For example, the query in Listing 1-21 will return every column reference from each query plan within the query store. Within the query method, we first declare the namespace for Microsoft's showplan schema. We can then easily specify the node that we wish to extract, as opposed to passing the node's full location within the hierarchy.

Listing 1-21. Using the query CROSS Method

```
SELECT
    CAST(query_plan AS XML).query('declare namespace
            qplan="http://schemas.microsoft.com/sqlserver/2004/07/showplan";
                        //qplan:ColumnReference') AS SQLStatement
FROM sys.query_store_plan ;
```

value and nodes Methods

The value method will extract a singleton value from an XML document, mapped to a SQL Server data type. The value method can be called against columns or variables of the XML data type in the format `XMLDoc.value('/path/to/node/@node[1]', 'int')`. Alternatively, you can also specify the schema that the XML document is bound to, in the format `XMLDoc.value('declare namespace alias=http://domain.com/schemalocation; (//alias:node[1]', 'int')`.

■ **Tip** Because the value method can only return a singleton value, it is mandatory to specify an index value in square brackets, even if the node only occurs once within the document.

Because the value method can only return an atomic (singleton) value, it can be used in conjunction with the nodes method to shred nodes into relational data. The nodes method returns a rowset that contains logical copies of the instances of a node. The value method can then be cross-applied to the results of the nodes method, in order to return multiple values from the same XML document. The query in Listing 1-22 will return a list of tables and columns that are accessed within each plan in the query store.

The subquery within Listing 1-22 simply converts the query_plan column to native XML, so that the nodes method can be called against it. The outer query cross-applies the nodes method to the native XML version of the query plan and then runs the value method against the logical representation of the node instances that have been returned by the nodes method. Note that because the value method is being called against the results returned by nodes, rather than the original XML document, there is no need to specify a path for the attributes. This is because the results returned by nodes begin at the level of the `<ColumnReference>` element, and the @Table and @Column nodes are attributes of this element. Therefore, as far as the value method is concerned, the attributes are at the top level of the document.

■ **Tip** When combining nodes with value, the schema is declared in the nodes method only. This is because the value method is run against the logical representation of instances, as opposed to the original XML document.

Listing 1-22. Using the value CROSS and nodes CROSS Methods

```
SELECT
    plan_id
    ,nodes.query_plan.value('@Table[1]', 'nvarchar(128)') AS TableRef
    ,nodes.query_plan.value('@Column[1]', 'nvarchar(128)') AS ColumnRef
FROM
(
    SELECT plan_id, CAST(query_plan AS XML) query_plan_xml
    FROM sys.query_store_plan
) base
CROSS APPLY query_plan_xml.nodes('declare namespace
        qplan="http://schemas.microsoft.com/sqlserver/2004/07/showplan";
                //qplan:ColumnReference') as nodes(query_plan) ;
```

exist Method

The exist method will run an XQuery expression against an XML document. It will then return a bit (Boolean) value to denote the success of the expression. 0 is returned when the result of the XPath expression is empty; 1 is returned if the result is not empty; and NULL is returned if the result is NULL.

The exist method is usually used in a WHERE clause. For example, you may have noticed that the queries in Listings 1-21 and 1-22 return many results for many internal queries run by SQL Server and also for DBA activity, such as accessing backup metadata. The query in Listing 1-23 extends the query in Listing 1-22, to filter out any results where the @Schema attribute of the <ColumnReference> element is equal to either [sys] or [dbo]. This will result if only plans that access user tables are considered.

Listing 1-23. Using the exist CROSS Method

```
SELECT
    plan_id
    ,nodes.query_plan.value('@Table[1]', 'nvarchar(128)') AS index1
    ,nodes.query_plan.value('@Column[1]', 'nvarchar(128)') AS index2
FROM
(
    SELECT plan_id, CAST(query_plan AS XML) query_plan_xml
    FROM sys.query_store_plan
) base
CROSS APPLY query_plan_xml.nodes('declare namespace
        qplan="http://schemas.microsoft.com/sqlserver/2004/07/showplan";
        //qplan:ColumnReference') as nodes(query_plan)
WHERE query_plan_xml.exist('declare namespace
        qplan="http://schemas.microsoft.com/sqlserver/2004/07/showplan";
            //qplan:Object[@Schema="[sys]"]') = 0
AND query_plan_xml.exist('declare namespace
        qplan="http://schemas.microsoft.com/sqlserver/2004/07/showplan";
            //qplan:Object[@Schema="[dbo]"]') = 0 ;
```

Pulling the Methods Together

In order to meet our original requirement, to examine the most expensive query plans, which use a scan operation, we will have to combine the value, query, and exist methods in a single query. The query in Listing 1-24 uses the exist method in the WHERE clause, to examine the <RelOp> element of each plan and filter out any operators that do not involve a scan operation. The WHERE clause will also use the exist method to filter any operations that are not against user tables.

The SELECT list uses the value method to extract the @Schema and @Table attributes, to help us to identify the tables where we may be missing indexes. It also uses the query method to extract the entire <Object> element, giving us full details of the table, in XML format.

As well as using XQuery methods, the query also returns the whole plan in native XML format and plan statistics from the sys.query_store_runtime_stats catalog view. The query uses TOP and ORDER BY to filter out all but the five most expensive plans, based on the average execution time of the plan, multiplied by the number of times the plan has been executed.

Listing 1-24. Finding the Most Expensive Plans with Scan Operations

```
SELECT TOP 5
    CAST(p.query_plan AS XML)
    , CAST(p.query_plan AS XML).value('declare namespace
```

```
                qplan="http://schemas.microsoft.com/sqlserver/2004/07/showplan";
                                (//qplan:Object/@Schema)[1]','nvarchar(128)')
      + '.'
      + CAST(p.query_plan AS XML).value('declare namespace
            qplan="http://schemas.microsoft.com/sqlserver/2004/07/showplan";
                                (//qplan:Object/@Table)[1]','nvarchar(128)') AS [Table]
    , CAST(p.query_plan AS XML).query('declare namespace
            qplan="http://schemas.microsoft.com/sqlserver/2004/07/showplan";
                                //qplan:Object') AS TableDetails
    , rs.count_executions
    , rs.avg_duration
    , rs.avg_physical_io_reads
    , rs.avg_cpu_time
FROM sys.query_store_runtime_stats rs
INNER JOIN sys.query_store_plan p
        ON p.plan_id = rs.plan_id
WHERE CAST(p.query_plan AS XML).exist('declare namespace
            qplan="http://schemas.microsoft.com/sqlserver/2004/07/showplan";
                                //qplan:RelOp[@LogicalOp="Index Scan"
                                or @LogicalOp="Clustered Index Scan"
                                or @LogicalOp="Table Scan"]') = 1
    AND CAST(p.query_plan AS XML).exist('declare namespace
            qplan="http://schemas.microsoft.com/sqlserver/2004/07/showplan";
                                //qplan:Object[@Schema="[sys]"]') = 0
    AND CAST(p.query_plan AS XML).exist('declare namespace
            qplan="http://schemas.microsoft.com/sqlserver/2004/07/showplan";
                                //qplan:Object[@Schema="[dbo]"]') = 0
ORDER BY rs.count_executions * rs.avg_duration DESC ;
```

Efficient Looping

One of the most common hosting standards enforced upon developers by DBAs is to disallow the use of cursors. At the same time, the majority of DBAs will use a cursor, whenever they need to iterate through a set of objects. The argument is normally that their script only runs once per day, and writing a cursor is the quickest way to achieve their means. That argument, of course, has some merit, but I always feel that it is better to lead by example. There have been several times when I have had "the cursor debate" with development teams and won the argument by virtue of the fact that I have implemented my own scripts without the use of cursors, and developers should be able to do the same.

Imagine that we need a script to kill all active sessions. This is a useful script for any DBA to have in his or her armory, as there will always be occasions when you have to disconnect all users quickly. The script in Listing 1-25 achieves this by using a cursor, but it will be slow and resource-intensive, especially in a highly transactional environment with many active sessions.

Listing 1-25. Kill All Sessions with a Cursor

```
DECLARE @session_id INT ;

DECLARE C_Sessions CURSOR
FOR
    SELECT Session_id
```

```
    FROM sys.dm_exec_sessions
    WHERE session_id <> @@SPID
        AND is_user_process = 1 ;

OPEN C_Sessions ;

FETCH NEXT FROM C_Sessions
INTO @Session_id ;

DECLARE @SQL NVARCHAR(MAX) ;

WHILE @@FETCH_STATUS = 0
BEGIN
    SET @SQL = 'Kill ' + CAST(@Session_id AS NVARCHAR(4)) ;
    EXEC(@SQL) ;
    FETCH NEXT FROM C_Sessions
    INTO @Session_id ;
END

CLOSE C_Sessions ;

DEALLOCATE C_Sessions ;
```

A much more efficient way of achieving the same results (and adhering to your own hosting standards!) is to use a trick with FOR XML. The query in Listing 1-26 uses a subquery to populate a variable. The subquery returns the string 'Kill ' concatenated to the Session_id for each row that is returned in the result set. This is then converted into XML format, using FOR XML PATH. The data() method is used to strip out the XML tags and characters, leaving only the text. This text is then passed back up to the outer query, where it is implicitly converted into NVARCHAR by virtue of the data type of the variable. The variable can then be executed using dynamic SQL.

The benefit of this approach is that the query is only executed once, as opposed to once for every active session. This means less disk activity. There is also less memory used in this approach, compared to other techniques, such as @SQL = @SQL + approach.

Listing 1-26. Kill All Sessions Efficiently

```
DECLARE @SQL NVARCHAR(MAX) ;

SELECT DISTINCT @SQL =
(
    SELECT 'Kill ' + CAST(session_id AS NVARCHAR(4)) AS [data()]
    FROM sys.dm_exec_sessions
    WHERE session_id <> @@SPID
        AND is_user_process = 1
    FOR XML PATH('')
) ;

EXEC(@SQL) ;
```

Summary

The DBA who is serious about reducing workload by scripting and automating tasks has to be familiar with some advanced T-SQL techniques. Using the APPLY operator allows you to apply a function to each row in a results set. When the CROSS APPLY operator is used, only rows that do not cause the function to return a NULL value will be returned. When the OUTER APPLY operator is used, all rows in the result set will be returned. DBAs can use this technique for applying Dynamic Management Functions to Dynamic Management Views.

XML is an ever increasingly important technology for a DBA to understand and be able to work with. The two main concepts relating to XML within SQL Server are converting XML to relational values and converting a result set to an XML document. The FOR XML clause of a SELECT statement can be used to produce XML documents from results sets. XQuery, which is based on XPath, can be used to extract values from XML documents.

Many DBAs still use cursors to iterate through objects, but using the XQuery data() method within a subquery provides a far more optimal solution. It also promotes good practice from developers, by showing that you lead by example.

CHAPTER 2

■ ■ ■

PowerShell Fundamentals

PowerShell is a scripting language, developed by Microsoft, that is capable of managing virtually every aspect of Windows and resources that sit on Windows, such as SharePoint and SQL Server. It is object-based and integrated with the .NET Framework. It can be used to run scripts both locally and remotely. The following sections will discuss the fundamentals of PowerShell, before a closer look is taken at the `sqlps` module and how to navigate an instance.

Getting Started with PowerShell

The following sections will introduce the PowerShell Command Line Interface and Integrated Scripting Environment. You will also learn how to enable PowerShell script execution on your local machine.

PowerShell Environments

Windows supplies two environments for working with PowerShell. One of these environments is the CLI (Command Line Interface) and the other is the ISE (Integrated Scripting Environment). In Windows Server 2012 R2, the PowerShell CLI is pinned to the Start menu by default. (The tile is illustrated in Figure 2-1.) It can also be found via its file location `C:\ProgramData\Microsoft\Windows\Start Menu\Programs\System Tools`.

Figure 2-1. *PowerShell CLI tile*

The CLI can be thought of as the PowerShell equivalent of the command prompt, in that it can be used for issuing single commands. The difference, of course, is that the command prompt is based on DOS (Disk Operating System), as opposed to PowerShell.

PowerShell can also be accessed from the command prompt. When in the command prompt, enter the command powershell to access the PowerShell command line. You can enter the command exit to return to the command prompt at any time. Just as when you are accessing the PowerShell CLI from the GUI, using PowerShell at the command line is useful for entering single commands.

The PowerShell ISE is useful for developing scripts, which contain multiple commands and can be reused or scheduled to run automatically. In Windows Server 2012 R2, the ISE can be accessed from Administrative Tools. The ISE is illustrated in Figure 2-2.

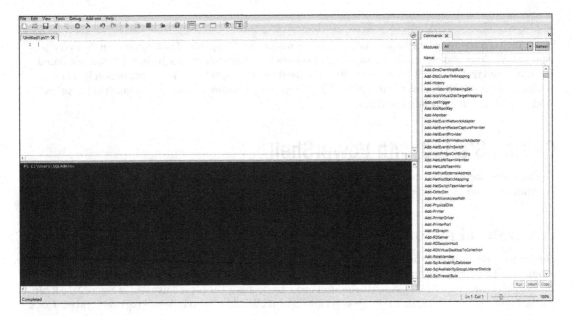

Figure 2-2. *PowerShell ISE*

The top pane is the script pane. You can use this pane for developing your scripts. The bottom pane is the command pane. You can type single commands into the command pane for immediate execution, as you would with the CLI. Additionally, when you execute a script that you have written in the script pane, the commands and outputs will be shown in the command pane.

On the right is the Commands tab. In this tab, you can search for cmdlets by name filter by module. If you click a cmdlet (providing the relevant module is loaded), you will be shown the cmdlet's parameters, as illustrated in Figure 2-3.

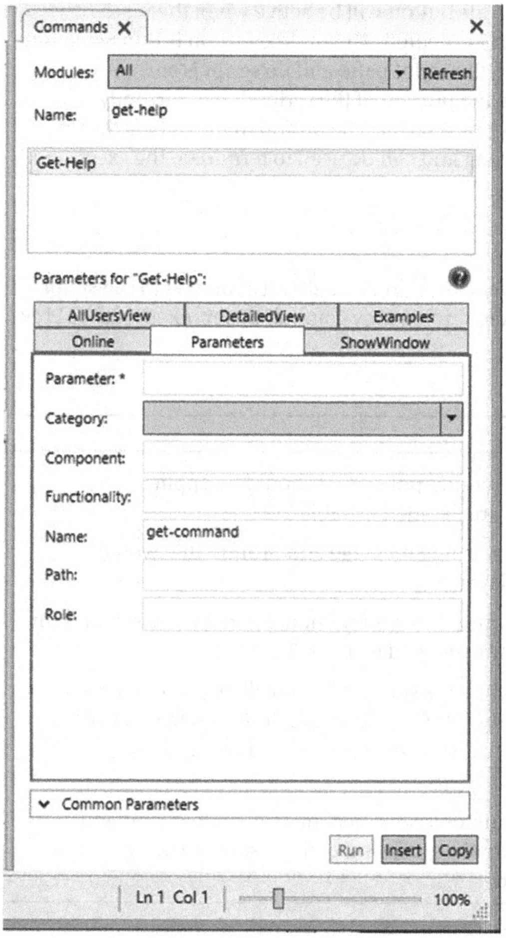

Commands ✕	✕

Modules: All ▼ Refresh

Name: get-help

Get-Help

Parameters for "Get-Help": ❓

AllUsersView	DetailedView	Examples
Online	Parameters	ShowWindow

Parameter: *

Category: ▼

Component:

Functionality:

Name: get-command

Path:

Role:

˅ Common Parameters

Run Insert Copy

Ln 1 Col 1 ──▯──────── 100%

Figure 2-3. cmdlet parameters

Here, you can see the parameters for the get-help command, which will display help. get-command has been added as the Name parameter, so we can now hit Run, to run the command, or Insert, to copy the command, including our parameters to the command pane. From the command pane, the command can either be executed or copied into the script pane.

At the top of the PowerShell ISE window, you will find the toolbar. The three buttons that I would like to discuss are Run, Run Selection, and Stop, which are illustrated in Figure 2-4.

Figure 2-4. Toolbar

The leftmost of these three buttons is the Run button. This button will be active when there are commands in the script pane and no script is currently being executed. The middle button is Run Selection. This button will also be active when there are commands in the script pane and no script is currently running. The difference is that this button will only execute the portion of the script that is currently highlighted. I find this button very useful when I am debugging a script. The button to the right is the Stop button. This button is active when a script is currently running and can be used to terminate the execution.

Enabling Script Execution

Windows Server 2012 R2 is the first version of Windows Server where PowerShell will allow you to run script by default. This behavior can be controlled using the `set-executionpolicy` command. `set-executionpolicy` accepts the parameters listed in Table 2-1.

Table 2-1. `set-executionpolicy` *Parameters*

Parameter	Description
`-ExecutionPolicy<ExecutionPolicy>`	Specifies the execution policy that should be applied. The possible values are detailed in Table 2-2.
`-Force`	Suppresses the warning message and prompt that would usually be displayed
`-Scope<ExecutionPolicyScope>`	Specifies the scope of the policy application. Possible values for this parameter are detailed in Table 2-3.
`-Confirm`	When this parameter is specified, you will be prompted to confirm the change, before the configuration is made. Unless `-Force` is specified, you will be prompted twice when specifying this parameter.
`-Whatif`	When this parameter is specified, instead of the command being run, a textual description of the resultant configuration will be provided.

Table 2-2 explains the execution policies that can be configured.

■ **Tip** When specifying a parameter by name, it should always be prefixed with a hyphen.

Table 2-2. *Execution Policies*

Execution Policy	Description
`Restricted`	PowerShell will not allow any scripts to run. Default value prior to Windows Server 2012 R2
`AllSigned`	Only allows scripts to run, if they have been signed by a trusted authority
`RemoteSigned`	Allows locally created scripts to run, but downloaded scripts must be signed by a trusted authority
`Unrestricted`	Allows all scripts to run, but you will be prompted before running unsigned downloaded scripts
`Bypass`	Allows all scripts to run. No prompts will be received.
`Undefined`	Removes the specified execution policy

Table 2-3 details the possible scopes to which the policy can be applied.

Table 2-3. *Policy Scopes*

Scope	Description
Process	The policy will only apply to the current process. All other processes continue to use the original execution policy. When the process terminates, the configuration is deleted.
CurrentUser	The policy will be applied to the current user. All other users will be unaffected.
LocalMachine	The policy will be applied across the entire machine. All users will be affected. This is the default value.

To configure the server to allow downloaded scripts, only if they have been signed, or locally created scripts, use the command in Listing 2-1. Here, set-executionpolicy is the cmdlet; -ExecutionPolicy is the name of the parameter; and RemoteSigned is the value being passed to the parameter.

■ **Tip** To enable PowerShell to run scripts, you will have to run the CLI with Administrator privileges. To do this, right-click PowerShell and choose Run As Administrator. When running the command, the user will be prompted to confirm.

Listing 2-1. Setting Execution Policy

```
Set-ExecutionPolicy -ExecutionPolicy RemoteSigned
```

Language Fundamentals

The following sections will discuss comments, standards and aliases, data types, and variables. You will then discover how to use piping and control execution flow, before finally discovering how to import modules into PowerShell.

Comments

PowerShell supports both inline comments and block comments. An inline comment is denoted by the # symbol. Anything to the right of this symbol is treated as a comment and is not executed. For example, the command in Listing 2-2 is functionally equivalent to the command in Listing 2-1.

Listing 2-2. Inline Comments

```
Set-ExecutionPolicy -ExecutionPolicy RemoteSigned #Set execution policy to RemoteSigned
```

Block comments begin with <# and end with #>. Anything between these character sequences is regarded as a comment and is not executed. The script in Listing 2-3 demonstrates the use of block comments.

Listing 2-3. Block Comments

```
<# This script
Demonstrates block
comments #>

Set-ExecutionPolicy <# Code to the right comment will execute #> -ExecutionPolicy RemoteSigned
```

Standards and Aliases

While there are exceptions, most cmdlets follow a naming convention, by which the first part of the command's name describes the action that you will be performing, such as the following prefixes:

- Add
- Clear
- Complete
- Connect
- Convert
- ConvertFrom
- ConvertTo
- Copy
- Disable
- Disconnect
- Dismount
- Enable
- Export
- Format
- Get
- Import
- Install
- Invoke
- Join
- Mount
- Move
- New
- Out
- Publish
- Read
- Receive
- Register
- Remove
- Rename
- Reset

- Resize

- Restart

- Restore

- Resume

- Revoke

- Save

- Select

- Send

- Set

- Show

- Start

- Stop

- Suspend

- Switch

- Test

- Undo

- Unregister

- Update

- Wait

- Write

This prefix is followed by a hyphen (-) and ends with a description of the resource that you will be performing the action upon. For example, `get-childitem` can be used to list the contents of the current PowerShell location. This location could be a folder in the file system or it could be a table inside an SQL Server instance. Navigating a SQL Server instance is discussed later in this chapter. The logical and consistent naming convention, combined with intellisence, makes learning and finding commands a relatively easy process, in the PowerShell ISE.

To make learning PowerShell even easier, many commands have aliases, which map to DOS or LINUX commands. This means that if you have any experience using DOS, Windows Command Prompt (which is based on DOS), or LINUX, you can continue to use many commands that you are already familiar with.

■ **Tip** Aliases can enhance productivity when you are operating interactively with PowerShell, but it is considered bad practice to use aliases within scripts.

Let's consider `get-childitem` as an example of this. As mentioned earlier, `get-childitem` can be used to list the contents of a folder, in the file system. Many new PowerShell users unfamiliar with this command will be familiar with `dir` from DOS or `ls` from LINUX. Therefore, PowerShell provides both of these aliases. For example, all of the commands in Listing 2-4 are functionally equivalent.

Listing 2-4. Using Aliases

```
dir *.txt #Using the DOS alias

ls *.txt #Using the LINUX alias

gci *.txt #Using gci alias

Get-ChildItem . *.txt #Using the PowerShell command
```

The get-childitem cmdlet accepts the parameters detailed in Table 2-4.

Table 2-4. *get-childitem Parameters*

Parameter	Description
-Path / -LiteralPath	Specifies the location to be searched. It is possible to specify multiple locations. If LiteralPath is used, the location will be interpreted exactly as typed. This means that wildcards are not permitted. If Path is used, wildcards and environmental variables can be included. Use . to designate PowerShell's current location.
-Filter	Limits the results returned by the command. The filter is applied by the provider (such as the file system or SQL Server, as opposed to PowerShell). The supported wildcards are provider-specific.
-Include	A whitelist of results that should be returned. The filter is applied by PowerShell, after results have been returned by the provider.
-Exclude	A blacklist of results that should not be returned. The filter is applied by PowerShell, after results have been returned by the provider.
-Force	While it will not override security settings and permissions, -Force will allow you to return results that you would not normally see. This is provider-specific, but in regards to the file system, this would include hidden files and system files.
-Name	Causes the command to return the file name only and not additional attributes, such as length or the last date that the item was updated
-Recurse	Causes child locations to be searched, as well as the specified location. When searching the file system, this means that subdirectories would also be searched.
-UseTransaction	Only applies if there is an active transaction and includes the command within that transaction. A transaction causes all actions within that transaction to be processed as an atomic unit, meaning that either all actions succeed or all actions fail.*

Transactions are supported by PowerShell only when they are also supported natively by the underlying provider. Transactions are most commonly used for database operations.

Data Types

PowerShell uses the data types provided by the .NET Framework. Every data type in the .NET framework is derived from the Object data type. Therefore, the Object data type is the root of the type hierarchy, as well as being a data type in its own right.

The base types listed in Table 2-5 are derived directly from the Object type. From these base types, literally hundreds of data types are derived. Some of these derived types are complex, such as XML, DateTimeOffset (which stores a date and time with an offset against UTC), and Array.

Table 2-5. *Base Data Types*

Base Data Type	Description
Byte	8-bit unsigned integer
SByte	Non-CLS-compliant 8-bit signed integer
Int16	16-bit signed integer
Int32	32-bit signed integer
Int64	64-bit signed integer
UInt16	16-bit unsigned integer
UInt32	32-bit unsigned integer
UInt64	Non-CLS-compliant 64-bit unsigned integer
Single	32-bit floating-point number
Double	64-bit floating-point number
Boolean	Boolean/Bit value
Char	Unicode (16-bit) character
Decimal	Decimal (128-bit) value
IntPtr	A signed integer that has a 32-bit value on a 32-bit platform and a 64-bit value on a 64-bit platform
UIntPtr	An unsigned integer that has a 32-bit value on a 32-bit platform and a 64-bit value on a 64-bit platform
String	A string of Unicode characters

Variables

As with all languages, variables contain values that are unknown until runtime or that change during execution. They are critical to writing flexible, powerful, and maintainable code. They are used for purposes such as storing user inputs and looping. Each variable maps to a data type, and because variables are objects derived from a .NET class, various methods can be called against them. For example, the ToString() method can be called against an Int32, to output the variable value as a string, as opposed to an integer.

A variable is always prefixed with a $, and when declaring a variable, you specify the data type in square brackets, immediately before the $, before finally declaring the name of the variable.

■ **Tip** Always give variables meaningful names. If you give variables names such as $i or $a, they become as meaningless as naming them %foo and %bar. Giving variables meaningful names makes your code easier to read and maintain.

The script in Listing 2-5 first creates two variables. One is an integer called $HelloWorldInt, and the other is a string called $HelloWorldText. The second part of the script assigns values to each of the variables, and the final part of the script clears the console of messages, before it outputs the results.

Listing 2-5. Declaring and Using Variables

```
#Declare the variables

[int]$HelloWorldInt
[string]$HelloWorldText

#Assign Values to the Variables

$HelloWorldInt = 123

$HelloWorldText = "Hello World"

#Print the Results to the Console

clear-host

"HelloWorldInt: " + $HelloWorldInt

"HelloWorldString: " + $HelloWorldText
```

You can also declare a variable without specifying a data type. When you do this, PowerShell will use the data type that it considers to be most appropriate. Be warned, however, that PowerShell is not psychic! It can only guess what data type the variable should be. For example, consider the script in Listing 2-6. Here, we declare six variables without specifying a data type. We then use the GetType() method to extract the data type for each. As you can see from the results, which are listed in Listing 2-7, the data types are not as you might expect.

Listing 2-6. Declaring Variables Without Data Types

```
#Declare Variables In-line

$StringVariable1 = "Hello World"
$StringVariable2 = 123
$StringVariable3 = "123"
$Int32Variable = 123
$SingleVariable = 3.3
$XMLVariable = '<root><MyElement>MyValue</MyElement></root>'

#Extract Data Types
```

```
Clear-Host

"StringVariable1: " + $StringVariable1.GetType()
"StringVariable2: " + $StringVariable2.GetType()
"StringVariable3: " + $StringVariable3.GetType()
"Int32Variable: " + $Int32Variable.GetType()
"SingleVariable: " + $SingleVariable.GetType()
"XMLVariable: " + $XMLVariable.GetType()
```

Listing 2-7. Declaring Variables Without Data Types—Results

```
StringVariable1: string
StringVariable2: int
StringVariable3: string
Int32Variable: int
SingleVariable: double
XMLVariable: string
```

You can see that $StringVariable, $StringVariable3, and $Int32Variable have been assigned to the data types we wanted. We have not been so lucky with the other variables, however. $StringVariable2 has been created with an int data type, because we did not encase the assigned value within quotation marks. This is why $StringVariable3 did not suffer the same issue. $SingleVariable has been created with a data type of double. This is not the end of the world, but it does mean that we are using more memory resource than we require. $XMLVariable has been created with the string data type. This means that we will be unable to use XML-specific methods and cmdlets, such as the get-member method and the select-xml cmdlet.

To summarize, it is important to remember the potential complications of not specifying a data type, and if the data type is important to your script, it should always be specified. An additional factor to consider is code maintenance. If it is not easy for you (or another DBA) to reference the data type of a variable, it may slow you down when you come to troubleshoot, revise, or enhance the script.

Piping, Filtering, and Controlling Flow

If you are familiar with T-SQL, the idea of piping is probably new to you. In PowerShell, piping is the process of passing the results of one command into another command. Piping is a key concept of PowerShell, and one of the things that makes it so powerful. A simple example of piping can be found in Listing 2-8.

Listing 2-8. Basic Piping

```
# Return a list of running processes and then filter by the name of the process

$process = Get-Process | where {$_.ProcessName -like "*PowerShell*"}

# Print the filtered list of processes to the console

$process
```

The first line in this script pulls a list of running processes from the operating system. It then passes the results of this command into a where-object cmdlet (which has an alias of where). The where command uses the $_.constructor, which indicates "in the data stream." It uses the ProcessName property of the data stream to apply a filter, which removes any results in which the process's name does not include the string PowerShell. The asterisks are used as wildcards.

The operators supported by where-object are detailed in Table 2-6.

Table 2-6. where-object *Operators*

Operator	Description
-Contains	Any item in the property's value is equal to the value specified. This is useful if you must ensure that a specific value exists within an array.
-EQ	The property's value is equal to specified value.
-GE	The property's value is greater than or equal to the specified value.
-GT	The property's value is greater than the specified value.
-In	The property's value is equal to any of the list of values specified. The list of values specified should be separated by a comma.
-Is	The property's value is of the specified data type. The data type specified must be enclosed in square brackets.
-IsNot	The data type of the property's value is not the same as the specified data type. The data type specified must be enclosed in square brackets.
-LE	The property's value is less than or equal to the specified value.
-LT	The property's value is less than the specified value.
-Like	The property's value contains the specified value, following a wildcard match.
-Match	The property's value matches the regex pattern provided.
-NE	The property's value is not equal to the value specified.
-NotContains	No item in the property's value is equal to the value specified. This is useful if you have to ensure that a specific value does not exist within an array.
-NotIn	The property's value is not equal to any of the list of values specified. The list of values specified should be separated by a comma.
-NotLike	The property's value does not contain the specified value, following a wildcard match.
-NotMatch	The property's value does not match the regex pattern provided.
-CContains	As per -Contains, but case-sensitive
-CEQ	As per -EQ, but case sensitive
-CGE	As per -GE, but case-sensitive
-CGT	As per -GT, but case-sensitive
-CIn	As per -In, but case-sensitive
-CLE	As per -LE, but case-sensitive
-CLT	As per -LT, but case-sensitive
-CLike	As per -Like, but case-sensitive
-CMatch	As per -Match, but case-sensitive
-CNE	As per -NE, but case-sensitive
-CNotContains	As per -NotContains, but case-sensitive
-CNotIn	As per -NotIn, but case-sensitive
-CNotLike	As per -NotLike, but case-sensitive
-CNotMatch	As per -NotMatch, but case-sensitive

If you have any scripting or programming experience, you will already know how useful looping can be for iterating through objects, performing an action (or set of actions) a specified number of times, or performing an action (or set of actions) repeatedly, until a condition is met. PowerShell provides looping capability through a for statement, a foreach statement, and a while statement.

A for loop can be used for either repeating a set of actions a specified number of times or iterating through a subset of an array or collection. A foreach loop is useful when you have to iterate through every item in an array or collection, and a while loop is used to repeat a set of actions, until a condition is met.

Listing 2-9 demonstrates how a for loop could be used to implement error handling. The script will attempt to read the contents of a file three times, at 30-second intervals.

■ **Caution** Of course, the statement asserting how useful looping can be does not hold true for T-SQL, as set-based operations are always far more efficient than looping. Please refer to Chapter 1 for more details.

Listing 2-9. Using a for Loop

```
for($i=1
    $i -le 3
    $i++
    )
    {
    Try
        {
get-content c:\ExpertScripting.txt -ErrorAction Stop
        "Attempt " + $i + " Succeeded"
        Break
        }
    Catch
        {
        "Attempt " + $i + " Failed"
        Start-Sleep -s 30
        }
    }
```

■ **Tip** Although failing to read the file will always generate an error, it will not usually cause the script to terminate. As we need the script to terminate, for the flow to move to the catch block, we use the -OnErrorAction parameter, to force the script to terminate.

The behavior of the for loop is defined within parentheses. There are three definitions within the parentheses. The first initializes the variable that will control the loop. In our example, we create a variable named $i with an initial value of 1. The second definition specifies the condition that has to be met before our loop terminates. We specify that we will continue to loop, while $- is less than or equal to 3. The final definition controls the increment of the looping variable. $i++ is shorthand for $i = $i + 1.

The code to be repeated in each iteration of the loop is enclosed within braces. Here, we use a try...catch block to attempt to read the file. If the operation succeeds, we will write the success to the console and then exit the loop via the break command. If the operation fails, execution moves to the catch block. Here, we write the failure to the console and then pause the execution of the script for 30 seconds.

The script in Listing 2-10 demonstrates how a while loop can be used to refine the code in Listing 2-9, so that the script will continue to loop (potentially infinitely) until the read of the file exists.

■ **Note** If you are following along with the demonstrations, create a file named `ExpertScripting.txt` in the root of `c:\` while the script is running.

Listing 2-10. Using a while Loop

```
$i = 0
while (1 -eq 1)
    {
    Try
        {
        $i++
        get-content c:\ExpertScripting.txt -ErrorAction Stop
        "Attempt " + $i + " Succeeded"
        Break
        }
    Catch
        {
        "Attempt " + $i + " Failed"
        Start-Sleep -s 30
        }
    }
```

The while loop is defined within parentheses. In our example, we specify that the loop will continue while 1 is equal to 1. Of course, as 1 is a constant, as opposed to a variable, the while loop will continue infinitely. Once the contents of the file have been read successfully, however, the break command will exit the loop. This technique is particularly useful when you are scripting a middleware component, which requires a file to be written, before continuing.

The script in Listing 2-11 demonstrates how a foreach loop can be used to ensure that all SQL Server services are running and start them if they are not.

Listing 2-11. Using a foreach Loop

```
# Populate a new variable with the details all SQL Server services
$service = Get-Service | where {$_.Name -LIKE "*SQL*" -AND $_.Status -eq "Stopped"}

# Start each service

foreach ($name in $service)
    {
    Start-Service $name
    }
```

The final control of flow concept that we will discuss is IF...ELSE. An IF...ELSE block allows you to branch your code, based on a condition. You can also nest IF...ELSE blocks to implement complex logic (although you should consider code maintenance when doing so). It is only possible to have one IF block. To implement multiple IF conditions, you can add multiple ELSEIF blocks. The ELSE block always comes last (if you choose to use one) and is a catchall for any occurrences in which none of your IF and ELSEIF conditions is met. The conditions of IF and ELSEIF blocks are enclosed within parentheses. The code block to execute is enclosed within braces. Where ELSE is a catchall, you only have to specify a code block, with no condition.

The script in Listing 2-12 demonstrates how to implement an IF...ELSE block to check the status of a service.

Listing 2-12. Using IF, ELSEIF, and ELSE

```
$Service = "SQLBrowser"
$ServiceDetails = get-service | where{$_.Name -eq $Service}

IF ($ServiceDetails.Status -eq "Running")
{$Service + " is  working"}
ELSEIF ($ServiceDetails.Status -eq "Stopped")
{$Service + " is not working. Please check the Event Log"}
ELSEIF ($Service -notin $ServiceDetails.Name)
{$Service + " is not installed"}
ELSE
{$Service + " is changing state"}
```

Importing Modules

To make PowerShell fully extensible and able to manage virtually any application that Windows has access to, it has been written using a modular approach, with modules having to be imported to allow users access to the cmdlets that they contain. Some of the core modules are imported automatically when a command is executed. For example, using the get-ExecutionPolicy command causes the Microsoft.PowerShell. Security module to be imported.

Other modules, such as the sqlps module, which allow you to run SQL Server cmdlets and navigate the SQL Server object hierarchy, have to be imported manually. The import is performed using the import-module cmdlet. PowerShell will search for the module in a folder path stored in the PSModulePath environment variable. When you install SQL Server Management Tools, the module is placed in the default location (%SystemRoot%\system32\WindowsPowerShell\v1.0\Modules\;C:\Program Files (x86)\ Microsoft SQL Server\130\Tools\PowerShell\Modules\ on Windows Server 2012 R2). The command in Listing 2-13 imports the sqlps module.

Listing 2-13. Importing a Module

```
import-module sqlps
```

Some modules, including the sqlps module, can take a few seconds to load, so you can enhance the script so that the module is only imported if it is not already loaded. When using import to load the module, you will notice a warning about unapproved verbs. These warnings can be suppressed by using the -DisableNameChecking parameter. The script in Listing 2-14 demonstrates both of these techniques.

Listing 2-14. Enhancing the import-module Command

```
If ( ! (Get-module sqlps))
    {
    Import-Module sqlps -DisableNameChecking
    }
```

sqlps Module

The sqlps module contains the cmdlets described in Table 2-7. Many of the cmdlets will be discussed in further detail throughout the course of this book.

Table 2-7. sqlps cmdlets

cmdlet	Description
Decode-SqlName	Converts into hexadecimal references characters within delimited identifiers that are not supported by PowerShell
Disable-SqlAlwaysOn	Disables the availability group's functionality on an SQL instance
Enable-SqlAlwaysOn	Enables the availability group's functionality on an SQL instance
Encode-SqlName	Converts hexadecimal references into the characters that they represent
Get-SqlCredential	Retrieves a credential object and its properties
Get-SqlDatabase	Returns names and metadata for databases
Get-SqlInstance	Returns metadata about the instance(s) on the target server
Get-SqlSmartAdmin	Returns details of managed backups for the target instance
Invoke-PolicyEvaluation	Causes a SQL Server PBM (policy-based management) policy to be evaluated
Invoke-Sqlcmd	Exposes SQLCMD functionality to PowerShell
Join-SqlAvailabilityGroup	Adds a secondary replica to an AlwaysOn availability group
New-SqlAvailabilityGroup	Creates an AlwaysOn availability group
New-SqlAvailabilityGroupListener	Creates a new AlwaysOn availability group listener
New-SqlAvailabilityReplica	Used to create a replica. When the -AsTemplate parameter is used, the replica will not be created; instead, an in-memory template will be created. This template can then be applied during replica creation.
New-SqlBackupEncryptionOption	Defines a new certificate or key and encryption algorithm for use with encrypted backups
New-SqlCredential	Creates a Credential object, which is required to back up a database to Windows Azure
New-SqlHADREndpoint	Creates a TCP endpoint, which can be used by availability groups
Remove-SqlAvailabilityDatabase	Removes a database from an AlwaysOn availability group
Remove-SqlAvailabilityGroup	Removes an AlwaysOn availability group
Remove-SqlAvailabilityReplica	Removes a secondary replica from an AlwaysOn availability group
Remove-SqlCredential	Deletes a SQL Credential object
Remove-SqlFirewallRule	Disables a firewall rule (does not delete it)
Restore-SqlDatabase	Used to restore a database

(continued)

Table 2-7. (*continued*)

cmdlet	Description
Resume-SqlAvailabilityDatabase	Used to resume a database that is suspended within an availability group. Sets the state to SYNCHRONIZING
Save-SqlMigrationReport	Evaluates migration suitability of database objects. This feature is new in SQL Server 2016 and, in this first release version, only supports in-memory OLTP migration evaluation.
Set-SqlAuthenticationMode	Toggles the instance authentication mode between Windows and Mixed Mode
Set-SqlAvailabilityGroup	Used to set the properties of an AlwaysOn availability group and to take the availability group online or offline
Set-SqlAvailabilityGroupListener	Used to configure the properties of an availability group listener
Set-SqlAvailabilityReplica	Used to configure the properties of an AlwaysOn availability group replica. For example, it can be used to change the failover mode of a replica.
Set-SqlCredential	Used to configure the properties of a SQL Credential object
Set-SqlHADREndpoint	Alerts an existing TCP endpoint (used by availability groups)
Set-SqlNetworkConfiguration	Configures instance-level network configuration, such as protocol and port
Set-SqlSmartAdmin	Configures the properties of managed backups
Start-SqlInstance	Used to start a SQL Server instance's service
Stop-SqlInstance	Used to stop a SQL Server instance's service
Suspend-SqlAvailabilityDatabase	Used to suspend synchronization for a database that is participating in an AlwaysOn availability group
Switch-SqlAvailabilityGroup	Used to manually failover an AlwaysOn availability group
Test-SqlAvailabilityGroup	Used to assess the health of an AlwaysOn availability group, using PBM
Test-SqlAvailabilityReplica	Used to assess the health of a replica within an AlwaysOn availability group, using PBM
Test-SqlDatabaseReplicaState	Used to assess the health of a database participating in an AlwaysOn availability group, using PBM
Test-SqlSmartAdmin	Used to create custom health messaging for managed backups

Navigating an Instance

As well as navigating a folder structure with commands such as get-childitem and set-location, PowerShell can also be used to navigate the SQL Server object hierarchy of an instance. You can connect PowerShell to the SQL Server database engine provider by using set-location to navigate to SQLSERVER:\SQL. The information returned by get-childitem is dependent on the current location of the object hierarchy. Table 2-8 details what information is returned from each level of the hierarchy.

Table 2-8. *Details Returned at Each Hierarchy Level*

Location	Information Returned
SQLSERVER:\SQL	The name of the local machine
SQLSERVER:\SQL\ComputerName	The names of the database engine instances installed on the local machine
SQLSERVER:\SQL\ComputerName\InstanceName	Instance-level object types
Lower levels	Object types or objects contained within the current location

Once you have navigated to an appropriate level of the hierarchy, you are able to use PowerShell to perform basic operations against objects at that level. For example, the script in Listing 2-15 will navigate to the tables namespace within the AdventureWorks2016 database and rename the dbo.DatabaseLog table to dbo.DatabaseLogPS. The dir commands will display the original name and new name of the table.

Listing 2-15. Navigating Object Hierarchy and Renaming a Table

```
Import-Module sqlps

sl SQLSERVER:\SQL\ESASSMGMT1\MASTERSERVER\DATABASES\ADVENTUREWORKS2016\TABLES

dir | where{$_.name -like "*DatabaseLog*"}

rename-item -LiteralPath dbo.DatabaseLog -NewName DatabaseLogPS

dir | where{$_.name -like "*DatabaseLog*"}
```

■ **Tip** More complex tasks that do not have a specific cmdlet associated with them can be performed through the invoke-sqlcmd cmdlet. This cmdlet is discussed further throughout this book.

It is also possible to start PowerShell from within SSMS (SQL Server Management Studio). To do this, select Start PowerShell from the context menu of an object folder, within Object Explorer. This will cause the PowerShell CLI to be invoked, with the initial location matching the object folder that you used to invoke the CLI.

Summary

PowerShell provides two environments. The Command Line Interface can be used to immediately execute commands, in a similar manner to the Windows Command Prompt. The Integrated Scripting Environment allows you to build complex PowerShell scripts that involve many commands or be scheduled to run automatically.

The PowerShell language is implemented through modules, to make it extensible. Each module contains cmdlets, which provide the functionality. Commonly used cmdlets provide aliases, which can shorten the length of the command you have to type and help new PowerShell users with DOS or LINUX experience to learn the language.

Each variable in PowerShell is an object, with a data type associated with it. Because the objects map to .NET classes, methods such as `ToString()` are available. PowerShell also provides a rich framework for controlling the execution flow of your script. This includes piping, which allows you to pass the results of one command directly into the next.

The `sqlps` module provides support for SQL Server. Once the module has been loaded, it exposes a set of SQL Server–based cmdlets, which allow you to manage SQL Server from the command line or through automated scripts. It also allows you to navigate the object hierarchy of the SQL Server instance and perform basic tasks against objects.

CHAPTER 3

■ ■ ■

SQL Server Agent Multi-Server Environments

SQL Server includes useful features for managing the enterprise that allow you to run queries and policies against multiple instances and run SQL Server Agent jobs on multiple instances. These features are key to your automation efforts, as they provide a mechanism for scheduling and running your scripts across the enterprise.

Using Central Management Servers

A central management server is an instance of SQL Server that has been registered as a controller that will store the connection details for groups of servers. This allows a DBA to run a query or evaluate a policy against multiple instances. Servers must also be registered before they can form part of an SQL Server Agent multi-server environment. The following sections will discuss how to register a central management server and how to create server groups and register servers. You will also learn how central management servers can reduce your administrative overhead.

■ **Note**   Central management servers are a very useful feature, but their greatest limitation is that they are integrated into SSMS (SQL Server Management Studio) and, therefore, can only be used interactively and cannot be referenced in scripts. To script queries that run against multiple servers, you should either use SQL Server Agent multi-server jobs or PowerShell, to orchestrate the process. Using PowerShell to run a script against multiple instances is discussed and demonstrated in Chapter 4.

Registering a Central Management Server

To register a central management server, you will have to navigate to the Registered Servers window in SSMS. This can be found by drilling through View ➤ Registered Servers. Once in the Registered Servers window, select Register Central Management Server from the context menu of the Central Management Servers node. This will cause the New Server Registration dialog box to be displayed. This General tab of the dialog box is illustrated in Figure 3-1.

© Peter A. Carter 2016

P. A. Carter, *Expert Scripting and Automation for SQL Server DBAs*, DOI 10.1007/978-1-4842-1943-0_3

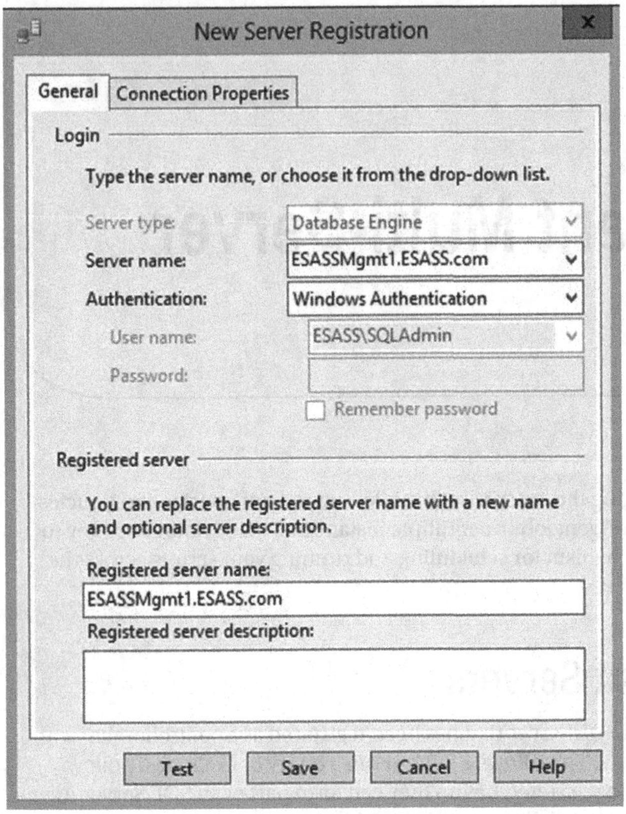

Figure 3-1. *New Server Registration window—General tab*

Here, we have entered the server/instance name of the instance that we want to register as the central management server, in the Server name field, and selected the appropriate authentication method. The Registered Server name column will be automatically populated, but we have the option of changing this name, if we so wish. We can also add a description, which is useful in a large topology, in which multiple central management servers are required.

On the Connection Properties tab of the dialog box, which is illustrated in Figure 3-2, you are able to configure the properties of the connection string that will be used to connect to the central management server. For slow connections, the connection and query time-outs may be extended. An initial catalog (or landing database) can be specified in the Connect to database drop-down, and in the Network section of the tab, you can configure the protocol and packet size to use. Custom colors can be useful when you are working with a mix of production and development or test servers, as you can color coordinate your environments, to avoid the risk of accidently running a test script against production—a mistake you tend never to make more than once in your career! The Encrypt connection check box is selected by default and will cause data to require encryption in transit. The Trust server certificate forces the certificate of the server to be trusted, even if it was not issued by a trusted authority.

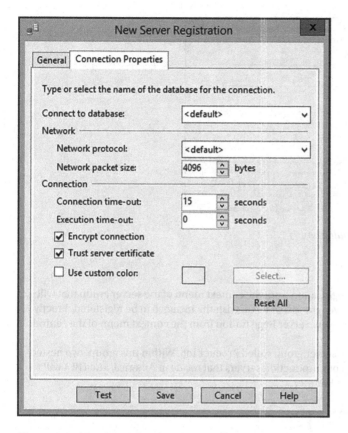

Figure 3-2. *New Server Registration window—Connection Properties tab*

The Test button at the bottom of the dialog box will test the authentication details that you have selected to connect to the central management server. It always makes sense to do this before saving the connection.

Creating Server Groups

If you plan to register many servers under your central management server, it is sensible to organize these servers into logical groups. For example, you will likely create different groups for Production, UAT, and Development. You may also choose to create groups per region or data center. A more granular grouping makes it easy to run a query or evaluate a policy against a targeted group of servers.

It is also possible to nest groups, which adds even more flexibility. For example, you may create a group called Production and then create further groups underneath the Production group, to further organize servers by region. This would allow you to evaluate a policy that checks that xp_cmdshell is disabled against all Production servers in the enterprise. At the same time, if you have a policy that checks the collation of your databases, you could evaluate this policy at the level of region, as each region may require a different standard collation.

To create a group, select New Server Group from the context menu of the central management server. This will cause the New Server Group Properties dialog to be invoked, as displayed in Figure 3-3. To create a nested server group, select New Server Group from the context menu of the server group you wish them to be nested under.

New Server Group Properties

Specify the name and description of the server group.

Group name: Production

Group description: ESProd(x) Servers

| OK | Cancel | Help |

Figure 3-3. New Server Group Properties dialog box

Registering Servers

To register an instance, select New Server Registration from the context menu of the server group that will contain the instance. If you are not using server groups, or if you wish the instance to be registered directly under the central management server, select New Server Registration from the context menu of the central management server.

Figure 3-4 shows that we have created a server group called Production. Within this group, two nested groups have been created. NTAM will contain our production servers that reside in America, and EMEA will contain our production servers that reside in Europe.

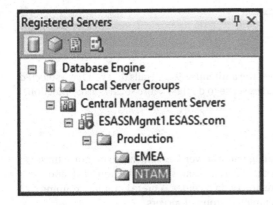

Figure 3-4. Server group hierarchy

We will register our ESPROD1 and ESPROD2 instances under the Production ➤ NTAM server group. As shown in Figure 3-5, the dialog box used to specify the connection details is the same as the dialog box we used to register the central management server.

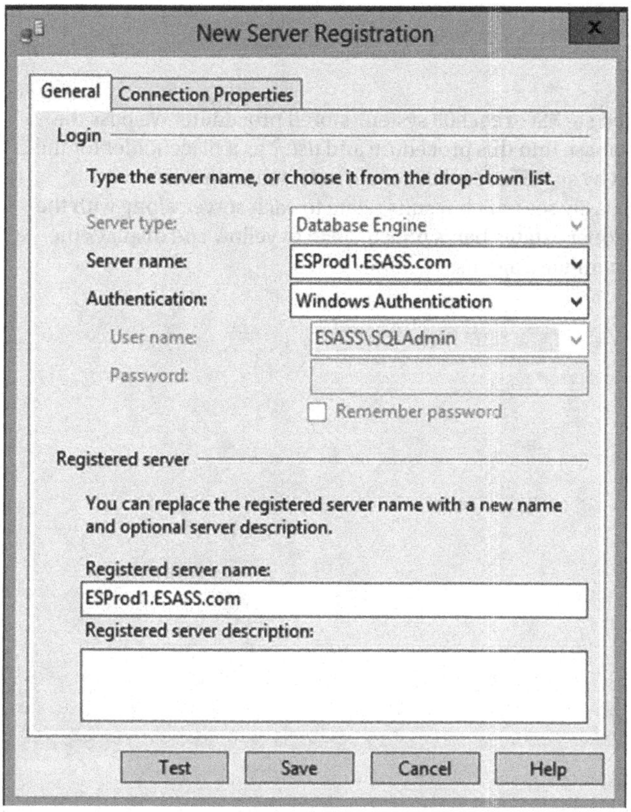

Figure 3-5. *Registering a server*

Using Central Management Servers

After both of our production servers are registered, we can begin to look at the advantages that central management servers can bring. The following sections will demonstrate how central management servers can be used with administrative queries and policies.

Running Queries with Central Management Servers

Imagine a scenario in which you have a number of SQL Server instances, wherein the database files are hosted on a SAN (Storage Area Network). You come into work one morning to find that there has been an issue with the production SAN, and you have to check all databases, on all instances, for corruption. This can be easily achieved, using central management servers.

Because you have a separate SAN for each environment, in each data center, you will only want to check the servers in the NTAM server group, as this is where the SAN issue occurred. Therefore, select New Query from the context menu of the NTAM server group. This will cause a new query window to be displayed, and we will use DBCC CHECKDB to check the consistency of all databases on both instances. This is demonstrated in Listing 3-1.

Listing 3-1. Checking Database Consistency

```
EXEC sp_MSforeachDB 'DBCC CHECKDB (?)' ;
```

This command executes the undocumented sp_MSForeachDB system-stored procedure. We pass the command that we want to run against each database into this procedure and use ? as a placeholder for the database name. This is automatically populated by sp_MSForeachDB for each database, in turn.

Figure 3-6 shows a partial output. You can easily see which results relate to each server, along with the execution context. You may also notice that the query status bar is pink instead of yellow and displays the name of the server group that we can pass the command against.

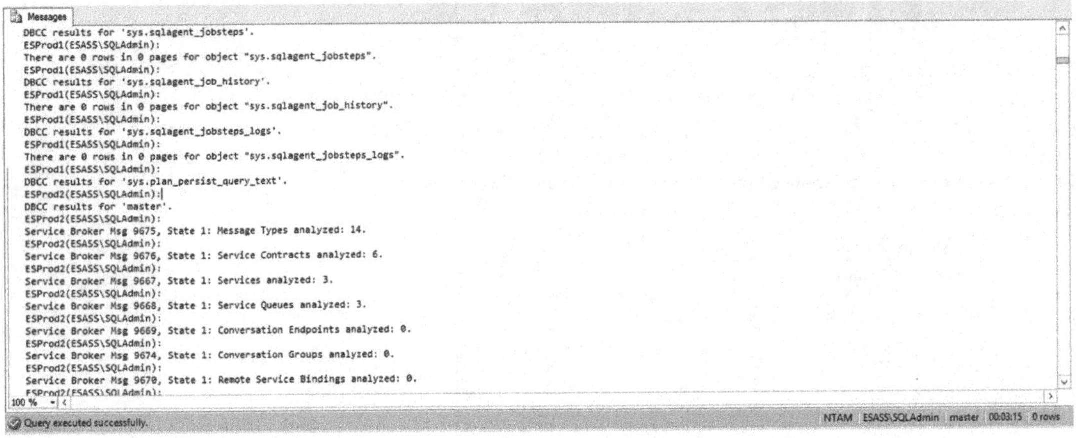

Figure 3-6. *DBCC CHECKDB results*

If you have discovered issues, you may decide to restore some databases. Because the integrity issues are caused by disk problems, you may want to check that all databases have been backed up with a checksum. To do this, we will query the sys.databasescatalog view, as demonstrated in Listing 3-2.

Listing 3-2. Checking Backup Page Verification Option

```
SELECT
        name
        ,recovery_model_desc
        ,page_verify_option_desc
FROM sys.databases ;
```

As you can see from the results, which are illustrated in Figure 3-7, an additional column has been added to the results set, so that the server that the row was generated from can be easily identified.

	Server Name	name	recovery_model_desc	page_verify_option_desc
1	ESProd2.ESASS.com	master	SIMPLE	CHECKSUM
2	ESProd2.ESASS.com	tempdb	SIMPLE	CHECKSUM
3	ESProd2.ESASS.com	model	FULL	CHECKSUM
4	ESProd2.ESASS.com	msdb	SIMPLE	CHECKSUM
5	ESProd2.ESASS.com	AdventureworksDW2016CTP3	SIMPLE	CHECKSUM
6	ESProd1.ESASS.com	master	SIMPLE	CHECKSUM
7	ESProd1.ESASS.com	tempdb	SIMPLE	CHECKSUM
8	ESProd1.ESASS.com	model	FULL	CHECKSUM
9	ESProd1.ESASS.com	msdb	SIMPLE	CHECKSUM
10	ESProd1.ESASS.com	AdventureWorks2016CTP3	SIMPLE	CHECKSUM

Figure 3-7. *Results of checking page verification option*

Evaluating Policies with Central Management Servers

■ **Note** I will assume that you understand the concepts of policy-based management (PBM) in SQL Server and how to create a policy. If you require a refresher, however, full details can be found in *Apress Pro SQL Server Administration*, which can be purchased at `www.apress.com/9781484207116?gtmf=s`.

To evaluate a policy against a server group, you will have to select Evaluate Policies from the context menu of the server group that you wish to evaluate the policy against. This will cause the Evaluate Policies dialog box to be displayed. Here, we can use the ellipse next to the Source field, to invoke the Select Source dialog box, which is illustrated in Figure 3-8.

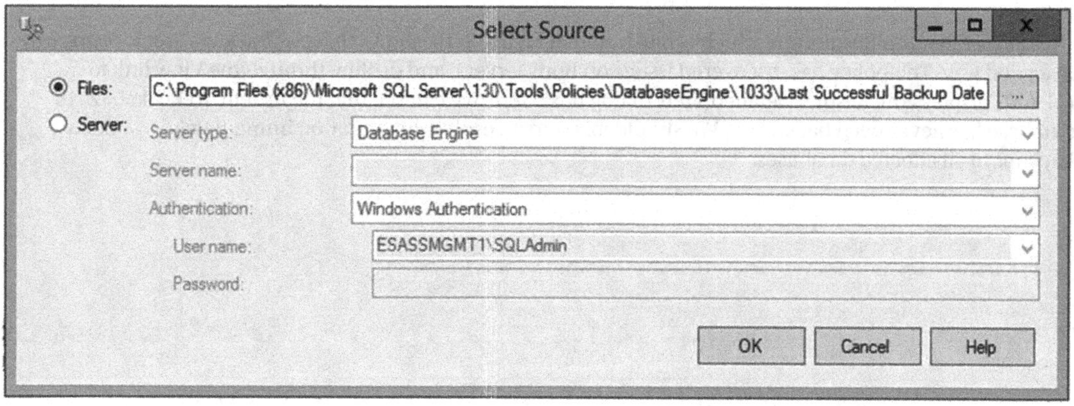

Figure 3-8. *Select Source dialog box*

In this dialog box, you can either connect to an SQL Server instance, or you can select a policy that is stored in the file system. For this demonstration, we will evaluate the Last Successful Backup Date policy, which is stored in the file system.

■ **Tip**   The Last Successful Backup Date policy is part of the best practice policies that are supplied by Microsoft. They will be added to your server when the database engine is installed.

Once we have navigated back to the Evaluate Policies dialog box (Figure 3-9) we can use the Evaluate button to evaluate the policy or policies that we have selected. The results will then be displayed on the Evaluation Results page of the dialog box.

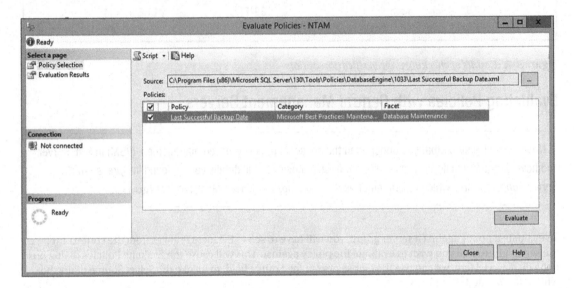

Figure 3-9. *Evaluate Policies dialog box*

The Evaluation Results tab, which is illustrated in Figure 3-10, shows that our backups are not currently in a good way. The policy has discovered issues on both servers, and drilling through the View link to ESPROD2 displays the Results Detailed View dialog box. Here, we can see that the AdventureWorksDW2016 database has never been backed up. We should, of course, resolve this situation immediately, by taking backups of all affected databases.

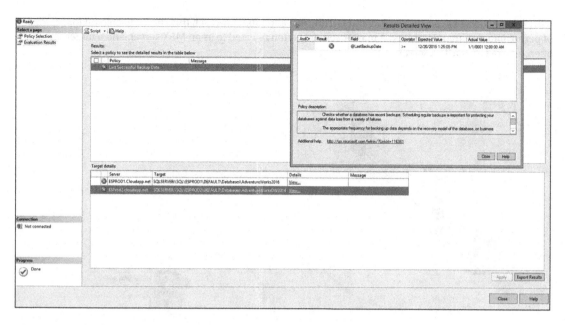

Figure 3-10. *Evaluation results*

PowerShell is a fantastic tool for creating scripts that loop around multiple servers and running commands against each. It even has dedicated cmdlets for working with policies. If you have an ad-hoc requirement, however, and if the script you require can be written entirely in T-SQL, it is much more time efficient to use central management servers as a method of script execution.

■ **Note**   Please refer to Chapter 4 for details of how to iterate through servers and databases, using PowerShell.

Configuring Server Agent for Multi-Server Environments

■ **Tip**   This section will assume that you are familiar with the concepts of Server Agent and experienced in using it on a local machine. If you require a refresher, full implementation details of SQL Server Agent can be found in *Apress Pro SQL Server Administration*, which can be purchased at www.apress.com/9781430239154?gtmf=s.

Multi-server jobs provide a great framework for automated administration, which provides a mechanism for executing your regular maintenance routines across the enterprise. An alternative to using multi-server jobs is to include the server agent jobs in your automated build (if you have one). Using multi-server jobs is a much more maintainable approach, however, because if you have to add, remove, or change a job, you can do so in a central location, as opposed to on every individual instance.

Conceptually, SQL Server Agent multi-server environments have the architecture detailed in Figure 3-11. The diagram shows that a master server stores the master copy of all jobs. Here, you can enlist target servers and configure which jobs will run on which servers. The target servers will periodically poll the master server and download the jobs that they should process. By default, the master and target server use

SSL (Secure Socket Layer) encryption and Certificate validation, however, this can be turned off for reasons of performance or manageability. A master server is often referred to as an MSX server, and a target server is often referred to as a TSX server.

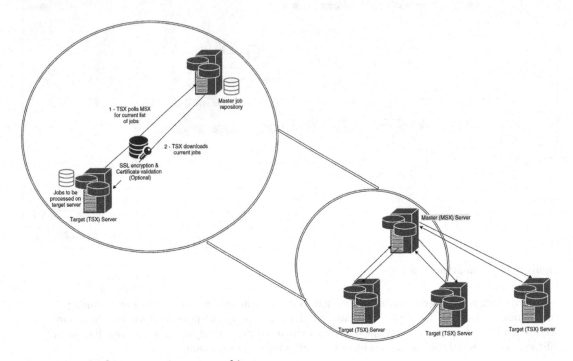

Figure 3-11. *Multi-server environment architecture*

MSDB Roles

As with local jobs, multi-server jobs are secured through database roles in the MSDB database. Table 3-1 provides a permissions matrix for SQL Server Agent roles in MSDB that pertain specifically to multi-server jobs. Tasks that are not possible through any of the roles can only be performed by a member of the sysadmin server role.

Table 3-1. *Multi-Server Permissions Assigned to MSDB Roles*

Permission	SQLAgentUserRole	SQLAgentReaderRole	SQLAgentOperatorRole
CREATE/ALTER/DROP multi-server job	No	No	No
View list of multi-server jobs	No	Yes	Yes
Enable/disable multi-server jobs	No	No	No
View multi-server job properties	No	Yes	Yes
Start/stop multi-server jobs	No	No	No
View multi-server job history	No	Yes	Yes
Delete multi-server job history	No	No	No

Configuring Master and Target Server

In this section, we will configure the ESASSMGMT1 instance as a master server, and we will enlist ESPROD1 and ESPROD2 as target servers. Before we can begin, however, we will have to configure the environment.

Prerequisite Tasks

The first step in this configuration is to edit the registry of the target server(s), to allow jobs on target servers to download and match the name of the Proxy account(s) used to run the job's steps, along with the job itself, from the master server. Failure to follow this step will mean that a Proxy account name cannot be matched, resulting in an error. We will configure this by setting the AllowDownloadedJobsToMatchProxyName REG_DWORD key to 1. This key can be found in the HKLM\Software\Microsoft\Microsoft SQL Server\MSSQL[VERSION NUMBER].[YOUR INSTANCE NAME]\SQL Server Agent key, and we can change the value from within SQL Server, using an undocumented stored procedure called xp_regwrite, as demonstrated in Listing 3-3.

■ **Caution**   The use of undocumented features is not supported by Microsoft, and you may not be able to raise a support case against their usage.

Listing 3-3. Configuring Target Jobs to Match Master Proxy Name

```
USE Master
GO

EXEC xp_regwrite
  @rootkey = N'HKEY_LOCAL_MACHINE'
 ,@key = N'Software\Microsoft\Microsoft SQL Server\MSSQL13.MSSQLSERVER\SQLServerAgent'
  -- If you have a default instance, the instance name is MSSQLSERVER by default
 ,@value_name = N'AllowDownloadedJobsToMatchProxyName'
 ,@type = N'REG_DWORD'
 ,@value = 1 ;
```

■ **Tip**   xp_regwrite will execute under the context of the database engine service account, as opposed to your own security context. Therefore, you must ensure that the account that is running the SQL Server Service has sufficient permissions to modify the registry.

Next, we will have to decide if we wish to use SSL encryption for the communication between the MSX and TSX servers. Encryption is enabled by default, so if it is not required, it will have to be turned off. This means another change to the registry on the target servers. This time, we will set the MsxEncryptChannelOptionsREG_SZ key to 0. This key can be found in HKLM\SOFTWARE\Microsoft\Microsoft SQL Server\MSSQL[VERSION NUMBER].[INSTANCENAME]\SQLServerAgent key. To turn encryption off, you should run the script in Listing 3-4 on each of the target servers.

■ **Tip**   Running a script against multiple servers can be achieved efficiently through the use of a PowerShell script. Chapter 4 demonstrates how to create such a script.

Listing 3-4. Disabling Encryption

```
EXEC xp_regwrite
  @rootkey='HKEY_LOCAL_MACHINE'
  ,@key = N'Software\Microsoft\Microsoft SQL Server\MSSQL13.MSSQLSERVER\SQLServerAgent'
  -- If you have a default instance, the instance name is MSSQLSERVER by default
  ,@value_name='MsxEncryptChannelOptions'
  ,@type='REG_DWORD'
  ,@value= 0 ;
```

Our next task will be to configure a Proxy Account on each instance. This will be used for accessing resources outside of the database engine and to allow us to reduce the security footprint of the account running the SQL Server Agent service. A proxy account maps to a credential, so we will create a credential that maps to a domain user named WinServiceAccount on ESSASMGMT1, by using the script in Listing 3-5. The credential should then be created on ESPROD1 and ESPROD2.

Listing 3-5. Creating a Credential

```
USE master
GO

CREATE CREDENTIAL WinUserCredential
      WITH IDENTITY = 'ESASS\WinServiceAccount'
      , SECRET = 'Pa$$w0rd'
GO
```

This script uses the CREATE CREDENTIAL command. The arguments that can be used with the WITH clause are described in Table 3-2.

Table 3-2. *CREATE CREDENTIAL Arguments*

Argument	Description
IDENTITY	The name of the security principle to which the credential will be mapped
SECRET	The password or secret that is used to authenticate the security principle
FOR CRYPTOGRAPHIC PROVIDER	If you are using Extensible Key Management (EKM), use this argument to provide the name of the EKM provider.

We will now create the Proxy account, which can be used by the PowerShell subsystem, by using the script in Listing 3-6. The script should be run against the MSX server and all TSX servers. This script uses the sp_add_proxy and sp_grant_proxy_to_subsystem system-stored procedures, which are located in the MSDB database. The sp_add_proxy procedure is used to create the proxy and accepts the parameters listed in Table 3-3.

Table 3-3. sp_add_proxy *Parameters*

Parameter	Description
@proxy_name	Defines the name that will be assigned to the new proxy account
@enabled	Specifies if the proxy should be enabled on creation • 0 indicates disabled • 1 indicates enabled
@description	Optionally, provides a textual description of the proxy account
@credential_name	The name of the credential that the proxy will map to. If @credential_id is NULL, this parameter must be specified.
@credential_id	The ID of the credential that the proxy will map to. If @credential_name is NULL, this parameter must be specified.
@proxy_id	An output parameter that provides the ID of the newly created proxy

The sp_grant_proxy_to_subsystem system-stored procedure is used to assign the proxy account permissions to use specific subsystems and accepts the parameters detailed in Table 3-4.

Table 3-4. sp_grant_proxy_to_subsystem *Parameters*

Parameter	Description
@proxy_id	The ID of the Proxy account to assign permissions to. If @proxy_name is NULL, this parameter must be supplied.
@proxy_name	The name of the Proxy account to assign permissions to. If @proxy_id is NULL, this parameter must be supplied.
@subsystem_id	The ID of the subsystem that the proxy should be assigned permissions to. If @subsystem_name is NULL, this parameter must be supplied.
@subsystem_name	The name of the subsystem that the proxy should be assigned permissions to. If @subsystem_id is NULL, this parameter must be supplied.

The mapping of subsystem IDs to subsystem names can be found in Table 3-5.

Table 3-5. *Subsystem ID to Subsystem Name Mappings*

Subsystem ID	Subsystem Name	Description
2	ActiveScripting	Runs ActiveX commands. This subsystem is deprecated and should not be used.
3	CmdExec	Runs operating system commands
4	Snapshot	Runs job steps for the snapshot replication agent
5	LogReader	Runs job steps for the replication log reader agent
6	Distribution	Runs job steps for the replication distribution agent
7	Merge	Runs job steps for the replication merge agent
8	QueueReader	Runs job steps for the replication queue reader agent
9	ANALYSISQUERY	Runs queries against an SSAS (SQL Server Analysis Services) instance
10	ANALYSISCOMMAND	Runs commands against an SSAS instance
11	Dts	Runs SSIS (SQL Server Integration Services) packages
12	PowerShell	Runs PowerShell commands

Listing 3-6. Creating a Proxy

```
USE msdb
GO

EXEC msdb.dbo.sp_add_proxy
        @proxy_name = 'WinUserProxy'
      , @credential_name = 'WinUserCredential'
      , @enabled = 1 ;
GO

EXEC msdb.dbo.sp_grant_proxy_to_subsystem
        @proxy_name = 'WinUserProxy'
      , @subsystem_name = 'PowerShell' ;
GO
```

Configuration Tasks

Now that our prerequisite tasks are complete, we can begin to configure the ESASSMGMT1 instance as the MSX Server. We will first look at how to achieve this through the GUI, before reviewing the system-stored procedures that can be used to achieve the same results.

Selecting Multi Server Administration ➤ Make this a master server, from the context menu of SQL Server Agent in Object Explorer, will cause the Master Server Wizard to be invoked. After passing through the Welcome page of the wizard, you will be presented with the Master Server Operator page, where you will be prompted to enter an e-mail address, pager address, or NET SEND address that will be used to notify an operator of the success or failure of multi-server jobs. It is important to note that multi-server jobs can only have a single operator, so it makes sense to use a distribution list or group mailbox, as opposed to an individual. Pager and NET SEND notifications are deprecated and should not be used. The Master Server Operator page is illustrated in Figure 3-12.

■ **Note**   SQL Server Agent notifications via e-mail rely on Database Mail. This feature should be configured before you test your multi-server topology.

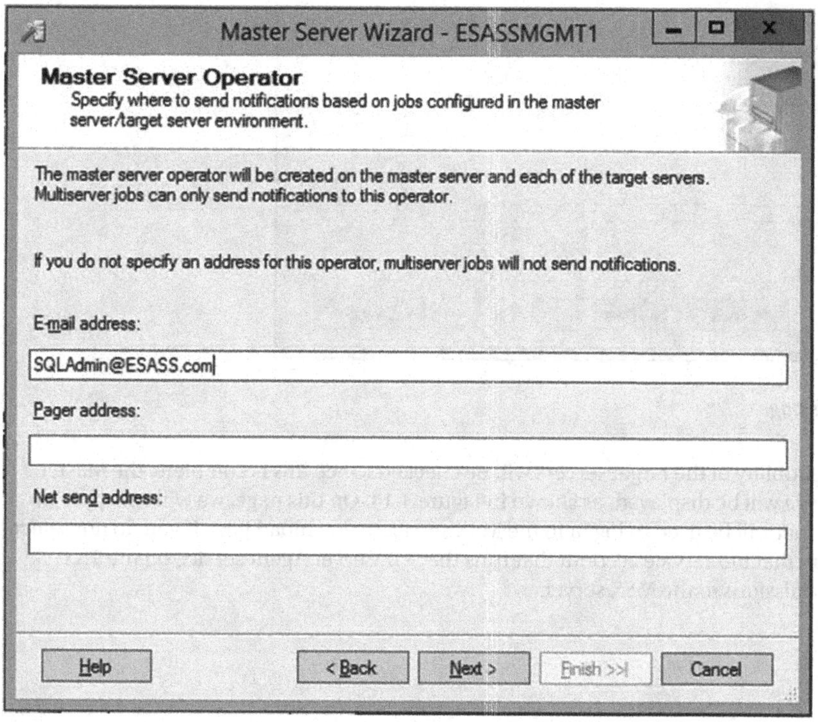

Figure 3-12. *Master Server Operator page*

The Target Servers page of the wizard is illustrated in Figure 3-13. On this page, you will specify the instances that will be enlisted as TSX servers. Because both of the servers that we want to register are in the NTAM server group, we can select the NTAM server group and use the right arrow to move all servers within that group.

Figure 3-13. Target Servers page

At this point, the compatibility of the target servers will be checked. Once this is complete, the Master Server Login Credentials page will be displayed, as shown in Figure 3-14. On this page, we will specify if an account should be created that will be used to log in to the MSX server, to download jobs. If you do not select this option, you must ensure that the service account that runs the SQL Server Agent service on the TSX servers has appropriate permissions to the MSX server.

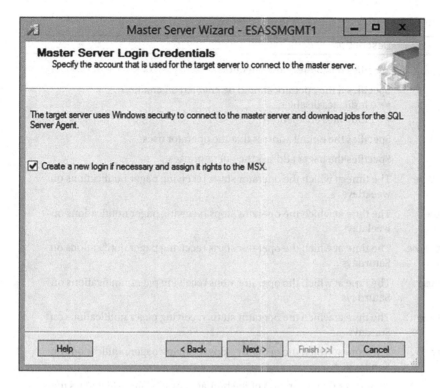

Figure 3-14. *Master Server Login Credentials page*

The complete Wizard page will provide a summary of the actions to be performed. After choosing Finish, the progress of each task will be displayed in real time.

To perform the tasks with T-SQL, we will enlist the server with the sp_msx_enlist and sp_add_operator system-stored procedures, which are located in the MSDB database. The parameters accepted by the sp_msx_enlist stored procedure are detailed in Table 3-6.

Table 3-6. *sp_msx_enlist Parameters*

Parameter	Description
@msx_server_name	The name of the instance that will become the MSX server
@location	Optionally, specifies the location of the MSX server

The sp_add_operator stored procedure accepts the parameters detailed in Table 3-7.

Table 3-7. sp_add_operator Parameters

Parameter	Description
@name	Specifies the name of the operator
@enabled	Specifies if the operator should be enabled on creation • 0 indicates disabled. • 1 indicates enabled.
@email_address	Specifies the e-mail address that the operator uses
@pager_address	Specifies the pager address the operator uses
@weekday_pager_start_time	The time at which the operator starts receiving pager notifications on weekdays
@weekday_pager_end_time	The time at which the operator stops receiving pager notifications on weekdays
@saturday_pager_start_time	The time at which the operator starts receiving pager notifications on Saturdays
@saturday_pager_end_time	The time at which the operator stops receiving pager notifications on Saturdays
@sunday_pager_start_time	The time at which the operator starts receiving pager notifications on Sundays.
@sunday_pager_end_time	The time at which the operator stops receiving pager notifications on Sundays
@pager_days	An integer representation of the bitmap that specifies which days the operator receives notifications. The following values represent each day: • 1 indicates Sunday • 2 indicates Monday • 4 indicates Tuesday • 8 indicates Wednesday • 16 indicates Thursday • 32 indicates Friday • 64 indicates Saturday When an operator is active for multiple days, these values should be added together. For example, if an operator should only receive notifications on Saturdays and Sundays, the value 96 should be passed to this parameter.
@netsend_address	The network address used by the operator
@category_name	Optimally, specifies a category to which the operator belongs

■ **Note** Table 3-7 includes details of pager and NET SEND–related parameters. Both of these notification methods are deprecated, however, so you should avoid using them.

The sp_msx_enlist procedure is also used to bring TSX servers under management, after the MSX server has been enlisted. Listing 3-7 demonstrates how these system-stored procedures can be used to configure the ESASSMGMT1 instance as an MSX Server and enlist ESPROD1 and ESPROD2 instances as TSX servers.

■ **Tip**   The script in Listing 3-7 must be run in SQLCMD mode, as it connects to multiple servers. If you have many servers that you must enlist, you could create a PowerShell script that loops around each required instance. This methodology is discussed in Chapter 4.

Listing 3-7. Enlisting the MSX Server

```
:connect ESASSMGMT1

USE MSDB
GO

EXEC msdb.dbo.sp_add_operator
                @name = 'MSXOperator2'
            ,  @enabled = 1
            ,  @email_address = 'SQLAdmin@ESASS.com' ;

EXEC sp_msx_enlist
        @msx_server_name = 'ESASSMGMT1'
, @location = 'NTAM - MGMT network block' ;

:connect ESPROD1

USE MSDB
GO

sp_msx_enlist
        @msx_server_name = 'ESASSMGMT1'
, @location = 'NTAM - PROD network block' ;

:connect ESPROD2

USE MSDB
GO

sp_msx_enlist
        @msx_server_name = 'ESASSMGMT1'
, @location = 'NTAM - PROD network block' ;
```

Creating Multi-Server Jobs

Multi-server jobs are created much like normal jobs, with the exception of specifying a list of target servers on which they should run. For example, imagine that we want to create a job that will run a PowerShell script on each target server, to ensure that all SQL Server–related services are running. The job should alert the MSXOperator if any services are not in a running state. The job will consist of a single job step, which runs a PowerShell script, shown in Listing 3-8.

Listing 3-8. CheckSQLServices.ps1

```
# Return SQL Server services to a variable, if they are not running

$services = Get-Service | where{$_.Name -like "*SQL*" -and $_.Status -ne "Running" }

# If the variable is non-empty, write a list of services that are not running and force the
script to fail

IF ($services.Length -gt 0)
{
write-warning "Warning! The following Services are not running"
    foreach ($service in $services)
{
write-warning $service.Name
}
    write-error "Please check services and start as required" -EA stop
}
```

■ **Tip**   Passing stop to the -EA parameter forces the error to terminate the script.

Creating the Job in Object Explorer

We will create the job using the New Job dialog box, which can be accessed by selecting New Job, from the context menu of SQL Server Agent, then Jobs ➤ Multi-Server Jobs in Object Explorer. On the general page of the wizard, which is illustrated in Figure 3-15, we will provide a name and owner for the job, as well as specifying the category. Because we are creating a multi-server job, the category will default to Uncategorized (Multi-server). We will also ensure that the Enabled check box is selected, so that our job will be enabled on creation.

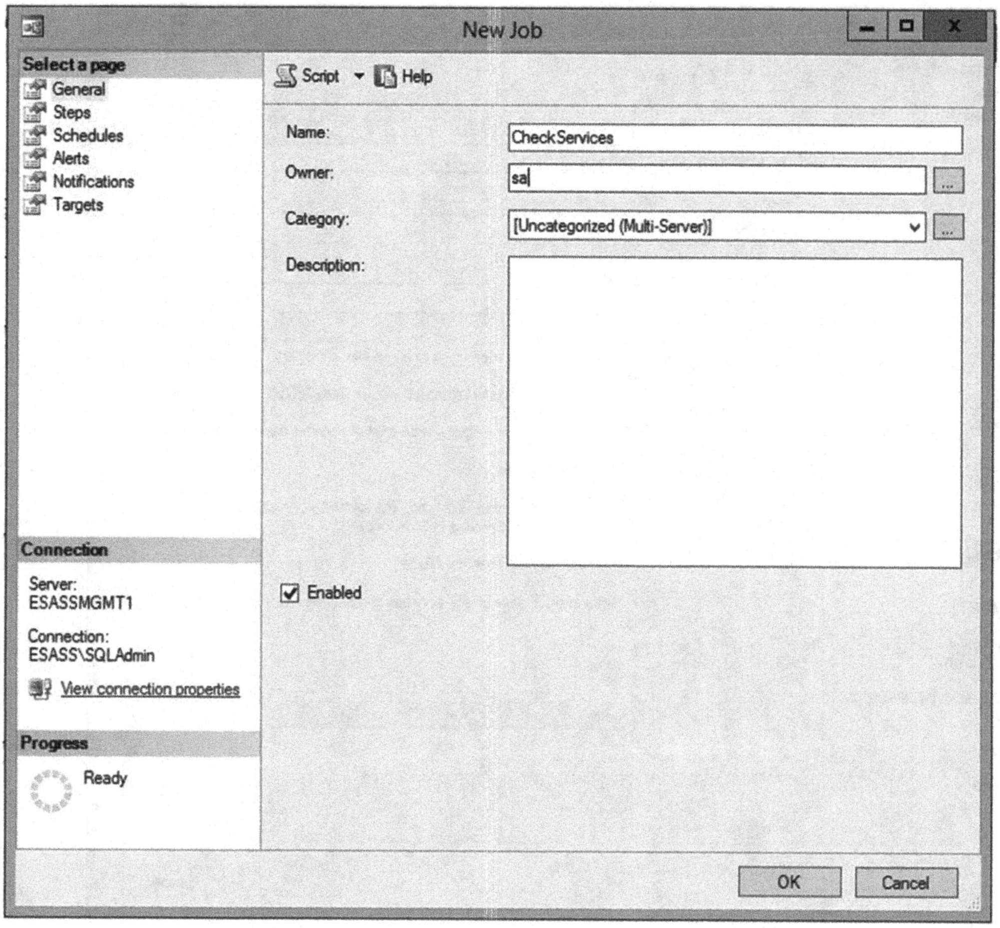

Figure 3-15. *General page*

On the Steps page of the wizard, we will use the New button to invoke the New Job Step dialog box. The General page of the New Job Step dialog box is illustrated in Figure 3-16. On this page, we have provided a name for the job step, specified the subsystem that will be used in the job step, selected the account that will be used to run the job step, and, finally, pasted our PowerShell script into the Command window.

■ **Tip** Selecting the job step type causes the page to be dynamically refreshed, revealing the appropriate options for the selected subsystem.

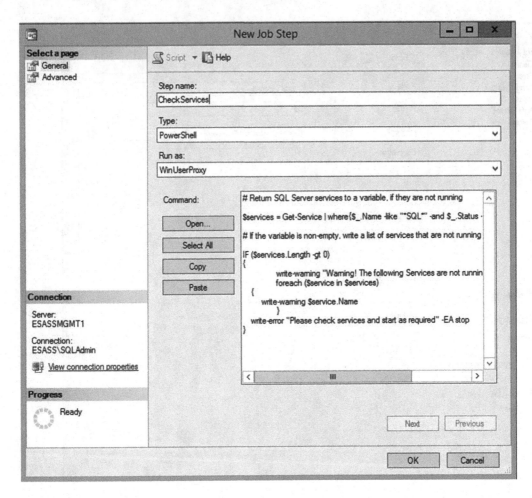

Figure 3-16. *New Job Step—General page*

The Advanced page of the New Job Step dialog box allows you to define the flow control of your job, which is useful when you have multiple steps, especially if some steps perform error handling for previous steps. Essentially, configuring the options on the Advanced page for each job step allows you to create a decision tree for your job steps.

As our job will have a single step, our requirements on this page are minimal. As shown in Figure 3-17, we have specified that if the step succeeds, the job will quit, returning success, and if it fails, the job will quit with failure. Because our PowerShell script generates a terminating error if any SQL Server–related services are not running, the job will also fail. We can then configure the MSXOperator to be notified. We have also specified that the output of the job step should be recorded in the job history.

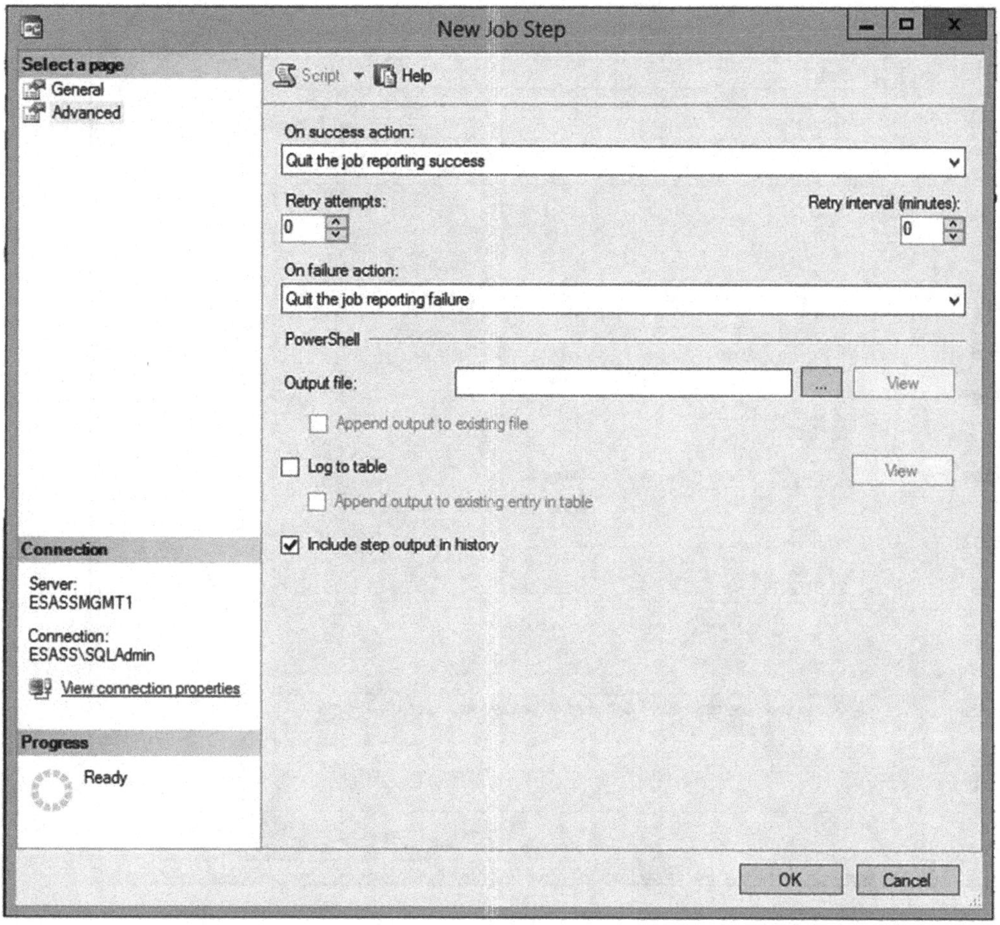

Figure 3-17. *New Job Step—Advanced page*

On the Schedules page of the New Job dialog box, we will use the New button to invoke the New Job Schedule dialog box and create a new schedule, which will run on a daily basis. As illustrated in Figure 3-18, we will name the schedule Daily and configure it to run at midnight every night.

■ **Tip** Changing the schedule frequency will cause the dialog box to be dynamically updated with the appropriate options.

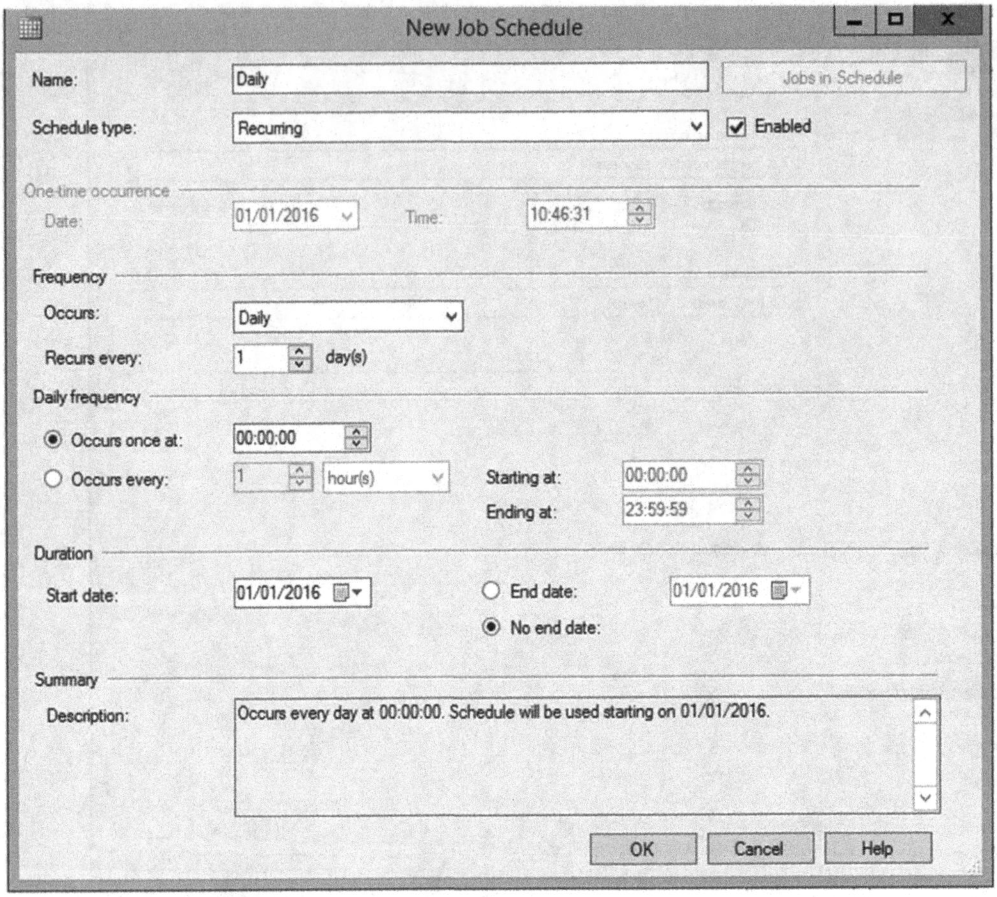

Figure 3-18. *New Job Schedule dialog box*

As shown in Figure 3-19, we will use the Notifications page of the New Job dialog box to configure the MSXOperator operator to be notified in the event that the job fails. This makes managing service checks easy, as the operator will only be notified in the event of a service not being in a running state.

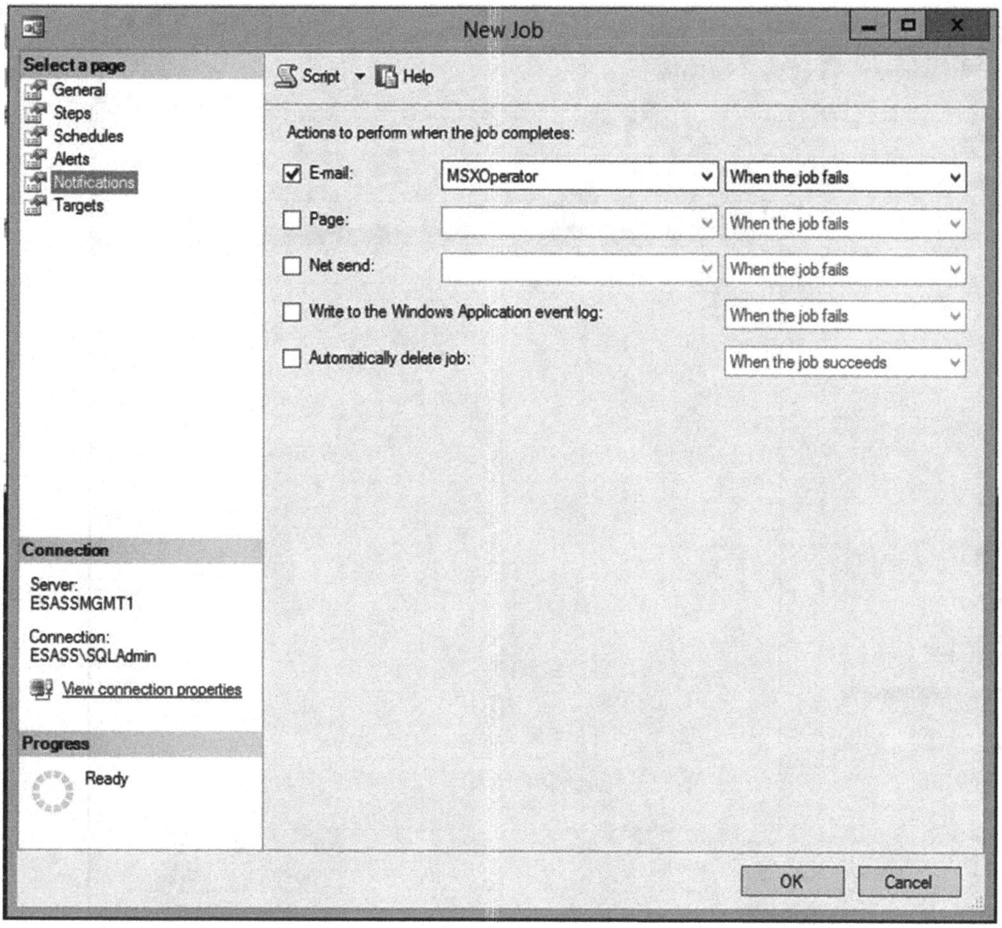

Figure 3-19. *Notifications page*

On the Targets page of the New Job dialog box, we will specify which of our TSX servers we want the job to run against. We would like this specific job to run against both of our target servers, so we will select both of them, as shown in Figure 3-20.

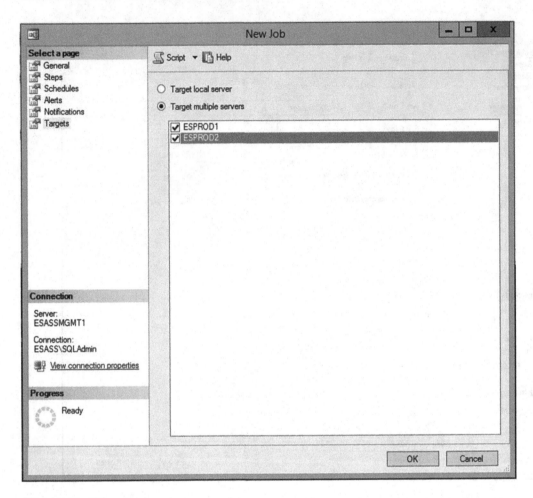

Figure 3-20. *Targets page*

Creating the Job with T-SQL

To use T-SQL to create the CheckServices job, we will have to use the sp_add_job, sp_add_jobserver, sp_
add_job_step, and sp_add_job_schedule system-stored procedures. All of these procedures can be located
in the MSDB database.

The sp_add_job procedure accepts the parameters detailed in Table 3-8.

Table 3-8. sp_add_job *Parameters*

Parameter	Description
@job_name	Specifies a name for the job
@enabled	Specifies if the job should be enabled on creation • 0 indicates disabled • 1 indicates enabled
@description	A textual description of the job
@start_step_id	The job step ID of the step that should be the first step executed
@category_name	Specifies the name of the category in which the job should be included
@category_id	Specifies the ID of the category in which the job should be included
@owner_login_name	Specifies the login that will own the job
@notify_level_eventlog	Specifies when the job status should be written to the Windows Application Event Log: • 0 indicates Never • 1 indicates On Success • 2 indicates On Failure • 3 indicates Always
@notify_level_email	Specifies when the job status should be sent as an e-mail notification: • 0 indicates Never • 1 indicates On Success • 2 indicates On Failure • 3 indicates Always
@notify_level_netsend	Specifies when the job status should be sent as a NET SEND notification: • 0 indicates Never • 1 indicates On Success • 2 indicates On Failure • 3 indicates Always
@notify_level_page	Specifies when the job status should be sent as a pager notification: • 0 indicates Never • 1 indicates On Success • 2 indicates On Failure • 3 indicates Always
@notify_email_operator_name	The name of the operator that should be notified via e-mail
@notify_netsend_operator_name	The name of the operator that should be notified via NETSEND
@notify_page_operator_name	The name of the operator that should be notified via pager
@delete_level	Specifies what status should result in the job being deleted: • 0 indicates Never • 1 indicates On Success • 2 indicates On Failure • 3 indicates Always
@job_id	An OUTPUT parameter that returns the ID of the job

■ **Note** For completeness, Table 3-8 details parameters used for configuring NET SEND and Pager notifications. These notification types are deprecated and should not be used.

We will use this procedure to create the CheckServices job, using the script in Listing 3-9.

Listing 3-9. Creating the Job

```
USE msdb
GO

EXEC msdb.dbo.sp_add_job
                @job_name = 'CheckServices'
                , @enabled = 1
                , @notify_level_email = 2
                , @category_name = '[Uncategorized (Multi-Server)]'
                , @owner_login_name = 'sa'
                , @notify_email_operator_name = 'MSXOperator' ;
GO
```

The sp_add_jobserver system-stored procedure accepts the parameters detailed in Table 3-9.

Table 3-9. sp_add_jobserver Parameters

Parameter	Description
@job_id	The GUID of the job. If omitted, @job_name must be specified.
@job_name	The name of the job. If omitted, @job_id must be specified.
@server_name	The name of the server on which you are registering the job

We will use the sp_add_jobserver procedure to target our job against the two TSX servers. The procedure has to be executed for every server the job will be targeted against. This is demonstrated in Listing 3-10.

Listing 3-10. Targeting the Job

```
USE msdb
GO

EXEC msdb.dbo.sp_add_jobserver
                @job_name = 'CheckServices'
                , @server_name = 'ESPROD1' ;
GO

EXEC msdb.dbo.sp_add_jobserver
                @job_name='CheckServices'
                , @server_name = 'ESPROD2' ;
GO
```

The `sp_add_job_step` system-stored procedure accepts the parameters detailed in Table 3-10.

Table 3-10. `sp_add_jobstep` *Parameters*

Parameter	Description
@job_id	Specifies the GUID of the job. If omitted, the @job_name parameter must be specified.
@job_name	Specifies the name of the job. If omitted, the @job_id parameter must be specified.
@step_id	The sequential ID of the job step within the job. This is used to define the order of the steps.
@step_name	Specifies a name for the job step
@subsystem	Specifies the subsystem to use for the job step. Table 3-4 lists the acceptable values.
@command	The command that should be executed
@cmdexec_success_code	The success code expected to be returned from the operating system
@on_success_action	Specifies the action that should be performed if the step succeeds: • 1 indicates Quit With Success • 2 indicates Quit With Failure • 3 indicates Go To Next Step • 4 indicates that the next step to be executed is specified by @on_success_step_id
@on_success_step_id	The step ID of the next step to be executed if a value of 4 has been passed to @on_success_action
@on_fail_action	Specifies the action that should be performed if the step fails: • 1 indicates Quit With Success • 2 indicates Quit With Failure • 3 indicates Go To Next Step • 4 indicates that the next step to be executed is specified by @on_success_step_id
@on_fail_step_id	The step ID of the next step to be executed, if a value of 4 has been passed to @on_fail_action
@database_name	If the subsystem is T-SQL, specifies the database name in which to execute the command
@database_user_name	If the subsystem is T-SQL, specifies the database user to use as the security context for executing the command
@retry_attempts	Specifies how many times the step should be retried in the event of failure
@retry_interval	Specifies an interval between retries in the event of failure
@output_file_name	Specifies the fully qualified file name of a file in which the output of the step should be saved

(continued)

71

Table 3-10. (*continued*)

Parameter	Description
@flags	Controls the behavior of the step output: • 0 indicates that the output file should be overwritten • 2 indicates that the output should be appended to the output file • 4 indicates that T-SQL job step output should be written to the step history • 8 indicates that the log should be written to a table and overwrite existing entries • 16 indicates that the log should be appended to the log table • 32 indicates that all output should be written to the job history • 64 indicates that a Windows event should be created to use as an abort signal when the subsystem is cmdexec
@proxy_id	The ID of the proxy that should run the job step
@proxy_name	The name of the proxy that should run the job step

We will use the sp_add_jobstep procedure to add our PowerShell job step, by using the script in Listing 3-11.

Listing 3-11. Creating the Job Step

```
USE msdb
GO

EXEC msdb.dbo.sp_add_jobstep
                @job_name = 'CheckServices'
            , @step_name = 'CheckServicesRunning'
            , @step_id = 1
            , @on_success_action = 1
            , @on_fail_action = 2
            , @subsystem = 'PowerShell'
            , @command = ' # Return SQL Server services to a variable,
        #if they are not running

$services = Get-Service | where{$_.Name -like "*SQL*" -and $_.Status -ne "Running" }

# If the variable is non-empty, write a list of services
        # that are not running and force the script to fail

IF ($services.Length -gt 0)
{
        write-warning "Warning! The following Services are not running"
        foreach ($service in $services)
{
write-warning $service.Name
        }
write-error "Please check services and start as required" -EA stop
}'
                , @flags = 32
                , @proxy_name = 'WinUserProxy' ;
GO
```

The sp_add_jobschedule procedure accepts the parameters detailed in Table 3-11.

Table 3-11. sp_add_jobschedule Parameters

Parameter	Description
@job_id	The ID of the job to which the schedule will be attached. This must be specified if @job_name is NULL.
@job_name	The name of the job to which the schedule will be attached. This must be specified if @job_id is NULL.
@name	Specifies a name for the schedule
@enabled	Specifies if the schedule should be enabled on creation: • 0 indicates disabled. • 1 indicates enabled
@freq_type	Specifies the type of schedule to use: • 1 indicates it should run once • 4 indicates it should run daily • 8 indicates weekly • 16 indicates monthly • 32 indicates it should run monthly, relative to @freq_interval and @freq_relative_interval—for example, every first Tuesday of the month • 64 indicates it should run when SQL Server Agent starts • 128 indicates that it should run when the server is idle
@freq_interval	Specifies when the schedule should run relative to the type of schedule used. Table 3-12 contains details of how to calculate this value.
@freq_subday_type	Specifies how frequently, within a day, the schedule should run, in relation to the subday interval
@freq_subday_interval	The frequency, within a day, that the schedule should run. For example, if @frequency_subday is configured as hours and @frequency_subday_interval is configured as 2, the schedule will run every two hours.
@freq_relative_interval	When a schedule is monthly, relative (32), this parameter is used in conjunction with @freq_interval to calculate the day of the month that it runs: • 1 indicates the first day of the month • 2 indicates the second • 4 indicates the third • 8 indicates the fourth • 16 indicates the last For example, if @freq_type is 32, @freq_relative_interval is 1, and @freq_interval is 4, the schedule runs on the first Tuesday of the month. This is because 1 for @freq_relative_interval implies "the first," and 4 for @freq_interval implies Tuesday.
@freq_recurrence_factor	For schedules that run weekly and monthly (relative to frequency interval), this specifies the number of weeks or months between executions.
@active_start_date	Specifies the date that the job is first scheduled to run
@active_end_date	Specifies the date that the job stops being scheduled
@active_start_time	Specifies the time that the job is first scheduled to run
@active_end_time	Specifies the time that the job stops being scheduled
@schedule_id	An OUTPUT parameter that returns the ID of the schedule

Table 3-12 describes how to calculate the value for @frequency_interval, based on the value supplied for @frequency_type.

Table 3-12. @frequency_interval *Values*

@frequency_type value	Usage of @frequency_interval
4	Specifies the number of days that should elapse before the schedule repeats. For example, 5 would mean the schedule runs every five days.
8	Specifies the day(s) of the week: • 1 for Sunday • 2 for Monday • 4 for Tuesday • 8 for Wednesday • 16 for Thursday • 32 for Friday • 64 for Saturday The value is a bitmask converted to an int, so if multiple days of the week are required, combine the values with a bitwise OR operator. For example, to run every weekday, the value would be 62. The math here is 2 (Mon) + 4 (Tue) + 8 (Wed) + 16 (Thur) + 32 (Fri) = 62.
16	Specifies the day (number) of the month
32	Specifies the day of the week: • 1 for Sunday • 2 for Monday • 3 for Tuesday • 4 for Wednesday • 5 for Thursday • 6 for Friday • 7 for Saturday • 8 for day • 9 for weekday • 10 for weekend day

We will use the sp_add_jobschedule procedure to create our Daily schedule and attach it to our job. The script in Listing 3-12 demonstrates this.

Listing 3-12. Creating the Job Schedule

```
USE msdb
GO

EXEC msdb.dbo.sp_add_jobschedule
                @job_name = 'CheckServices'
              , @name = 'Daily'
              , @enabled = 1
              , @freq_type = 4
              , @freq_interval = 1
              , @freq_subday_type = 1
              , @freq_subday_interval = 0
```

```
        , @freq_relative_interval = 0
        , @freq_recurrence_factor = 1
        , @active_start_date = 20160101
        , @active_end_date = 99991231
        , @active_start_time = 0
        , @active_end_time = 235959 ;
GO
```

Limitations of the PowerShell Job Step

The PowerShell subsystem is very powerful and allows your SQL Server Agent jobs to interact with external resources in a cleaner way than using the cmdexec subsystem. It does have limitations, as compared to using PowerShell interactively, or via scheduling scripts via alternative means.

Firstly, cmdlets such as write-host and write-debug cannot be used. This is because SQL Server Agent uses the SQLPS.exe stub to execute the commands, and this does not use a console. To return information to the job step, you have to use write-output or write-error.

Assemblies are not pre-loaded. Therefore, if you have to use an assembly, such as Microsoft. AnalysisServices or Microsoft.SharePoint.PowerShell, they must be manually loaded.

If your job step uses the sqlps module, a process will be spawned that consumes around 20MB of memory. Therefore, you should limit the number of concurrent jobs that run PowerShell job steps, to avoid performance issues.

Additionally, there is no scripting environment provided. This, combined with the limitations mentioned, means that you should create and test your scripts using the PowerShell ISE before testing them again inside your SQL Server Agent job.

Summary

Central Management Servers allow you to simplify administration, by registering servers, within groups, so that queries can be run or policies evaluated across a number of related servers at the same time. Servers must also be registered to allow an SQL Server Agent multi-server topology to be created.

Multi-server jobs are an important part of your overall automation strategy, as they provide the framework for running SQL Server Agent jobs across the enterprise. Just as with local jobs, a variety of subsystems are available, including T-SQL, operating system commands (cmdexec), SSIS packages (DTS), and PowerShell.

The ability to run PowerShell scripts from an SQL Server Agent job provides great power and flexibility. There are limitations, however, when compared to running PowerShell scripts by other methods. These limitations include the inability to use commands that require a console, such as write-host, and the potential performance implications caused by many concurrent jobs using the sqlps module.

CHAPTER 4

■ ■ ■

Metadata-Driven Automation

Metadata is data that describes other data. SQL Server exposes a large amount of metadata. This includes structural metadata, which describes every object, and descriptive metadata, which describes the data itself. Metadata is exposed through catalog views, information schema views, dynamic management views, dynamic management functions, system functions, and stored procedures. Metadata is the key to automation, as it allows you to create dynamic, intelligent scripts.

I will assume that you are familiar with basic metadata objects, such as `sys.tables` and `sys.databases`. Instead, this chapter will focus on interrogating some less commonly known metadata objects that can prove very useful to DBAs. It will demonstrate how these metadata objects can be used to play a key role in automating maintenance routines. It is important to remember, however, that a discussion of all metadata objects available within SQL Server would be worthy of several volumes in its own right. Therefore, I suggest that you do your own research on SQL Server metadata and identify objects that will prove useful to your individual environment. A good place to start is the Dynamic Management Views and Functions page on MSDN, which can be found at `https://msdn.microsoft.com/en-us/library/ms188754.aspx`.

Creating Intelligent Routines

The following sections will demonstrate how SQL Server metadata can be used, in conjunction with PowerShell, to write intelligent routines that can be used to make your enterprise more consistent and better-performing, with less DBA effort. I will discuss configuring consistent port numbers, profiling instance workloads, using query store metadata, dynamic index rebuilds, and enforcing policies that cannot be enforced using Policy-Based Management.

Configuring a Consistent Port Number

Assuming an instance is configured to use TCP, a default instance of SQL Server will automatically be configured to use Port 1433. (Named instances will be configured to use a dynamic port.) Many DBAs choose to change the port number to a number that is not commonly known. This is a security measure that helps to slow down potential attackers, who may be looking to exploit port 1433. It is also considered good practice in some organizations to avoid using the SQL Browser service. While I do not usually recommend turning off the SQL Browser service, in environments in which this is the policy, I recommend using a consistent port number across all servers, to ease both application development and operational support.

The port number that an instance is running on can be found by looking in the SQL Server log, just after the instance has started, or, more conveniently, it is also exposed through the `sys.dm_server_registry` DMV. This DMV returns the columns detailed in Table 4-1.

P. A. Carter, *Expert Scripting and Automation for SQL Server DBAs*, DOI 10.1007/978-1-4842-1943-0_4

Table 4-1. sys.dm_server_registry *Columns*

Column	Description
Registry_key	The name of the registry key
Value_name	The name of the key's value
Value_data	The data contained within the value

The script in Listing 4-1 will iterate through the instances within your SQL Server enterprise and check their port number configuration. It will then alert you if there is an instance configured to listen on the incorrect port. The ServerInstance parameter of the invoke-sqlcmd cmdlet should be specified as server\instance for named instances and simply server for default instances.

■ **Note**   The script in Listing 4-1 pulls a list of server names from an array. In a real-world scenario, these server names would be pulled from your inventory database. Creating an inventory database and using it to assist with the automation effort is discussed in depth in Chapter 6.

Listing 4-1. Checking Port Configuration

```
import-module sqlps

$Port = "6152"

[array]$Servers = "ESASSMGMT1", "ESPROD1", "ESPROD2"

foreach ($Server in $Servers)
{
    s$Results = invoke-sqlcmd -ServerInstance "$Server" -User "sa" -Password "Pa$$w0rd"
    -Query "SELECT *
FROM (
        SELECT
        CASE
                WHEN value_name = 'TcpPort' AND value_data <> ''
                        THEN value_data
                WHEN value_name = 'TcpPort' AND value_data = ''
                        THEN (
                                SELECT value_data
                                FROM sys.dm_server_registry
                                WHERE registry_key LIKE '%ipall'
                                        AND value_name = 'TcpDynamicPorts'
                                                        )
        END PortNumber
        FROM sys.dm_server_registry
        WHERE registry_key LIKE '%IPAll' ) a
    WHERE a.PortNumber IS NOT NULL ;"
```

```
IF ($Results.PortNumber -ne $Port)
    {
        "The default instance on " + $Server + " is incorrectly configured to listen on
        Port " + $Results.PortNumber
    }

}
"All other instances are correctly configured"
```

■ **Note**   The script will only work if your instance has the default network configuration, which uses IPAll. If the instance is listening on multiple IP addresses, then there will be no port configuration for IPAll.

The script begins by importing the sqlps module, which will allow us to use the invoke-sqlcmd cmdlet. The script then assigns a port number and defines a list of servers. These values would be pulled from your inventory database in a real-world scenario.

The script then uses a foreach loop, to iterate through every server in the array. It runs a query against each instance, which returns the current port number for that instance. The query runs against the sys.dm_server_registry DMV and attempts to return the static port number that is registered against IPAll. If this value is blank, it means that the instance is configured to use dynamic ports and, instead, returns the TCP dynamic port number.

Finally, the script uses an IF statement to determine if the instance's port number matches the value stored in the $Port variable. If they do not match, it displays a warning.

The invoke-sqlcmd cmdlet operates in a very similar manner to SQLCMD in the command line and can be used to run scripts against an SQL Server instance. While the functionality is very similar, not all functionality has been implemented, as it is not required in the richer PowerShell environment. Table 4-2 lists the parameters that are not implemented in invoke-sqlcmd.

Table 4-2. *Parameters Not Implemented*

Parameter	Description
-r	Outputs messages to stderr
-R	Uses client's regional settings
-q	Runs the specified query and remains running
-f	Codes page to use for output data
-z	Changes a password and remains running
-a	Packet size
-s	Column separator
-h	Controls output headers
-k	Specifies control characters
-Y	Fixed-length display width
-y	Variable length display width
-e	Echo input
-I	Enables quoted identifiers

(*continued*)

Table 4-2. (*continued*)

Parameter	Description
-W	Removes trailing spaces
-L	Lists instances
-u	Formats output as Unicode
-p	Prints statistics
-c	Command end
-E	Connects using Windows Authentication

■ **Tip** It is worth noting that some of the parameters are case-sensitive.

There are also two parameters that are new in the invoke-sqlcmd implementation that did not appear in the command-line version of SQLCMD. These parameters are listed in Table 4-3.

Table 4-3. *New Parameters*

Parameter	Description
-EncryptConnection	Connects using SSL encryption.
-OutputSqlErrors	Displays errors

Table 4-4 provides a description of the remaining invoke-sqlcmd parameters.

Table 4-4. *invoke-sqlcmd Parameters*

Parameter	Description
-ServerInstance	The server\instance name for invoke-sqlcmd to connect to
-Database	The landing database
-Query	The query or script that should be run against the database
-Username	When using second-tier authentication, specifies the security principle to use
-Password	When second-tier authentication is used, specifies the password associated with the security principle
-Variable	Specifies variable values that should be passed into the script
-QueryTimeout	Specifies the query time-out interval
-AbortOnError	Terminates the script in the event of an error
-DedicatedAdministratorConnection	Connects using the DAC, which is the "emergency door" into an SQL Server instance that is otherwise inaccessible
-DisableCommands	Disables interactive commands, startup script, and environment variables
-DisableVariables	Disables variable substitution
-SeverityLevel	Specifies the minimum severity level that should be reported

(*continued*)

Table 4-4. (*continued*)

Parameter	Description
-ErrorLevel	Specifies the minimum error level that should be reported
-ConnectionTimeout	Specifies the login time-out interval
-HostName	Specifies the hostname that the script will run on
-NewPassword	Changes the password and exits
-InputFile	Specifies the name and location of a file containing an SQLCMD script that you wish to execute
-MaxCharLength	Specifies the maximum length of character output
-MaxBinaryLength	Specifies the maximum length of binary output

■ **Tip**   An important note about invoke-sqlcmd is that the -variable parameter is expecting an array. This provides the ability to pass multiple scripting variables. Therefore, in order to pass scripting variables from PowerShell down to an SQLCMD script, you must first create an array containing the scripting variables and then pass this array into the -variable parameter. This holds true, even if you only have to pass a single variable.

Profiling an Instance Workload

There are occasions when it is important to understand the workload that your instance supports. For example, you may wish to find out the read/write ratio of your instances, across your instances. This can help in tasks such as consolidation planning or when planning the most optimally use of Buffer Cache Extensions.

A snapshot of this ratio can be obtained from the sys.dm_os_bufferdescriptors. It provides a point-in-time snapshot, however, so you will have to use the script at regular intervals, at different days and times, to build a true picture. The sys.dm_os_buffer_descriptors DMV returns the columns listed in Table 4-5.

Table 4-5. sys.dm_os_buffer_descriptors *Columns*

Column	Description
database_id	The ID of the database that the page is associated with
file_id	The ID of the data file that the page is associated with
page_id	The ID of the page
page_level	The level of the index that the page is used for
allocation_unit_id	The ID of the allocation unit, to which the page is associated
page_type	The type of page
row_count	The number of rows stored within the page
free_space_in_bytes	The amount of free space within the page, represented in bytes
is_modified	Marks if the page is dirty. A value of 0 implies that the page is clean (has not been modified since being read from disk). A value of 1 indicates that the page is dirty (has been modified since being read from disk).
numa_node	The NUMA (non-uniform memory access) node that the page is associated with
read_microsec	The time it takes to read the page from disk into its buffer, represented in microseconds

Every time a page is accessed, it is accessed in memory. All pages accessed are stored in an area of memory reserved by the SQL Server process, called the buffer cache. When a page is requested by a query, it can either be served up directly from the buffer cache, or if it is not already in memory, it is read from disk, into a buffer in the buffer cache and then served up from the cache. The sys.dm_os_buffer_descriptors DMV returns details of every page that is currently in the buffer cache.

In order to gain an idea of the ratio of reads to writes in our instance, we can make use of the is_modified flag, which indicates if the page is dirty. We will also filter on database_id and page_type. The filter of database_id will prevent system databases skewing the results, and the filter on page_type will prevent the results being skewed by system pages, such as GAM (Global Allocation Map), SGAM (Shared Global Allocation Map), PFS (Page Free Space), ML (Minimally Logged) MAP, and IAM (Index Allocation Map) pages, among others.

The script in Listing 4-2 demonstrates how we can extract the percentages of clean and dirty pages. The inner query uses PIVOT to extract the raw number of pages from sys.dm_os_buffer_descriptors and pivot the results from rows to columns. This makes it easy for the outer query to calculate the percentage of rows, by comparing the count of clean and dirty pages to a count of rows in the entire view.

■ **Tip**   A dirty page is a page that has been modified since the last time it was read from disk.

Listing 4-2. Extracting Percentage of Dirty Pages

```
SELECT
              CAST((Clean /
                      (SELECT CAST(COUNT(*) AS FLOAT)
                      FROM sys.dm_os_buffer_descriptors b
                      WHERE page_type IN
                          ('DATA_PAGE', 'INDEX_PAGE', 'TEXT_MIX_PAGE'))) * 100. AS
                          DECIMAL(4,2)
                      ) AS Clean_Percentage
            , CAST((
                      Dirty /
                      (SELECT CAST(COUNT(*) AS FLOAT)
                      FROM sys.dm_os_buffer_descriptors b
                      WHERE page_type IN
                          ('DATA_PAGE', 'INDEX_PAGE', 'TEXT_MIX_PAGE'))) * 100. AS
                          DECIMAL(4,2)
                      ) AS Dirty_Percentage
FROM
(
    SELECT 'Count' as is_modified
            , [0] AS Clean
            , [1] AS Dirty
    FROM
    (
    SELECT is_modified, 1 AS Page_Count
    FROM sys.dm_os_buffer_descriptors
    WHERE page_type IN ('DATA_PAGE', 'INDEX_PAGE', 'TEXT_MIX_PAGE')
        AND database_id > 4 ) SourceTable
    PIVOT
```

```
(
  COUNT(Page_Count)
  FOR is_modified IN ([0], [1])
) AS PivotTable
) a ;
```

If we call this script from PowerShell using the invoke-sqlcmd cmdlet, we can use the method demonstrated in Listing 4-1 to call the script against all servers in the enterprise. We can then schedule the PowerShell script to run at regular intervals, using SQL Server Agent, Windows Scheduled Tasks, or a third-party enterprise-scheduling tool, and save the results to a management database, from which we can later analyze the results and identify suitable candidates for a Buffer Cache Extension or targets for consolidation.

Query Store Metadata

The query store, introduced in SQL Server 2016, is a very exciting new feature for the serious DBA. It provides an interactive dashboard, which allows users to easily pinpoint problem queries, including those that have regressed in performance. It also stores historic query plans, which means that you can force a better performing query plan to be used, in the event of regression. This significantly reduces testing and remediation effort when deploying a new version of SQL Server or a new version of an application.

There are also great possibilities for DBAs who want to introduce or enhance their automation offering, as all query store data is also exposed through a set of catalog views. The following sections will discuss how this metadata can be used to remove unwanted ad hoc execution plans and how you can identify expensive queries across your estate.

Remove Ad Hoc Query Plans

Ad hoc query plans consume memory and can be of limited use. It is a good idea to remove ad hoc query plans if they are not being recused. The query in Listing 4-3 demonstrates how query store metadata can be used to clear unwanted ad hoc query plans from the cache.

The first part of the script runs a query against the sys.databases catalog view, to return a list of databases on the instance. The query store can be enabled or disabled at the database level and cannot be enabled on either master or TempDB system databases. Therefore, the query filters out databases with a database_id of less than three and any databases where query store is disabled.

■ **Tip** The output is piped into a select-object command, because, otherwise, PowerShell will treat each result as an object, as opposed to a string, which will result in the second part of the script attempting to set the database context to System.Data.DataRow, which, of course, will result in an error.

The second part of the script passes the database names into a foreach loop and executes an SQL script against each one. This technique provides a useful mechanism for running the same command against every database in an instance, and I would highly recommend this approach over the undocumented sp_MSForeachdb system stored procedure, which can be unreliable. We could also scale this script to run across all instances in the enterprise, by using the technique shown in Listing 4-3.

Listing 4-3. Removing Ad Hoc Query Plans

```
clear-host

import-module sqlps
```

```
$databases = @(invoke-sqlcmd -Query "SELECT name
                            FROM sys.databases
                            WHERE database_id > 2
                                    AND is_query_store_on = 1 ;") | select-object -expand
                            Name

foreach ($database in $databases)
{
Invoke-Sqlcmd -Database $database -Query "DECLARE @SQL NVARCHAR(MAX)

SELECT @SQL =
(
        SELECT 'EXEC sp_query_store_remove_query ' + CAST(qsq.query_id AS NVARCHAR(6)) + ';'
        AS [data()]
        FROM sys.query_store_query_text AS qsqt
        JOIN sys.query_store_query AS qsq
                ON qsq.query_text_id = qsqt.query_text_id
        JOIN sys.query_store_plan AS qsp
                ON qsp.query_id = qsq.query_id
        JOIN sys.query_store_runtime_stats AS qsrs
                ON qsrs.plan_id = qsp.plan_id
        GROUP BY qsq.query_id
        HAVING SUM(qsrs.count_executions) = 1
                AND MAX(qsrs.last_execution_time) < DATEADD (HH, -24, GETUTCDATE())
        ORDER BY qsq.query_id
        FOR XML PATH('')
) ;
EXEC(@SQL) ;" }
```

The query that is run against each database uses the data() method approach to iteration, to build a string that can be executed using dynamic SQL, before finally executing the script, using the EXEC statement. The metadata objects used by the query are described in the following sections.

sys.query_store_query_text

The sys.query_store_query_text catalog view exposes the text and handle of each T-SQL statement in the store. It returns the columns detailed in Table 4-6.

Table 4-6. *Columns Returned by* sys.query_store_query_text

Column	Description
query_text_id	The primary key
query_sql_text	The T-SQL text of the query
statement_sql_handle	The SQL handle of the query
is_part_of_encrypted_module	The SQL text that is part of an encrypted programmable object
has_restricted_text	The SQL text that includes sensitive information that cannot be displayed, such as a password

sys.query_store_query

The sys.query_store_query catalog view joins to the sys.query_store_query_text catalog view on the query_text_id column in each view. It also joins to sys.query_context_settings on the context_settings_id column in each object. sys.query_store_query returns details of the queries, including aggregated statistics. The columns returned are detailed in Table 4-7.

Table 4-7. *Columns Returned by* sys.query_store_query

Column	Description
query_id	The primary key
query_text_id	Foreign key that joins to sys.query_store_query_text
context_settings_id	Foreign key that joins to sys.query_context_settings
object_id	The object ID of the programmable object, of which the query is a part. 0 represents ad hoc SQL.
batch_sql_handle	The ID of the batch of which the query is a part. This field is only populated when the query uses table variables or temp tables.
query_hash	The query tree represented as an MD5 hash value
is_internal_query	Indicates if the query is a user or internal query: • 0 indicates a user query • 1 indicates an internal query
query_parameterization_type	The parameterization used for the query: • 0 indicates none • 1 indicates user parameterization • 2 indicates simple parameterization • 3 indicates forced parameterization
query_parameterization_type_desc	Description of the parameterization type
initial_compile_start_time	The date and time that the query was compiled for the first time
last_compile_start_time	The data and time of the most recent compilation of the query
last_execution_time	The date and time of the most recent execution of the query
last_compile_batch_sql_handle	The handle of SQL batch of which the query was a part on the most recent occurrence of the query being executed
last_compile_batch_offset_start	The offset of the start of the query from the beginning of the batch that is represented by last_compile_batch_sql_handle
last_compile_batch_offset_end	The offset of the end of the query from the beginning of the batch that is represented by last_compile_batch_sql_handle
count_compiles	A count of how many times that the query has been compiled
avg_compile_duration	The average length of time that it has taken the query to compile, recorded in milliseconds

(continued)

Table 4-7. *(continued)*

Column	Description
last_compile_duration	The duration of the most recent compilation of the query, recorded in milliseconds
avg_bind_duration	The average time it takes to bind the query. Binding is the process of resolving every table and column name to an object in the system catalog and creating an algebrization tree.
last_bind_duration	The time it took to bind the query on its most recent execution
avg_bind_cpu_time	The average CPU time that has been required to bind the query
last_bind_cpu_time	The amount of CPU time required to bind the query on its most recent compilation
avg_optimize_duration	The average length of time that the query optimizer takes to generate candidate query plans and select the most efficient
last_optimize_ duration	The time it took to optimize the query during its most recent compilation
avg_optimize_cpu_time	The average CPU time that has been required to optimize the query
last_optimize_cpu_ time	The amount of CPU time that was required to optimize the query on its most recent compilation
avg_compile_memory_kb	The average amount of memory used to compile the query
last_compile_memory_ kb	The amount of memory used to compile the query during its most recent compilation
max_compile_memory_kb	The largest amount of memory that has been required on any compilation of the query
is_clouddb_internal_ query	Indicates if the query is a user query or generated internally. This column only applies to the Azure SQL Database. It will always return 0 if the query is not run against the Azure SQL Database. When run on the Azure SQL Database: • 0 indicates a user query • 1 indicates an internal query

sys.query_store_plan

The sys.query_store_plan catalog view exposes details about the execution plans. The view joins to sys.query_store_query catalog view on the query_id column in each table. The columns returned by this view are detailed in Table 4-8.

Table 4-8. *Columns Returned by sys.dm_query_store_plan*

Column	Description
plan_id	The primary key
query_id	Foreign key that joins to sys.query_store_query
plan_group_id	The ID of the plan group that the plan is part of. This is only applicable to queries involving a cursor, as they require multiple plans.
engine_version	The version of the database engine that was used to compile the plan
compatibility_level	The compatibility level of the database that the query references
query_plan_hash	The plan represented in an MD5 hash
query_plan	The XML representation of the query plan
is_online_index_plan	Indicates if the plan was used during an online index rebuild: • 0 indicates that is was not • 1 indicates that it was
is_trivial_plan	Indicates if the optimizer regarded the plan as trivial: • 0 indicates that it is not a trivial plan • 1 indicates that it is a trivial plan
is_parallel_plan	Indicates if the plan is parellelised. • 0 indicates that it is not a parellel plan • 1 indicates that it is a parellel plan
is_forced_plan	Indicates if the plan is forced: • 0 indicates it is not forced • 1 indicates that it is forced
is_natively_compiled	Indicates if the plan includes natively compiled stored procedures: • 0 indicates that it does not • 1 indicates that it does
force_failure_count	Indicates the number of times an attempt to force the plan has failed
last_force_failure_reason	The reason for the failure in forcing the plan. Further details can be found in Table 4-9.
last_force_failure_reason_desc	Text describing the reason for the failure in forcing the plan. Further details can be found in Table 4-9.
count_compiles	A count of how many times that the query has been compiled
initial_compile_start_time	The date and time that the query was compiled for the first time
last_compile_start_time	The data and time of the most recent compilation of the query
last_execution_time	The date and time of the most recent execution of the query
avg_compile_duration	The average length of time that it has taken the query to compile, recorded in milliseconds
last_compile_duration	The duration of the most recent compilation of the query, recorded in milliseconds

If plan forcing fails, then last_force_failure_reason and last_force_failure_reason_desc columns describe the reasons for the failure. Table 4-9 defines the mapping between codes and reasons.

Table 4-9. *Plan Forcing Failure Reasons*

Reason Code	Reason Text	Description
0	N/A	No failure
8637	ONLINE_INDEX_BUILD	The query attempted to update a table while an index on the table was being rebuilt
8683	INVALID_STARJOIN	The start join included in the plan is invalid
8684	TIME_OUT	While searching for the force plan, the optimizer exceeded the threshold for allowed operations.
8689	NO_DB	The plan references a database that does not exist.
8690	HINT_CONFLICT	The plan conflicts with a query hint. For example, FORCE_INDEX(0) is used on a table with a clustered index.
8694	DQ_NO_FORCING_SUPPORTED	The plan conflicts with the use of full-text queries or distributed queries.
8698	NO_PLAN	Either the optimizer could not produce the forced plan, or it could not be verified.
8712	NO_INDEX	An index used by the plan does not exist.
8713	VIEW_COMPILE_FAILED	There is an issue with an indexed view that the plan uses.
Other values	GENERAL_FAILURE	An error not covered by the other codes

sys.query_store_runtime_stats

The sys.query_store_runtime_stats catalog view exposes the aggregated runtime statistics for each query plan. The view joins to sys_query_store_plan using the plan_id column in each table and joins to the sys.query_store_runtime_stats_interval catalog view, using the runtime_stats_interval_id column in each object. The columns returned by the catalog view are described in Table 4-10.

Table 4-10. *Columns Returned by* sys.query_store_runtime_stats

Column	Description
runtime_stats_id	The primary key
plan_id	Foreign key, joining to sys.query_store_plan
runtime_stats_interval_id	Foreign key, joining to store_runtime_stats_interval
execution_type	Specifies the execution status: • 0 indicates a regular execution that finished successfully • 1 indicates the client aborted the execution • 2 indicates that the execution was aborted because of an exception
execution_type_desc	A textual description of the execution_type column
first_execution_time	The date and time that the plan was first executed

(continued)

Table 4-10. (*continued*)

Column	Description
last_execution_time	The date and time of the most recent execution of the plan
count_executions	The number of times that the plan has been executed
avg_duration	The average length of time that the query has taken to execute, expressed in microseconds
last_duration	The time that the query took to execute on its most recent execution, expressed in microseconds
min_duration	The shortest length of time that the plan has taken to execute, expressed in microseconds
max_duration	The longest amount of time that the plan has taken to execute, expressed in microseconds
stdev_duration	The standard deviation of time spent executing of the plan, expressed in microseconds
avg_cpu_time	The average amount of CPU time used by executions of the plan, expressed in microseconds
last_cpu_time	The amount of CPU time used by the most recent execution of the plan, expressed in microseconds
min_cpu_time	The minimum amount of CPU time used by any execution of the plan, expressed in microseconds
max_cpu_time	The maximum amount of CPU time used by any execution of the plan, expressed in microseconds
stdev_cpu_time	The standard deviation of CPU time used by executions of the plan, expressed in microseconds
avg_logical_io_reads	The average number of logical reads required by the plan
last_logical_io_reads	The number of logical reads required by the most recent execution of the plan
min_logical_io_reads	The smallest number of logical reads required by any execution of the plan
max_logical_io_reads	The maximum number of logical reads required by any execution of the plan
stdev_logical_io_reads	The standard deviation of logical reads required by executions of the plan
avg_logical_io_writes	The average number of logical writes required by the plan
last_logical_io_writes	The number of logical writes required by the most recent execution of the plan
min_logical_io_writes	The smallest number of logical writes required by any execution of the plan
max_logical_io_writes	The maximum number of logical writes required by any execution of the plan
stdev_logical_io_writes	The standard deviation of logical writes required by executions of the plan
avg_physical_io_reads	The average number of reads from disk required by the plan

(*continued*)

Table 4-10. (*continued*)

Column	Description
last_physical_io_reads	The number of reads from disk required by the most recent execution of the plan
min_physical_io_reads	The smallest number of reads from disk required by any execution of the plan
max_physical_io_reads	The maximum number of reads from disk required by any execution of the plan
stdev_physical_io_reads	The standard deviation of reads from disk required by executions of the plan
avg_clr_time	The average CLR (Common Language Runtime) time required by executions of the plan, expressed in microseconds
last_clr_time	The CLR time required on the most recent execution of the plan, expressed in microseconds
min_clr_time	The smallest amount of CLR time required by any execution of the plan., expressed in microseconds
max_clr_time	The longest CLR time spent by any execution of the plan, expressed in microseconds
stdev_clr_time	The standard deviation of CLR time required by executions of the plan, expressed in microseconds
avg_dop	The average degree of parallelism used by execution of the plan
last_dop	The degree of parallelism used on the most recent execution of the plan
min_dop	The lowest degree of parallelism used by any execution of the plan
max_dop	The largest degree of parallelism used by any execution of the plan
stdev_dop	The standard deviation of the degree of parallelism used by executions of the plan
avg_query_max_used_memory	The average number of memory grants issued for any execution of the plan, expressed as a count of 8KB pages*
last_query_max_used_memory	The number of memory grants issued during the most recent execution of the plan, expressed as a count of 8KB pages*
min_query_max_used_memory	The smallest number of memory grants issued for any execution of the plan, expressed as a count of 8KB pages*
max_query_max_used_memory	The largest amount of memory grants issued for any execution of the plan, expressed as a count of 8KB pages*
stdev_query_max_used_memory	The standard deviation of memory grants issued during the executions of the plan, expressed as a count of 8KB pages*
avg_rowcount	The average number of rows affected by executions of the plan
last_rowcount	The number of rows affected by the most recent execution of the plan
min_rowcount	The minimum number of rows affected by any execution of the plan
max_rowcount	The largest number of rows affected by any execution of the plan
stdev_rowcount	The standard deviation of rows affected, across executions of the plan

Returns 0 for queries using natively compiled stored procedures

Identifying the Most Expensive Queries

Imagine a scenario in which you have a private cloud infrastructure that is supporting a number of data-tier applications. The Hyper-V farm supporting the private cloud is coming under generalized CPU pressure, and you want to identify the most expensive queries across the whole environment, in order to focus a query-tuning effort. This data is at hand, through query store metadata.

The script in Listing 4-4 demonstrates how you can retrieve the five most expensive queries and plans in the current database, based on the average CPU time required to execute them. The query filters out any queries that have not been executed in the previous seven days, because if the queries are being run infrequently, you are probably not going to be very interested in them.

Listing 4-4. Retrieving the Most Expensive Queries

```
SELECT TOP 5
        qsqt.query_sql_text
        ,qsp.query_plan
        ,CAST(AVG(qsrs.avg_duration) AS NUMERIC(10,2)) Avg_Duration
        ,CAST(AVG(qsrs.avg_cpu_time) AS NUMERIC(10,2)) Avg_CPU
        ,CAST((AVG(qsrs.avg_cpu_time) / AVG(qsrs.avg_duration)) * 100 AS NUMERIC(5,2)) Avg_
CPU_Percent
FROM sys.query_store_query_text AS qsqt
        JOIN sys.query_store_query AS qsq
                ON qsq.query_text_id = qsqt.query_text_id
        JOIN sys.query_store_plan AS qsp
                ON qsp.query_id = qsq.query_id
        JOIN sys.query_store_runtime_stats AS qsrs
                ON qsrs.plan_id = qsp.plan_id
WHERE qsq.is_internal_query = 0
        AND qsp.last_execution_time >= GETUTCDATE() - 7
GROUP BY qsqt.query_sql_text
                ,qsp.query_plan
ORDER BY AVG(qsrs.avg_cpu_time) ;
```

We can use the technique that you learned in Listing 4-2 to iterate through each database on the instance and the technique that you learned in Listing 4-1 to iterate through every instance in the enterprise. We will achieve this using a nested foreach loop. The final PowerShell script can be found in Listing 4-5. You will notice that we have added an additional two columns, so that the instance and database can easily be identified in the combined results. We are also piping the results to a file called SQLResults.txt.

Listing 4-5. Finding the Most Expensive Queries in the Enterprise

```
import-module sqlps

[array]$Servers = "ESASSMGMT1", "ESPROD1", "ESPROD2"

foreach ($Server in $Servers)
{
    $databases = @(invoke-sqlcmd -serverinstance $server -Query "SELECT name
                        FROM sys.databases
                        WHERE database_id > 2
                            AND is_query_store_on = 1") | select-object -expand Name
```

```
    foreach ($database in $databases)
    {
        Invoke-Sqlcmd -serverinstance $server -Database $database -Query "SELECT TOP 5
                @@SERVERNAME AS ServerName
            ,DB_NAME() AS DatabaseName
            ,qsqt.query_sql_text
                ,qsp.query_plan
                ,CAST(AVG(qsrs.avg_duration) AS NUMERIC(10,2)) Avg_Duration
                ,CAST(AVG(qsrs.avg_cpu_time) AS NUMERIC(10,2)) Avg_CPU
                ,CAST((AVG(qsrs.avg_cpu_time) / AVG(qsrs.avg_duration)) * 100 AS
                NUMERIC(5,2)) Avg_CPU_Percent
        FROM sys.query_store_query_text AS qsqt
            JOIN sys.query_store_query AS qsq
                    ON qsq.query_text_id = qsqt.query_text_id
            JOIN sys.query_store_plan AS qsp
                    ON qsp.query_id = qsq.query_id
            JOIN sys.query_store_runtime_stats AS qsrs
                    ON qsrs.plan_id = qsp.plan_id
        WHERE qsq.is_internal_query = 0
                AND qsp.last_execution_time >= GETUTCDATE() - 7
        GROUP BY qsqt.query_sql_text
                        ,qsp.query_plan
        ORDER BY AVG(qsrs.avg_cpu_time) ;" > C:\SQLResults.txt
    }
}
```

■ **Tip** As well as assisting in the diagnosis and remediation of issues such as CPU pressure in a private cloud, you may also want to consider setting up a weekly report to identify the most expensive queries across the enterprise. It is this kind of proactive administration that will allow you to troubleshoot issues before the business even knows about them and offer an outstanding platform service.

Dynamic Index Rebuilds

SQL Server does not provide out-of-the-box functionality for intelligently rebuilding indexes. If you use a Maintenance Plan to rebuild or reorganize all indexes in your database, every index will be rebuilt or reorganized, whether it needs it or not. Unfortunately, this can be a resource-intensive and time-consuming process, and it may be that only a fraction of your indexes need to be rebuilt.

To work around this issue, you can use index-related metadata to evaluate the fragmentation level in each index and take the appropriate action (rebuild, reorganize, or leave alone). To achieve this, we will use the sys.dm_db_index_physical_stats dynamic management function. This function returns fragmentation statistics for indexes, with one row returned for every level of every index within scope (based on the input parameters). The parameters required to call this function are detailed in Table 4-11.

■ **Tip** This book assumes that you are familiar with B-Tree indexes and fragmentation (both internal and external). If you require a refresher, full details can be found in *Apress Pro SQL Server Administration*, which can be purchased at www.apress.com/9781484207116?gtmf=s.

Table 4-11. *Parameters Required by* sys.dm_db_index_physical_stats

Parameter	Description
Database_ID	The ID of the database that the function will run against. If you do not know it, you can pass in DB_ID('DatabaseName').
Object_ID	The Object ID of the table that you want to run the function against. If you do not know it, pass in OBJECT_ID('TableName'). Pass NULL to run the function against all tables in the database.
Index_ID	The index ID of the index you want to run the function against. 1 is always the ID of a table's clustered index. Pass NULL to run the function against all indexes on the table.
Partition_Number	The ID of the partition that you want to run the function against. Pass NULL if you want to run the function against all partitions, or if the table is not partitioned.
Mode	Acceptable values are LIMITED, SAMPLED, or DETAILED. • LIMITED only scans the non-leaf levels of an index. • SAMPLED scans 1% of pages in the table, unless the table or partition has 10,000 pages or less, in which case DETAILED mode is used. • DETAILED mode scans 100% of the pages in the table. For very large tables, SAMPLED is often preferred, due to the length of time it can take to return data in DETAILED mode.

The columns returned by sys.dm_db_index_physical_stats are detailed in Table 4-12.

Table 4-12. *Columns Returned by* sys.dm_db_index_physical_stats

Column	Description
database_id	The database ID of the database, in which the index resides
object_id	The object ID of the table or index view to which the index is associated
index_id	The ID of the index within the table or indexed view. The ID is only unique within its associated parent object. 0 is always the index ID of a heap, and 1 is always the index ID of a clustered index.
partition_number	The partition number. This always returns 1 for non-partitioned tables and indexed views.
index_type_desc	Text defining the index types. Possible return values are as follows: • HEAP • CLUSTERED INDEX • NONCLUSTERED INDEX • PRIMARY XML INDEX • SPATIAL INDEX • XML INDEX (Referring to a secondary XML index) There are also some index types used for internal use only. These are as follows: • COLUMNSTORE MAPPING INDEX • COLUMNSTORE DELETE BUFFER INDEX • COLUMNSTORE DELETE BITMAP INDEX
hobt_id	The ID of the heap or B-Tree

(continued)

Table 4-12. (*continued*)

Column	Description
alloc_unit_type_desc	Text describing the type of location unit that the index level resides in
index_depth	The number of levels that the index consists of. If 1 is returned, the index is either a heap or LOB data or row overflow data.
index_level	The level of the index that is represented by the row returned
avg_fragmentation_in_percent	The average percentage of external fragmentation within the index level (lower is better)
fragment_count	The number of fragments within the index level
avg_fragment_size_in_pages	The average size of each fragment, represented as a count of 8KB pages
page_count	For in-row data, the page count represents the number of pages at the level of the index that is represented by the row. For a heap, the page count represents the number of pages within the IN_ROW_DATA allocation unit. For LOB or row overflow data, the page count represents the number of pages within the allocation unit.
avg_page_space_used_in_percent	The average amount of internal fragmentation within the index level that the row represents (higher is better...usually)
record_count	For in-row data, the record count represents the number of records at the level of the index that is represented by the row. For a heap, the record count represents the number of records within the IN_ROW_DATA allocation unit. For LOB or row overflow data, the record count represents the number of records within the allocation unit.
ghost_record_count	A count of logically deleted rows that are awaiting physical deletion by the ghost cleanup task
version_ghost_record_count	The number of rows that have been retained by a transaction using the snapshot isolation level
min_record_size_in_bytes	The size of the smallest record, expressed in bytes
max_record_size_in_bytes	The size of the largest record, expressed in bytes
avg_record_size_in_bytes	The average record size, expressed in bytes
forwarded_record_count	The number of records that have forwarding pointers to other locations. Only applies to heaps. If the object is an index, NULL is returned.
compressed_page_count	A count of the compressed pages within the index level represented by the row
hobt_id	New in SQL Server 2016, this column only applies to columnstore indexes. It represents the ID of the heaps or B-Trees that are used to track internal columnstore data.
column_store_delete_buffer_state	New in SQL Server 2016, this column only applies to columnstore indexes. It represents the state of the columnstore delete buffer.
column_store_delete_buff_state_desc	New in SQL Server 2016, this column only applies to columnstore indexes. It is a textual description of the value returned in the column_store_delete_buffer_state column.

The script in Listing 4-6 demonstrates how you can use this dynamic management function to determine which indexes have more than 25% external fragmentation and rebuild only those indexes.

Listing 4-6. Dynamic Index Rebuilds

```
clear-host

import-module sqlps

[array]$Servers = "ESASSMGMT1", "ESPROD1", "ESPROD2"

foreach ($Server in $Servers)
{
    $databases = @(invoke-sqlcmd -serverinstance $server -Query "SELECT name
                        FROM sys.databases
                        WHERE database_id > 4 ;") | select-object -expand Name

    foreach ($database in $databases)
    {
        Invoke-Sqlcmd -serverinstance $server -Database $database -QueryTimeout 7200 -Query "

            DECLARE @SQL NVARCHAR(MAX)

            SET @SQL =
            (
                SELECT 'ALTER INDEX '
                        + i.name
                        + ' ON ' + s.name
                        + '.'
                        + OBJECT_NAME(i.object_id)
                        + ' REBUILD ; '
                FROM sys.dm_db_index_physical_stats(DB_ID(),NULL,NULL,NULL,'DETAILED') ps
                INNER JOIN sys.indexes i
                        ON ps.object_id = i.object_id
                            AND ps.index_id = i.index_id
                INNER JOIN sys.objects o
                        ON ps.object_id = o.object_id
                        INNER JOIN sys.schemas s
                                ON o.schema_id = s.schema_id
                WHERE index_level = 0
                        AND avg_fragmentation_in_percent > 25
                        FOR XML PATH('')
            ) ;

            EXEC(@SQL) ;"
    }
}
```

This script uses the XML data() method technique to build and execute a string that contains ALTER INDEX statements for every index in the specified database that has more than 25% external fragmentation at the leaf level. The script joins sys.dm_db_index_physical_stats to sys.schemas to obtain the name of the schema that contains the index. There is no direct join between these objects, so the join is implemented through an intermediate catalog view (sys.objects). The script also joins to sys.indexes to retrieve the object_id, which is then passed into the OBJECT_NAME() function, to determine the name of the index.

Enforcing Policies

Policy-Based Management (PBM) is a great tool for ensuring that your policies are met across the Enterprise. It does have limitations, however. Specifically, some facets only allow you to report on policy violation but not actually to prevent the change that will cause the violation. Therefore, many DBAs will choose to enforce some of their key policies by using custom scripting.

xp_cmdshell is a system-stored procedure that allows you to run operating system commands from within an SQL Server instance. There seems to be some debate between DBAs about whether this is a security hole or not, but I have always found it cut and dried. The argument for xp_cmdshell not being a security risk generally revolves around "Only my team and I are allowed to use it." But what if the instance is compromised by a malicious user? In this case, you really do not want to reduce the number of steps hackers have to take before they can start spreading their attack out to the network.

PBM can report on xp_cmdshell, but it cannot prevent it being enabled. You can, however, create a PowerShell script that will check for xp_cmdshell being enabled and disable it, if required. The script can then be scheduled to run on a regular basis.

The script in Listing 4-7 demonstrates how to use the techniques that I have already discussed in this chapter to loop around every instance and disable xp_cmdshell, if required. The script discovers if the feature is incorrectly configured, by checking its status in the sys.configurations catalog view. It will then use sp_configure to reconfigure the setting. There are two calls of sp_configure, because xp_cmdshell is an advanced option, and the show advanced options property must be configured before the setting can be changed. The RECONFIGURE command forces the change.

There are two commands to reconfigure the instance, following a change made by sp_configure. The first is RECONFIGURE. The second is RECONFIGURE WITH OVERRIDE. RECONFIGURE, will change the running value of the setting, as long as the newly configured value is regarded as "sensible" by SQL Server. For example, RECONFIGURE will not allow you to disable contained databases when they exist on the instance. If you use RECONFIGURE WITH OVERRIDE, however, this action will be allowed, even though your contained databases will no longer be accessible. Even with this command, however, SQL Server will still run checks to ensure that the value you have entered is between the allowable minimum and maximum values for the setting. It will also not allow you to perform any operations that will cause fatal errors in the database engine. As an example of this, the procedure will not allow you to configure the Min Server Memory (MB) setting to be higher than the Max Server Memory (MB) setting.

Listing 4-7. Disable xp_cmdshell Throughout the Enterprise

```
import-module sqlps

[array]$Servers = "ESASSMGMT1", "ESPROD1", "ESPROD2"

foreach ($Server in $Servers)
{
    invoke-sqlcmd -ServerInstance "$Server" -Query "IF
        (
                        --Check if xp_cmdshell is enabled
```

```
                    SELECT value_in_use
                    FROM sys.configurations
                    WHERE name = 'xp_cmdshell'
            ) = 1
    BEGIN
            --Turn on advanced options
            EXEC sp_configure 'show advanced options', 1 ;
            RECONFIGURE

            --Turn off xp_cmdshell
            EXEC sp_configure 'xp_cmdshell', 0 ;
            RECONFIGURE

    END"
}
```

This approach can be used to configure many aspects of your enterprise's surface area. In SQL Server 2016, the features that can be configured with this methodology are detailed in Table 4-13.

Table 4-13. *Settings That Can Be Changed with* sp_configure

Setting	Description
recovery interval (min)	Maximum recovery interval in minutes
allow updates	Allows updates to system tables
user connections	Number of user connections allowed
locks	Number of locks for all users
open objects	Number of open database objects
fill factor (%)	Default fill factor percentage
disallow results from triggers	Disallows returning results from triggers
nested triggers	Allows triggers to be invoked within triggers
server trigger recursion	Allows recursion for server level triggers
remote access	Allows remote access
default language	Default language
cross db ownership chaining	Allows cross db ownership chaining
max worker threads	Maximum worker threads
network packet size (B)	Network packet size
show advanced options	Shows advanced options
remote proc trans	Creates DTC transaction for remote procedures
c2 audit mode	c2 audit mode
default full-text language	Default full-text language
two digit year cutoff	Two-digit year cutoff
index create memory (KB)	Memory for index create sorts (KBytes)
priority boost	Priority boost

(continued)

Table 4-13. (*continued*)

Setting	Description
remote login timeout (s)	Remote login time-out
remote query timeout (s)	Remote query time-out
cursor threshold	Cursor threshold
set working set size	Sets working set size
user options	User options
affinity mask	Affinity mask
max text repl size (B)	Maximum size of a text field in replication
media retention	Tape retention period in days
cost threshold for parallelism	Cost threshold for parallelism
max degree of parallelism	Maximum degree of parallelism
min memory per query (KB)	Minimum memory per query (KBytes)
query wait (s)	Maximum time to wait for query memory (s)
min server memory (MB)	Minimum size of server memory (MB)
max server memory (MB)	Maximum size of server memory (MB)
query governor cost limit	Maximum estimated cost allowed by query governor
lightweight pooling	User mode scheduler uses lightweight pooling
scan for startup procs	Scan for startup stored procedures
affinity64 mask	Affinity64 mask
affinity I/O mask	Affinity I/O mask
affinity64 I/O mask	Affinity64 I/O mask
transform noise words	Transforms noise words for full-text query
precompute rank	Uses precomputed rank for full-text query
PH timeout (s)	DB connection time-out for full-text protocol handler (s)
clr enabled	CLR user code execution enabled in the server
max full-text crawl range	Maximum crawl ranges allowed in full-text indexing
ft notify bandwidth (min)	Number of reserved full-text notifications buffers
ft notify bandwidth (max)	Maximum number of full-text notifications buffers
ft crawl bandwidth (min)	Number of reserved full-text crawl buffers
ft crawl bandwidth (max)	Maximum number of full-text crawl buffers
default trace enabled	Enables or disables the default trace
blocked process threshold (s)	Blocked process reporting threshold
in-doubt xact resolution	Recovery policy for DTC transactions with unknown outcome
remote admin connections	Dedicated Admin Connections are allowed from remote clients

(*continued*)

Table 4-13. (*continued*)

Setting	Description
common criteria compliance enabled	Common Criteria compliance mode enabled
EKM provider enabled	Enables or disables EKM provider
backup compression default	Enables compression of backups by default
filestream access level	Sets the FILESTREAM access level
optimize for ad hoc workloads	When this option is set, plan cache size is further reduced for a single-use ad hoc OLTP workload.
access check cache bucket count	Defaults hash bucket count for the access check result security cache
access check cache quota	Defaults quota for the access check result security cache
backup checksum default	Enables checksum of backups by default
automatic soft-NUMA disabled	Automatic soft-NUMA is enabled by default
external scripts enabled	Allows execution of external scripts
Agent XPs	Enables or disables Agent XPs
Database Mail XPs	Enables or disables Database Mail XPs
SMO and DMO XPs	Enables or disables SMO and DMO XPs
Ole Automation Procedures	Enables or disables Ole Automation Procedures
xp_cmdshell	Enables or disables command shell
Ad Hoc Distributed Queries	Enables or disables Ad Hoc Distributed Queries
Replication XPs	Enables or disables Replication XPs
contained database authentication	Enables contained databases and contained authentication
hadoop connectivity	Configures SQL Server to connect to external Hadoop or Microsoft Azure storage blob data sources through PolyBase
polybase network encryption	Configures SQL Server to encrypt control and data channels when using PolyBase
remote data archive	Allows the use of the REMOTE_DATA_ARCHIVE data access for databases
polybase mode	Configures the mode this node should operate in when using the PolyBase feature

The sys.configurations catalog view returns the columns detailed in Table 4-14.

Table 4-14. *Columns Returned by* sys.configurations

Column	Description
configuration_id	The primary key
name	The name of the setting
value	The currently configured value of the setting
minimum	The minimum value that can be configured for the setting

(*continued*)

Table 4-14. (*continued*)

Column	Description
maximum	The maximum value that can be configured for the setting
value_in_use	The value that is currently in use. This can differ from the value column, if the setting has been changed but the instance has not been reconfigured or restarted.
description	A description of the setting
is_dynamic	Specifies if the setting is dynamic: • 1 indicates that the setting can be applied using RECONFIGURE • 0 indicates that the instance must be restarted
is_advanced	Specifies if the setting can only be changed when show advanced options is set to 1: • 0 indicates it is not an advanced option • 1 indicates that it is an advanced option

The parameters accepted by sp_configure are detailed in Table 4-15.

Table 4-15. *Parameters Accepted by* sp_configure

Parameter	Description
@configname	The name of the setting to change
@configvalue	The value to be configured for the setting

Analyzing Performance Counters

In many environments, DBAs are not allowed access to the Operating System and become heavily reliant on the Windows Administrators to use tools such as Perfmon. What many DBAs are unaware of is that all Perfmon counters are actually exposed at the SQL Server level, which allows you to work around this issue and reduce the time to resolution for many performance issues experienced by the business.

These performance counters are exposed through the sys.dm_os_performance_counters DMV. The columns returned by this DMV are detailed in Table 4-16.

Table 4-16. *Columns Returned by* sys.dm_os_performance_counters

Column	Description
object_name	The category of the counter
counter_name	The name of the counter
instance_name	The instance of the counter. For example, database-related counters have an instance for each database.
cntr_value	The value of the counter
cntr_type	The type of counter. Counter types are described in Table 4-17.

The cntr_type column informs you of the type of counter. There are size types of counter exposed by the DMV, and each type is detailed in Table 4-17.

Table 4-17. *Counter Type*

Counter Type	Description
1073939712	Use `PERF_LARGE_RAW_BASE` as a base value in conjunction with the `PERF_LARGE_RAW_FRACTION` type to calculate a counter percentage or with `PERF_AVERAGE_BULK` to calculate an average.
537003264	Use `PERF_LARGE_RAW_FRACTION` as a fractional value in conjunction with `PERF_LARGE_RAW_BASE` to calculate a counter percentage.
1073874176	`PERF_AVERAGE_BULK` is a cumulative average that you use in conjunction with `PERF_LARGE_RAW_BASE` to calculate a counter average. The counter, along with the base, is sampled twice, to calculate the metric over a period of time.
272696320	`PERF_COUNTER_COUNTER` is a 32-bit cumulative rate counter. The value should be sampled twice, to calculate the metric over a period of time.
272696576	`PERF_COUNTER_BULK_COUNT` is a 64-bit cumulative rate counter. The value should be sampled twice, to calculate the metric over a period of time.
65792	`PERF_COUNTER_LARGE_RAWCOUNT` returns the last sampled result for the counter.

The query in Listing 4-8 demonstrates how to capture metrics of the type `PERF_COUNTER_LARGE_RAWCOUNT`, which is the simplest form of counter. The query returns the number of memory grants that are currently pending.

Listing 4-8. Using Counter Type 65792

```
SELECT *
FROM sys.dm_os_performance_counters
WHERE counter_name = 'Memory Grants Pending' ;
```

The script in Listing 4-9 demonstrates capturing metrics of type `PERF_COUNTER_BULK_COUNT` and `PERF_COUNTER_COUNTER`. The script records the number of lock requests that are occurring, by capturing the value twice, with a one-minute interval. It then subtracts the first value from the second value and divides by 60, to obtain the rate per second.

Listing 4-9. Using Counter Types 272696576 and 272696320

```
DECLARE @cntr_value1 BIGINT = (
SELECT cntr_value
FROM sys.dm_os_performance_counters
WHERE counter_name = 'Lock Requests/sec'
        AND instance_name = '_Total') ;

WAITFOR DELAY '00:01:00'

DECLARE @cntr_value2 BIGINT = (
SELECT cntr_value
FROM sys.dm_os_performance_counters
WHERE counter_name = 'Lock Requests/sec'
        AND instance_name = '_Total') ;

SELECT (@cntr_value2 - @cntr_value1) / 60 'Lock Requests/sec' ;
```

101

The script in Listing 4-10 demonstrates how to capture a counter of type 537003264. The plan cache hit ratio counter is of this counter. As it is a percentage value, in order to extract a meaningful value, we must multiply the value by 100 and divide by the base counter, to calculate the percentage.

■ **Tip**   If you are running the script against a named instance, you will have to replace SQLServer: with MSSQL$InstanceName:.

Listing 4-10. Using Counter Type 537003264

```
SELECT
        100 *
        (
        SELECT cntr_value
        FROM sys.dm_os_performance_counters
        WHERE object_name = 'SQLServer:Plan Cache'
                AND counter_name = 'Cache hit ratio'
                AND instance_name = '_Total')
        /
        (
        SELECT cntr_value
        FROM sys.dm_os_performance_counters
        WHERE object_name = 'SQLServer:Plan Cache'
                AND counter_name = 'Cache hit ratio base'
                AND instance_name = '_Total') [Plan cache hit ratio %] ;
```

The PERF_AVERAGE_BULK counter type is the most complex to use. We will have to capture the value and its corresponding base counter twice. We must then deduct the first capture of the counter from the second capture, deduct the first capture of the base counter from the second capture, and then divide the fractional counter value by its base value, to calculate the average over the time period.

The script in Listing 4-11 demonstrates how to achieve this for the Average Latch Wait Time (ms) counter. Because it is possible that no latches will be requested within the time period, we have wrapped the SELECT statement in an IF...ELSE block, to avoid the possibility of a divide-by-0 error being thrown.

Listing 4-11. Using Counter Type 1073874176

```
DECLARE @cntr TABLE
(
    ID                      INT                     IDENTITY,
    counter_name            NVARCHAR(256),
    counter_value           BIGINT,
    [Time]                  DATETIME
) ;

INSERT INTO @cntr
SELECT
        counter_name
        ,cntr_value
        ,GETDATE()
        FROM sys.dm_os_performance_counters
        WHERE counter_name IN('Average Latch Wait Time (ms)',
                                'Average Latch Wait Time base') ;
```

```
        WAITFOR DELAY '00:01:00' ;

INSERT INTO @cntr
SELECT
        counter_name
        ,cntr_value
        ,GETDATE()
        FROM sys.dm_os_performance_counters
        WHERE counter_name IN('Average Latch Wait Time (ms)',
                              'Average Latch Wait Time base') ;

IF (SELECT COUNT(DISTINCT counter_value)
    FROM @cntr
    WHERE counter_name = 'Average Latch Wait Time (ms)') > 2
BEGIN
SELECT
        (
                (
                SELECT TOP 1 counter_value
                FROM @cntr
                WHERE counter_name = 'Average Latch Wait Time (ms)'
                ORDER BY [Time] DESC
                )
                -
                (
                SELECT TOP 1 counter_value
                FROM @cntr
                WHERE counter_name = 'Average Latch Wait Time (ms)'
                ORDER BY [Time] ASC
                )
        )
        /
        (
                (
                SELECT TOP 1 counter_value
                FROM @cntr
                WHERE counter_name = 'Average Latch Wait Time base'
                ORDER BY [Time] DESC
                )
                -
                (
                SELECT TOP 1 counter_value
                FROM @cntr
                WHERE counter_name = 'Average Latch Wait Time base'
                ORDER BY [Time] ASC
                )
        ) [Average Latch Wait Time (ms)] ;
END
ELSE
BEGIN
        SELECT 0 [Average Latch Wait Time (ms)] ;
END
```

Being able to retrieve these performance counters allows a DBA to quickly tackle an issue without the involvement of Windows engineers. In some environments, in which enterprise monitoring solutions such as SOC (System Operations Center) are not available, this methodology can also be used toward creating a tactical monitoring solution. This will be discussed in depth in Chapter 9.

Summary

Using SQL Server metadata to create intelligent routines can drastically reduce your workload and help improve consistency and performance throughout your enterprise. PowerShell provides the ability to iterate through every instance in your environment, or even every database in every instance. This is implemented through the simple use of nested foreach loops.

SQL Server metadata can also be interrogated to retrieve performance statistics that are pertinent to the instance. This can reduce resolution times of performance-related incidents, as it removes the reliance on the Windows administration team, for configuring Perfmon traces.

CHAPTER 5

■ ■ ■

Automation Techniques with SSIS

Although its primary purpose is as an ETL (Extract, Transform, and Load) tool, SSIS (SQL Server Integration Services) provides many automation possibilities for database administrators. In fact, maintenance plans and the Copy Database Wizard are implemented using SSIS. There are many other features that are available in the full SSIS application that can drastically enhance your automation toolset. Additionally, when an automated routine requires a complex flow, an SSIS package can be much easier to develop and maintain than a flow that is implemented through SQL Server Agent job steps. This chapter will discuss the concepts and functionality of SSIS, before demonstrating how DBAs can use the tool to automate common maintenance tasks. Finally, I will discuss some recipes for other automation scenarios.

■ **Note** The demonstrations in this chapter require SQL Server Data Tools BI (SSDT BI) to be installed.

SSIS Concepts

SSIS provides a mechanism for orchestrating workflow processes as well as data movement and transformation. All of the artifacts within a process flow are encapsulated within a package. When you first create a package, it is an empty object, and subsequently adding flows and artifacts to the package provide its functionality. Packages can be created via a graphical design surface, providing drag-and-drop functionality, within SSDT, or can also be constructed programmatically, using C# or VB.NET.

■ **Note** A full discussion on creating packages programmatically is beyond the scope of this book; however, further information can be found at https://msdn.microsoft.com/en-GB/library/ms135946.aspx.

SSIS Components

The primary components within an SSIS package are the control flow and the data flow. The control flow provides the orchestration for the package and also contains the common administrative tasks. Therefore, the control flow will be the major focus of this chapter. The data flow provides data extraction, transformation, and load capabilities. A package will always contain a control flow and can contain zero or more data flows.

Up to and including SQL Server 2008 R2, deployment followed a package deployment model, whereby the package was the top-level object that could be deployed. In SQL Server 2012, SSIS underwent a major overhaul, with one of the major differences being a transition to a project-deployment model.

© Peter A. Carter 2016
P. A. Carter, *Expert Scripting and Automation for SQL Server DBAs*, DOI 10.1007/978-1-4842-1943-0_5

In the project-deployment model, a project containing one or more packages is deployed, as opposed to deploying individual packages. While the package-deployment model can still be used, the project-deployment model offers several benefits, including the implementation of project parameters, which map to variables within a package. This provides a simple and robust mechanism for passing values to a package at runtime. This simplifies deployment to different environments, such as Dev, QA, OAT, UAT, and Production.

Packages are control flow centric, meaning that they always have a control flow, and data flows are optional. Packages also normally have one or more connection managers. A connection manager provides a connection mechanism to a data source, such as an SQL Server instance or a folder in the file system. Packages can also be extended, by using logging and event handlers. Figure 5-1 shows the high-level architecture of a package.

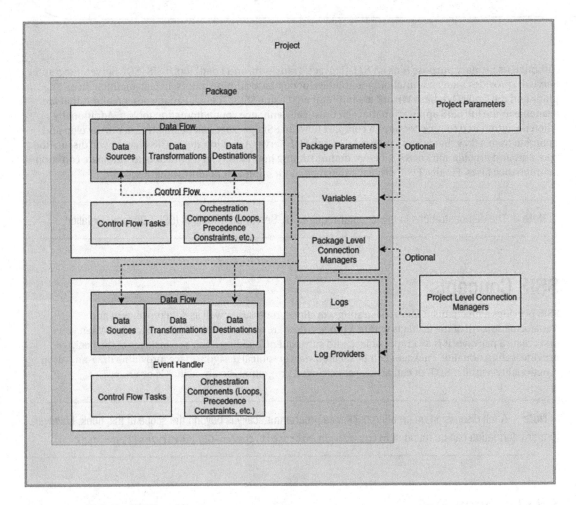

Figure 5-1. *High-level SSIS architecture*

Getting Started

To demonstrate the concepts and basic functionality of SSIS, we will create a simple package that will check the integrity of all databases on ESPROD1. If this task succeeds, it will perform a full backup of all databases on ESPROD1. If either of the tasks fail, an operator will be notified.

To initially create the project, launch SSDT and select File ➤ New ➤ Project, to invoke the New Project dialog box, which is illustrated in Figure 5-2. Here, we will choose the Integration Service Project template and provide the name SimpleSSISPackage as the project name. This will cause the Solution Name to be automatically updated, but you can overwrite this, if required. You can also select a folder in which the project will be stored, if you do not want to use the default location.

■ **Tip**   A solution is a container for multiple related projects.

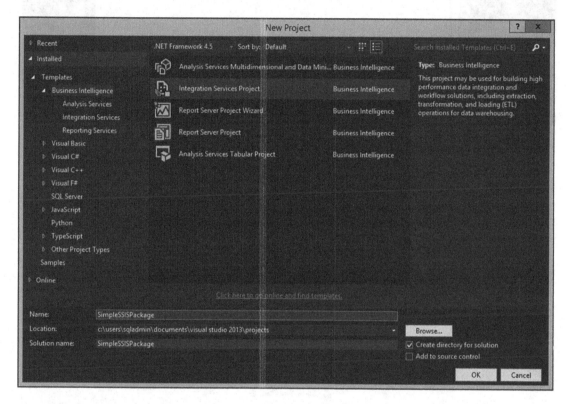

Figure 5-2. New Project dialog box

After the package has been created, you will see the SSIS design surface, as displayed in Figure 5-3. The design surface has tabs for the control flow, data flow, package parameters, event handlers, and the package explorer, which provides a hierarchical view of package artifacts.

To the left of the design surface, you will see the SSIS toolbox. Scrolling down to the other tasks section will expose tasks that are used by maintenance plans, as well as other tasks that are useful for DBAs. If you switch to the data flow, the control flow tasks in the toolbox will be replaced with data sources, transformations, and destinations.

To the right of the design surface, you will notice Solution Explorer, which provides a hierarchical view of artifacts within the solution and the projects that it contains. You will also see the properties window, which is context-sensitive and will display the properties of the artifact that you currently have in scope.

Selecting the tab for Team Explorer will allow you to provide a connection to your TFS (Team Foundation Server), to allow your project to be brought under source control.

Figure 5-3. *SSIS design surface*

Creating a Simple Package

We will now begin to develop our package by dragging the tasks that we require (Check Database Integrity Task, Back Up Database Task, and Notify Operator Task) onto the design surface. This will result in the design surface looking similar to that illustrated in Figure 5-4.

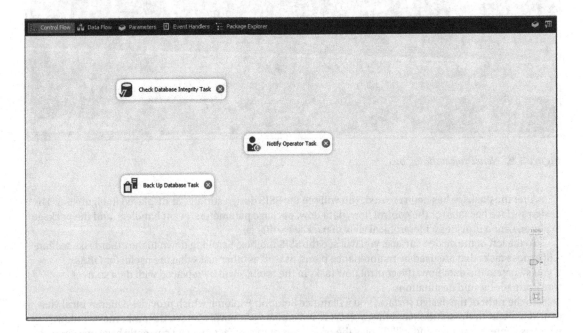

Figure 5-4. *Drag required tasks*

To configure the Check Database Integrity Task, we will double-click the task, causing the task's properties dialog box, known as a Task Editor, to be invoked. Here, we will use the New button to create a new connection manager to ESPROD1, as shown in Figure 5-5.

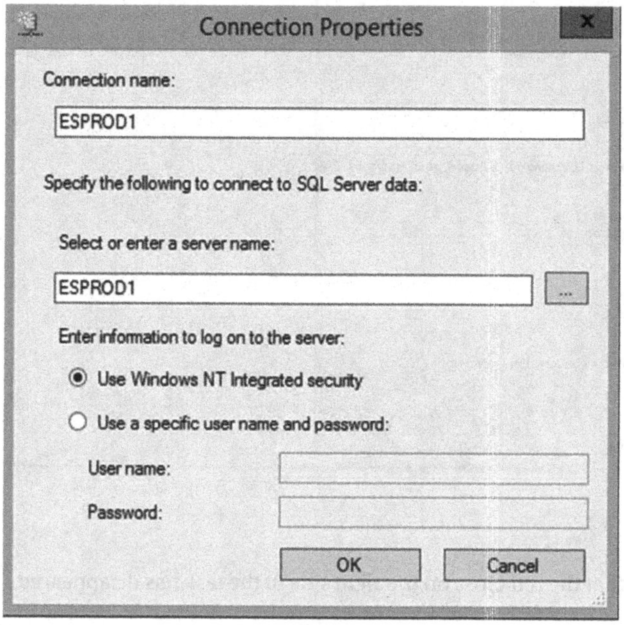

Figure 5-5. *New Connection dialog box*

Back in the Check Database Integrity Task dialog box, we will use the ellipse to specify which databases to run DBCC CHECKDB against. We will select the option to run against All user databases. This means that, currently, only AdventureWorks2016 will be selected, but if more databases are added to the instance, the task will also run against these new databases, without a need to change the package. We will also choose the option to ignore databases that are not currently online. This is demonstrated in Figure 5-6.

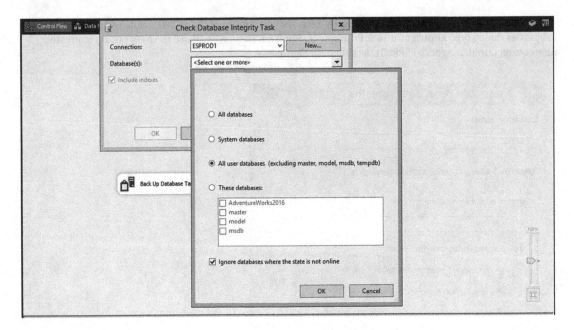

Figure 5-6. Selecting databases

After configuring the task, you will notice that the red cross on the right side of the task has disappeared, as shown in Figure 5-7.

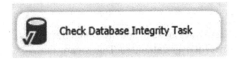

Figure 5-7. Task—post configuration

The Back Up Database Task dialog box contains three tabs. The first of these is the General tab, which is shown in Figure 5-8. Here, our ESPROD1 connection was automatically selected, but we could again use the New button to create a second connection manager, if required. We have specified that the task will be performing a FULL backup and that the backup device type will be Disk (as opposed to Tape or URL). As with the Check Database Integrity Task, we have specified that all user databases should be affected, meaning that new databases will be backed up, without the need to modify the package.

■ **Tip** Tape backup functionality is deprecated and should not be used. If already in use, you should look to move to a new implementation. Back up to URL is used for backups to Windows Azure.

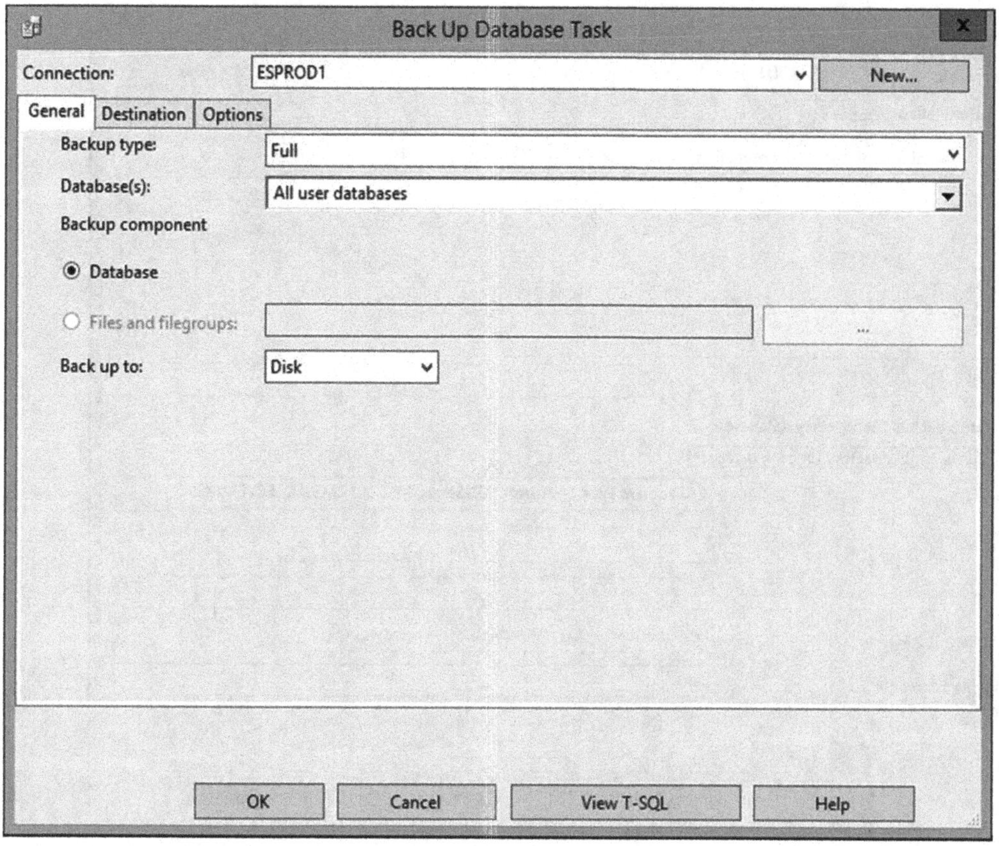

Figure 5-8. *Back Up Database Task—General tab*

On the Destination tab (Figure 5-9) we can configure the particulars of the backup destination, such as striping across multiple files and if a sub-folder should be created for each database. If we had selected back up to URL, then we would also use this tab to configure the connection details to the Azure blob storage. In our scenario, we have configured the backups to be taken to the default backup location but a sub-folder to be created for each unique database.

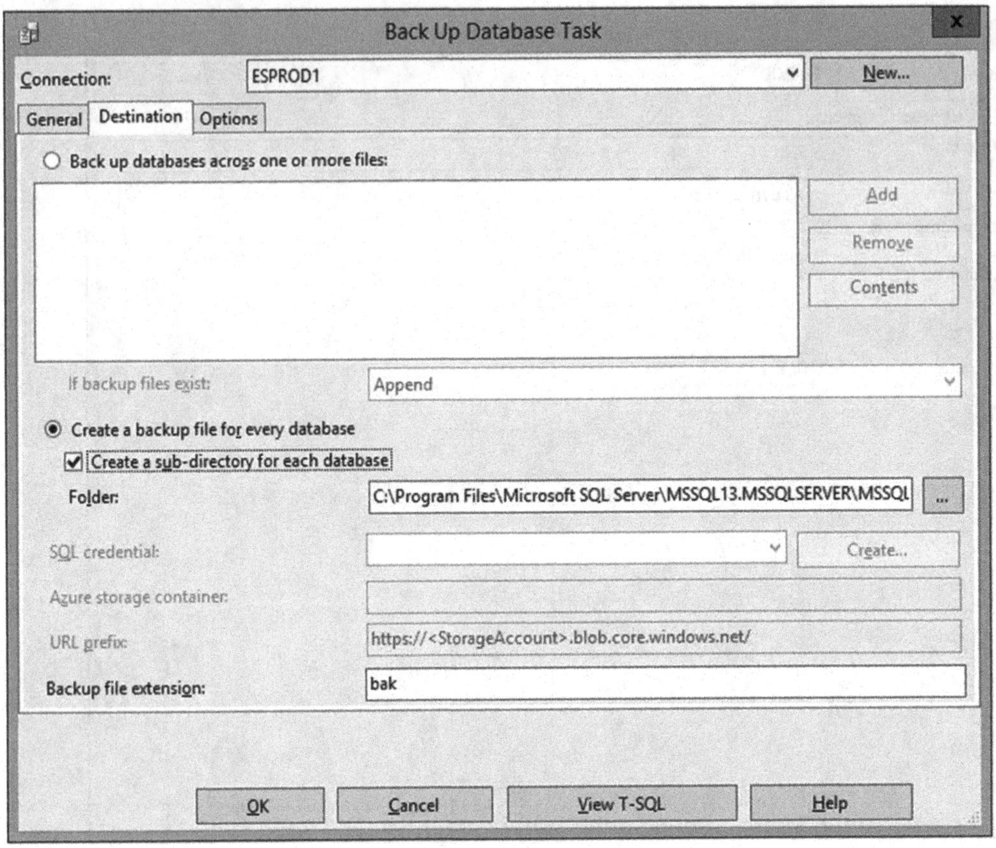

Figure 5-9. Back Up Database Task—Destination tab

On the Options tab, which is illustrated in Figure 5-10, we can configure options that are related to aspects of the backup that are not related to the destination. These options include the compression and encryption settings for the backup, if and when the backup will expire, if the backup should be verified against a checksum, and if the backup should be copy-only (which takes a backup, without affecting the restore sequence). If the database participates in an AlwaysOn availability group, you can also choose whether replica priority settings should be adhered to.

For the purpose of our scenario, we will specify that the backups should always be compressed, regardless of the instance level setting, and that the backup should be verified against a checksum.

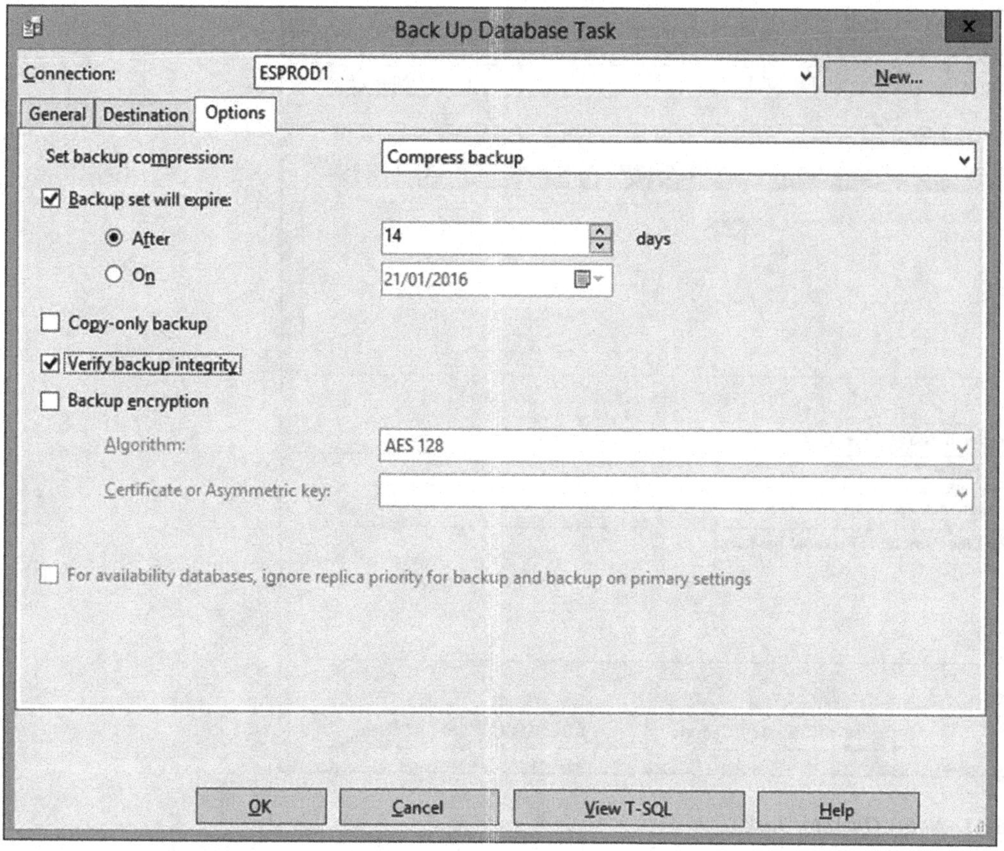

Figure 5-10. *Back Up Database Task—Options tab*

The Notify Operator Task will automatically select our ESPROD1 connection manager and display a list of operators that are in use on the instance. Because we created MSXOperator in Chapter 3, we are able to select this operator from the list, as shown in Figure 5-11. We will then provide a subject and message body for the e-mail that will be sent. Our specification states that an e-mail will only be sent if one of the tasks fails, so we will warn of failure in the notification.

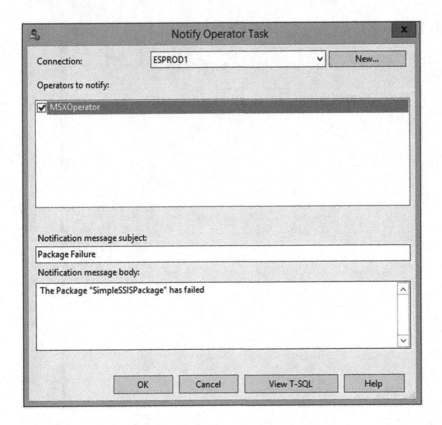

Figure 5-11. *Notify Operator Task*

Configuring Precedence Constraints

Now that our tasks are configured, we will configure precedence constraints between the tasks. Precedence constraints enforce the order in which tasks will be executed, as well as allowing you to implement decision trees within the package. The decision tree that we need our package to follow is illustrated in Figure 5-12.

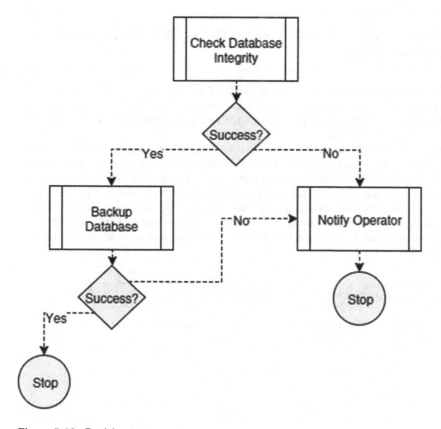

Figure 5-12. *Decision tree*

There are three types of precedence constraints available within SSIS: Success, Failure, and Completion. If a task is joined to its predecessor using a Success constraint, then it will only be executed if its preceding task completes without error. A task that is joined to its predecessor using a Failure constant will only execute if its predecessor fails. A task that is joined to its predecessors using a Completion constraint will execute after its predecessor, regardless of the predecessor's success or failure.

Any tasks that are not joined to a predecessor will execute in parallel when the package first executes. It is also possible to run tasks in parallel downstream within the flow. This is achieved by connecting multiple tasks to a single predecessor.

Precedence constraints can also include expressions. This is useful if you wish to change the flow of a package based on the value of a variable. For example, if you use a follow the sun support model, you may want a different operator to be notified, based on the time of day. In this instance, you could configure three Notify Operator tasks, with one configured to alert your NTAM operator, another configured to notify your EMEA operator, and the Notify Operator Task configured to notify your APAC operator. You could then join all of them to the Check Database Integrity Task using Failure constraints, but add an expression on each, based on the value of the System::StartTime variable. When configuring constraints and expressions, you have a choice of Expression only, Constraint only, Expression and Constraint (which means that the constraint must evaluate to true and the expression must also evaluate to true), or Expression or Constraint (which means that if either the constraint or the expression evaluates to true, the task will be executed).

If a task is connected to two or more preceding tasks, you can configure the constraints as AND constraints or OR constraints. When AND constraints are used, all constraints to preceding tasks must evaluate to true for the task to be executed. When OR constraints are used, if any of the constraints evaluates to true, the task will be executed.

■ **Tip** All constraints of the same type (Success, Failure, or Completion) must all be configured as either OR constraints or all configured as AND constraints.

To configure the Success constraint that we require, between the Check Database Integrity Task and the Back Up Database Task, we will hover the mouse over the bottom center of the Check Database Integrity Task, which will cause a green arrow to appear. We will then drag this arrow to the Back Up Database Task. A green constraint indicates a Success constraint.

To configure the Failure constraint between the Check Database Integrity Task and the Notify Operator Task, we will once again drag a green arrow from the bottom of the Check Database Integrity Task, this time connecting it to the Notify Operator Task. We will then double-click the constraint, to invoke the Precedence Constraint Editor, which is illustrated in Figure 5-13. As we require a simple Failure constraint, we will leave the Evaluation operation value as Constraint and change the Value to Failure. Because the Notify Operator Task should execute if either the Check Database Integrity Task or Back Up Database Task fails, we will also have to specify that the constraint is an OR constraint. If we kept it as an AND constraint, which is the default value, it would never be possible for the task to run.

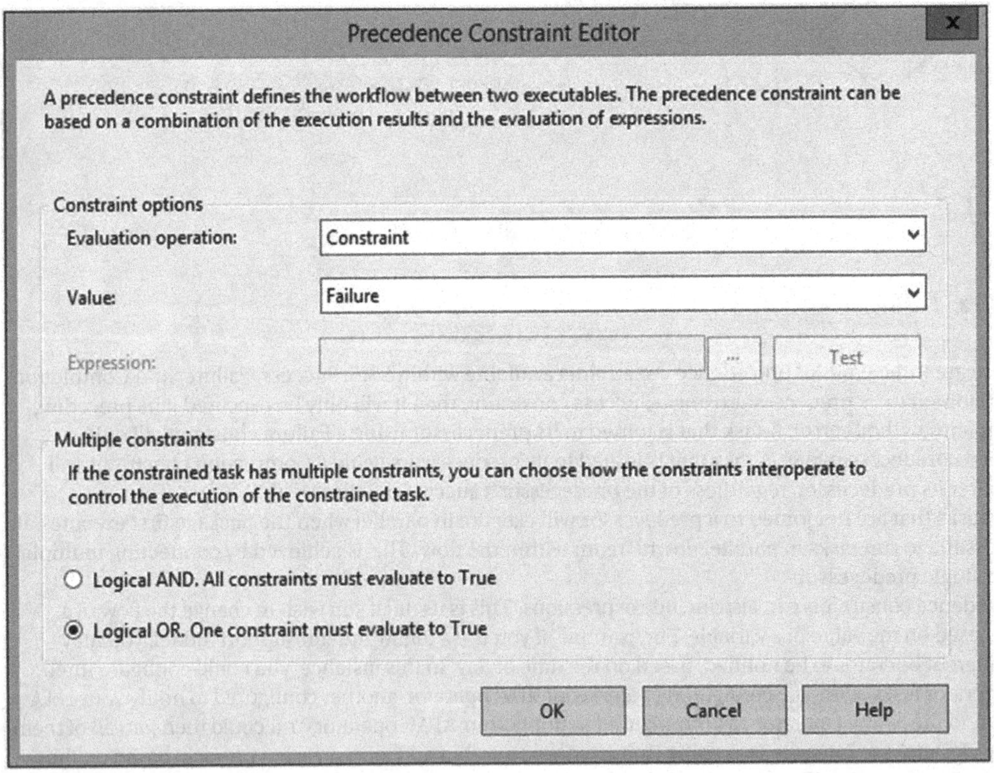

Figure 5-13. Precedence Constraint Editor

■ **Tip** If constraints are configured to use OR logic, they will be displayed as a dashed line, as opposed to a solid line.

We will create the final precedence constraint, which will be a Failure constraint, connecting the Back Up Database Task to the Notify Operator Task, by following the same steps that we used previously to create the Failure constraint that connects the Check Database Integrity Task to the Notify Operator Task. The resulting control flow is shown in Figure 5-14.

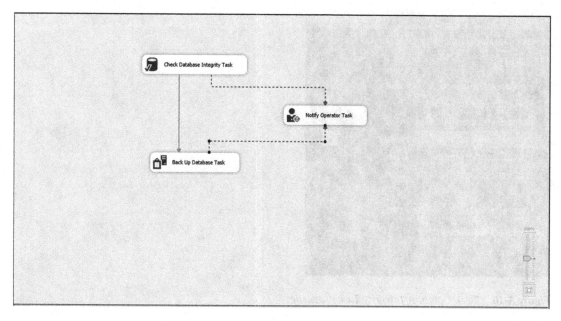

Figure 5-14. *Final control flow*

Testing the Package

The first step in testing the package is to run it! This will instantly call out any initial issues. We will click the Start (Play) button on the SSDT toolbar. This will cause the package to run. While a task is running, an amber wheel will turn, at the top right-hand corner of the task. When the task completes, the wheel will turn to a green tick, to indicate success, or a red cross, to indicate failure. When complete, we can press the Stop button on the SSIS toolbar, to end execution. You will notice in Figure 5-15 that the Notify Operator Task does not have a tick or cross. This is because the other two tasks completed successfully, and, therefore, it was never executed.

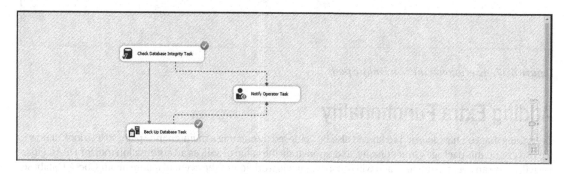

Figure 5-15. *Package after successful execution*

The package succeeded, which is a great start, but it is important to test all paths within the package, which means that we will have to force either the Check Database Integrity Task or the Back Up Database Task to fail, so that the Notify Operator Task is executed. We can achieve this by setting the ForceExecutionResult property of the Check Database Integrity Task to Failure, as shown in Figure 5-16.

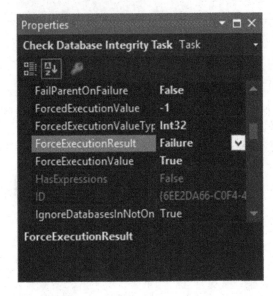

Figure 5-16. *Check Database Integrity Task properties*

We will now run the package again. This time, the Check Database Integrity Task will fail, which will cause the Notify Operator Task to be executed, instead of the Back Up Database Task. The results are shown in Figure 5-17.

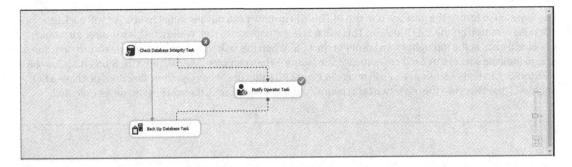

Figure 5-17. *Execution results on Failure path*

Adding Extra Functionality

Everything that you have learned so far can also be achieved by creating a maintenance plan, so let's look at how we can extend this package's functionality, to demonstrate the value of SSIS as an automation tool for DBAs. First, we will create an event handler, which will run a diagnostic workflow in the event of failure of our Check Database Integrity Task. Second, we will implement a ForEach loop, which will iterate through all servers in the enterprise.

Creating Event Handlers

Event handlers create additional control flows within the package that are only executed when a certain condition occurs. When the event is an error, you could choose to use precedence constraints and additional tasks within the main control flow, as you have already seen. The benefits of using event handlers, however, are listed following.

- Event handlers allow you to encapsulate logic within a separate container. This means that the code is more easily reused. It also dramatically simplifies the main control flow, allowing for faster code maintenance. This is similar to a procedural or modular approach to coding.

- Event handlers can be created at multiple levels of the package hierarchy. This means that a single event handler can be created to respond to issues with multiple tasks.

- Event handlers can be fired in response to more than just errors. They can also fire in response to conditions including the following:

  - On information

  - On warning

  - On error

  - On progress

  - On execution status changed

  - On pre-execution

  - On post-execution

  - On variable value changed

  - On pre-validation

  - On post-validation

  - On task failed

  - On query canceled

For our package, we will create one event handler. This event handler will be fired if the Check Database Integrity Task fails. For this reason, we will remove the Failure constraint that connects the Check Database Integrity Task to the Notify Operator Task.

We will begin by navigating to the Event Handlers tab of the design surface, which is illustrated in Figure 5-18. Here, we have used the Executable drop-down, to associate the event handler with the Check Database Integrity Task. As we want the event handler to be executed if this task fails, we will leave the default setting for the Event handler drop-down as its default value of OnError. You can now click the link in the center of the screen, to create the event handler.

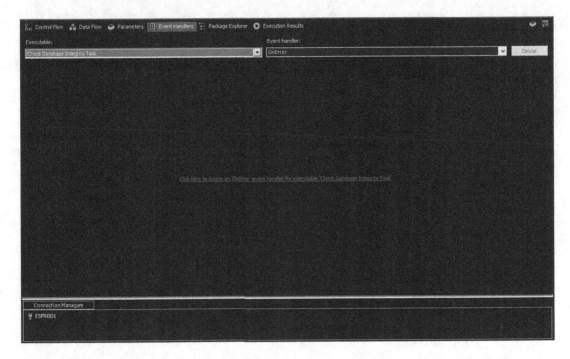

Figure 5-18. *Create OnError event handler*

We can now create the orchestration for our first event handler. The tasks that we will want our event handler to follow are represented in Figure 5-19.

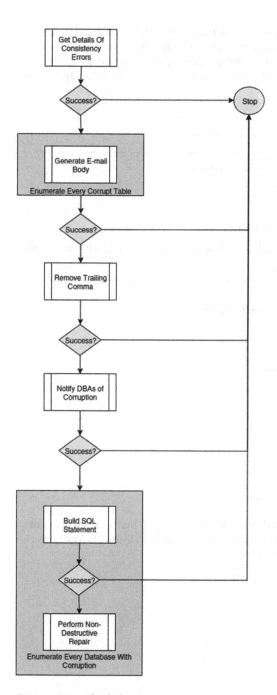

Figure 5-19. *Check database integrity on error event handler orchestration*

This process flow diagram shows that we will first find out the details of the corrupt database(s) that have caused the database consistency checks to fail. We will perform this action using an Execute SQL Task, to run a query against the dbo.suspect_pages table in the MSDB database. This table records details of corrupt pages that have been identified on the instance. The columns in the MSDB.dbo.suspect_pages table are detailed in Table 5-1.

Table 5-1. suspect_pages Columns

Column	Description
Database_id	The ID of the database that contains the suspect page
File_id	The ID of the file that contains the suspect page
Page_id	The ID of the page that is suspect
Event_Type	The nature of the event that caused the suspect pages to be updated
Error_count	An incremental counter, recording the number of times that the event has occurred
Last_updated_date	The last time the row was updated

The possible values in the Event_Type column are detailed in Table 5-2.

Table 5-2. Event Types

Event_type	Description
1	823 or 824 error
2	Bad checksum
3	Torn page
4	Restored
5	Repaired
7	Deallocated by DBCC CHECKDB

The details that we have to return from this table will determine the database(s) that we need to repair and also provide information about the afflicted tables, which will be sent to the DBA team. The query that we will use to return this information can be found in Listing 5-1.

Listing 5-1. Query Corruption Details

```
DECLARE @SQL NVARCHAR(MAX) ;

DECLARE @SQLXML XML ;

CREATE TABLE #TEST

(

    ParentObject        NVARCHAR(16),

    [Object]            NVARCHAR(32),

    Field               NVARCHAR(32),
```

```
    VALUE                    NVARCHAR(128)
) ;
SELECT @SQL = (
    SELECT 'INSERT INTO #TEST(ParentObject, [Object], Field, Value) EXEC(''DBCC PAGE ('
        + CAST(database_id AS NVARCHAR(3))
        + ','
        + CAST(file_id AS NVARCHAR(16))
        + ','
        + CAST(page_id AS NVARCHAR(32))
        + ',0) WITH TABLERESULTS''); ' AS [data()]
    FROM msdb.dbo.suspect_pages
    WHERE event_type NOT IN (4,5)
    FOR XML PATH('')
) ;
EXEC(@SQL) ;
CREATE TABLE #CorruptTables
(
    DatabaseName NVARCHAR(128),
    TableName NVARCHAR(128)
) ;
SELECT @SQL = (
    SELECT 'INSERT INTO #CorruptTables SELECT DISTINCT ''' + db_name(database_id) + '''
DatabaseName, t.Name TableName FROM '
        + DB_NAME(database_id)
        + '.sys.tables t INNER JOIN #TEST tt ON tt.VALUE = t.object_id AND tt.field =
''Metadata: ObjectId'' INNER JOIN #TEST tt2 ON tt2.Object = tt.Object WHERE (SELECT VALUE
FROM #test WHERE field = ''bdbid'' AND object = (SELECT object FROM #test WHERE field =
''bpage'' AND VALUE = SUBSTRING(tt2.object,7,len(tt2.object)-6)     ) ) = '
        + CAST(database_id AS NVARCHAR(4)) AS [data()]
    FROM msdb.dbo.suspect_pages
    WHERE event_type NOT IN (4,5)
```

```
    FOR XML PATH('')

) ;

EXEC(@SQL) ;

SELECT *

FROM #CorruptTables ;

DROP TABLE #test ;

DROP TABLE #CorruptTables ;
```

Before configuring the Execute SQL Task itself, we will have to create three variables. One of these variables will be of the object data type and will be passed the results of our query by the Execute SQL Task. The other two variables will be created with the string data type and will be used inside a Foreach Loop Container, one of which will hold the name of the corrupt table, and the other will store the name of the database that the corrupt table resides in.

To create the variables, we will have to invoke the Variables window, which can be found by drilling through the SSIS menu and selecting Variables. We will then use the Add Variable button to create each variable in turn, provide a name for the variable, and specify its data type. The scope of the variable should also be defined. The variables scope determines where within the package the variable can be accessed. Variables can be accessed by the component in which they are defined by their scope and by any elements that are at lower levels of that package hierarchy, within the executables branch. For example, if we set the scope at the level of the OnError event handler, then it could only be accessed within this event handler or a subcomponents of the event handler, such as data flows created within the event handler. If we configure the scope at the level of the package, however, the variable could be accessed by any component in the whole package. The Variables window is illustrated in Figure 5-20.

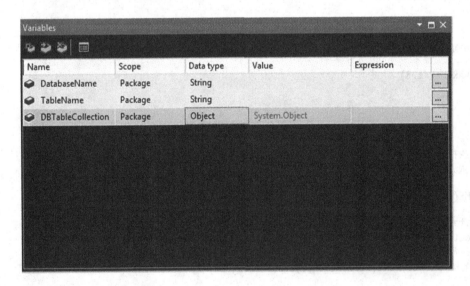

Figure 5-20. *Variables window*

We will now drag an Execute SQL Task onto the design surface and double-click it to enter the Execute SQL Task Editor. The General page of the editor is shown in Figure 5-21.

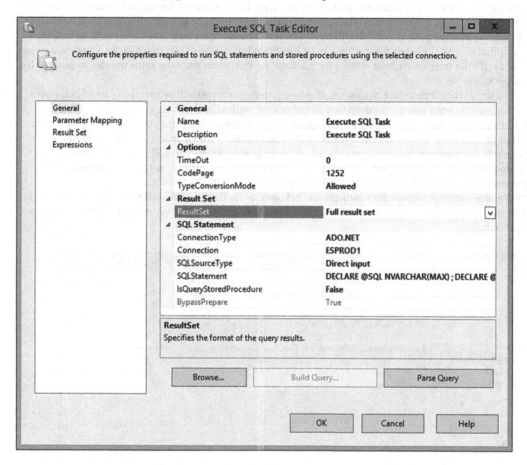

Figure 5-21. *Execute SQL Task Editor—General page*

On this page, we will use the ConnectionType and Connection properties to configure our ESPROD1 connection as the data source for the task. We will then use the ellipse on the SQLStatement property to open the query dialog box and paste our query. Additionally, we will need to configure the ResultSet property. This property is used to define the result set (if any) that will be output from the task and directly impacts the variable(s) that can be used to accept the output. If None is selected, it is not possible to map any variables for receiving output. If Single row is selected, then you will need to map a variable for each column, with an appropriate data type, which aligns with the data type of the column returned. If Full result set is selected, then a single variable, with the object data type must be mapped to results index 0. If XML is selected, then the parameter used will depend on the data returned. If a single XML document or XML fragment is returned, then you can map either a single string parameter or a single object parameter. If multiple XML documents are returned, the variable must be an object. If you are using native connection managers, such as OLEDB, the results will be returned as the MSXML6.IXMLDOMDocument object type. If you are using a managed connection manager, such as ADO.NET, however, the results will be returned as the System.Xml.XmlDocument object type.

The SQLSourceType and IsQueryStoredProcedure properties are also important, although we will be leaving them with their default values for this particular example. The SQLSourceType property allows you to define if the query will be input manually, as we have just seen, if the query will be stored in a variable or if the query is stored in a file in the file system. The option to use a variable can be helpful if the query will be used in multiple tasks, within the package, or if the query will be build, based upon outputs of other tasks or variables.

The option to read the query from a file is used less often but can be useful in scenarios where you need to be able to edit the queries, without editing the package, or where you want the same queries to be used by multiple packages.

The IsQueryStoredProcedure parameter allows you to define if you will be executing an ad hoc query or if you wish to execute a store procedure that already exists within the database you are connecting to. Using stored procedures, as opposed to ad hoc SQL is always the best policy from the angle of the database engine, but this does not always hold true within SSIS. The benefit of SSIS is that it will allow you to dynamically build query strings at runtime, based on package execution values. This benefit is lost when using stored procedures. Additionally, if your package will run against multiple servers or environments, then you need to ensure that the stored procedures exist on every instance.

The Parameters page of the editor is displayed in Figure 5-22. This page is used to map SSIS variables to parameters inside our Execute SQL Task. This is used when you are using an Execute SQL Task to execute a stored procedure.

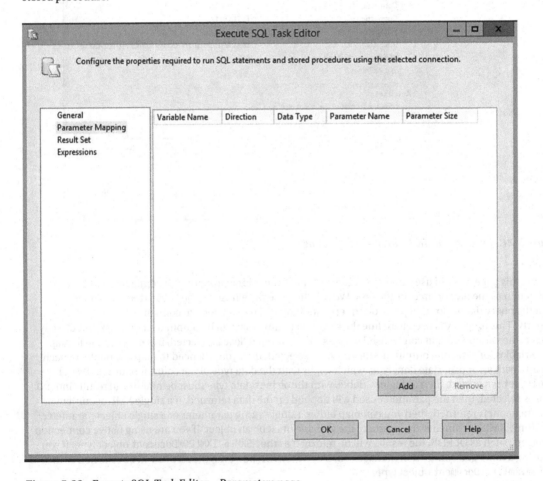

Figure 5-22. Execute SQL Task Editor—Parameters page

On the Result Set page, which is shown in Figure 5-23, we will configure the variable(s) that our results will be passed into. Because we will be returning a full result set, this will have to be a single variable, with the object data type. When a single row is returned, result names can be specified by name or ordinal position. When the result set is XML or a full result set, the parameter name is always 0.

■ **Tip** Ordinal Result Names are zero-based. This means that the first column is always 0, the second column is always 1, and so on.

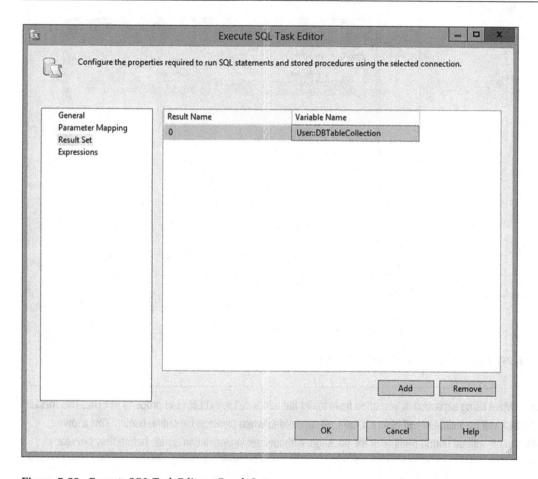

Figure 5-23. *Execute SQL Task Editor—Result Set page*

The Expressions page, which is illustrated in Figure 5-24, provides access to the Expression Editor for the task and allows you to configure the task's properties, using expressions, as opposed to hard-coded values. This is a great feature, which helps you create very dynamic, reusable packages.

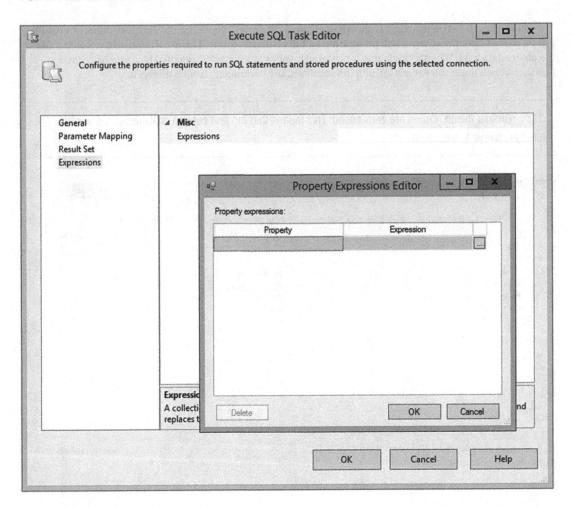

Figure 5-24. Execute SQL Task—Expressions page

■ **Tip** When using expressions, you often have to set the task's DelayValidation property to true. This means that the task will be validated just before it runs, as opposed to when package execution begins. This allows variables to be built up during runtime of the package, without causing validation issues before they are ready.

We will now have to add a Foreach Loop Container to the flow. This container will process each row of our result set in turn, until all results have been processed. The General page of the Foreach Loop Editor allows us to configure a name and description for the loop. The Collection page of the editor allows us to configure the enumeration and is illustrated in Figure 5-25.

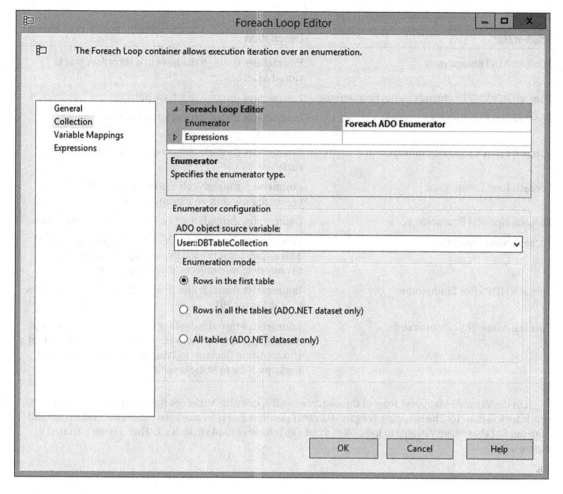

Figure 5-25. *Foreach Loop—Collection page*

On this page, we have selected Foreach ADO Enumerator as the enumerator type. This will accept our ADO.NET table and loop around each row within the table. A description of other enumerators can be found in Table 5-3. We will then specify our variable as the source variable that contains the rowset.

Table 5-3. *Foreach Loop Enumeration Types*

Enumerator	Description
Foreach ADO Enumerator	Enumerates through the rows in a recordset that is stored as an object
Foreach ADO.NET Schema Rowset Enumerator	Enumerates through database objects
Foreach File Enumerator	Enumerates through files stored in the Operating System
Foreach From Variable Enumerator	Enumerates through objects contained in an SSIS variable
Foreach Item Enumerator	Enumerates through collections, such as the executables within an Execute Process Task
Foreach Nodelist Enumerator	Enumerates through the results of an XPath expression
Foreach SMO Enumerator	Enumerates through SQL Server Management Objects. This enumerator is used by the Copy Database wizard to copy database objects as an online operation.
Foreach HDFS File Enumerator	Enumerates through files in an Hadoop file system. New in SQL Server 2016
Foreach Azure Blob Enumerator	Enumerates through the files in an Azure BLOB storage container. Can be used to enumerate backup files when you are using Backups to Windows Azure or Managed Backups. New in SQL Server 2014

On the Variable Mappings page of the editor, we will specify the variables that each column in our result set will map to. The mapping is against ordinal position and is a zero-based index. Therefore, we will map our DatabaseName variable to index 0 and our TableName variable to index 1. This is demonstrated in Figure 5-26.

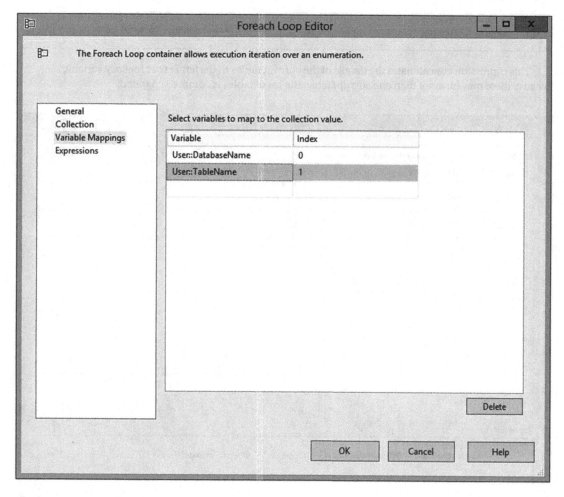

Figure 5-26. *Foreach Enumerator—Variable Mappings page*

The Expressions page, which is common to many tasks, allows us to configure the properties of the Foreach Loop Container via expressions, as opposed to hard-coding them. We will also drag a Success precedence constraint between the Execute SQL Task and the Foreach Loop Container.

Our next task will be to create another new variable. We will call it NotificationBody and define it as a string, at the package level. We will also give the variable an initial value of "The following table(s) are corrupt: ." This variable will be used to hold the e-mail message that is sent to the DBA team.

We can now drag an Expression Task into the Foreach Loop Container. In the editor, we will add the expression in Listing 5-2, as demonstrated in Figure 5-27. The expression can be tested, using the Evaluate Expression button.

Listing 5-2. Expression to Build E-mail Body

```
@[User::NotificationBody] =
        @[User::NotificationBody] + @[User::TableName] + "in database " + @
[User::DatabaseName] + ", "
```

> ■ **Tip** Variable names and functions can be dragged into the Expression window, to avoid unnecessary typing.

This expression concatenates the details of the corrupt tables to the `NotificationBody` variable. Because there may be more than one corrupt table, the list of tables is comma-separated.

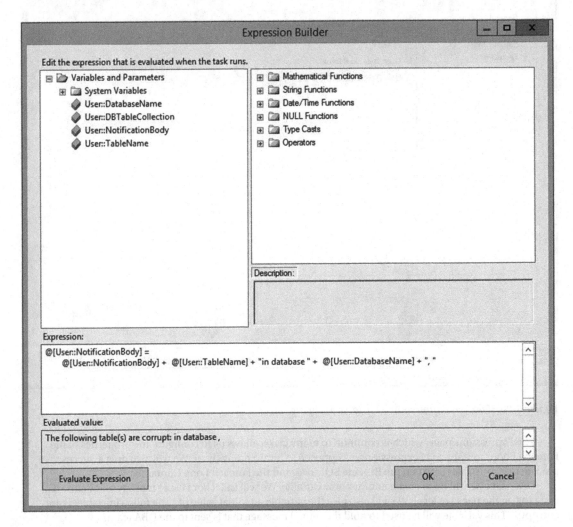

Figure 5-27. *Expression editor*

> ■ **Tip** The Expression editor offers a wide selection of built-in functions that can speed up development. Some of these will be discussed in this chapter, but I encourage you to explore as many as possible.

The Foreach Loop Container is an executable in its own right (every container and every task is an executable in its own right, as well as the package), and because the Expression Task is the first (and only) task to be executed inside the container, there is no need to attach a precedence constraint to the task.

We will now add another Expression Task, this time, outside of the Foreach Loop Container, and attach a Success constraint from the Foreach Loop Container to our new task. This task will be used to remove the final comma from the NotificationBody variable. Because the Expression Task inside the Foreach Loop Container is building up a comma-separated list of corrupt tables, and the expression ends with a comma, there will be a single unused comma at the end of the string, which should be removed. The expression that we will use to perform this task can be found in Listing 5-3.

Listing 5-3. Remove Trailing Comma Expression

```
@[User::NotificationBody] =
    SUBSTRING(@[User::NotificationBody]
        + @[User::TableName]
        + "in database "
        + @[User::DatabaseName]
        + ","
, 1
, LEN(@[User::NotificationBody]
        + @[User::TableName]
        + "in database "
        + @[User::DatabaseName]
        + ",") - 1)
```

We will now drag a Send Mail Task to the design surface and attach a Success precedence constraint from the Expression Task. The General page of the Send Mail Task Editor allows you to define a name and description for the task. There is also an Expressions page. On the Mail page of the editor, the properties of the task can be changed. The first property pertains to the connection manager. Here, we will use the ellipse to invoke the SMTP Connection Manager Editor, as shown in Figure 5-28.

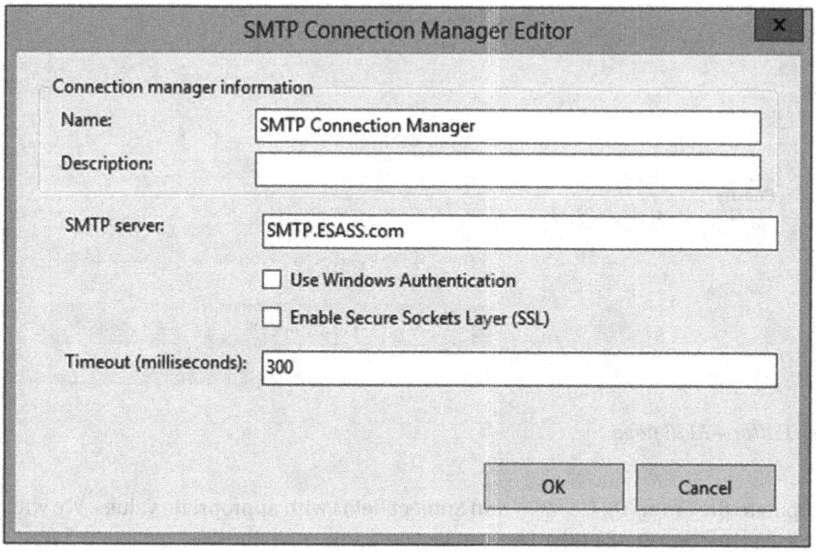

Figure 5-28. SMTP Connection Manager Editor

In this dialog box, we will specify the SMTP server, which will be used for sending the notification mails. If the SMTP server requires authentication, we should check the Use Windows Authentication box and ensure that the service account that will run the package has sufficient permissions to send mails from the SMTP server. If a secure connection is required by the SMTP server, we should also check the Enable Secure Socket Layer (SSL) box, which will force the message to be sent to the SMTP server via an encrypted authentication. Additionally, a time-out can be specified. We have specified this value as five minutes (300 milliseconds). When we exit this dialog box, the connection manager will be created, and we will be returned to the Mail page of the Send Mail Task Editor, which is displayed in Figure 5-29.

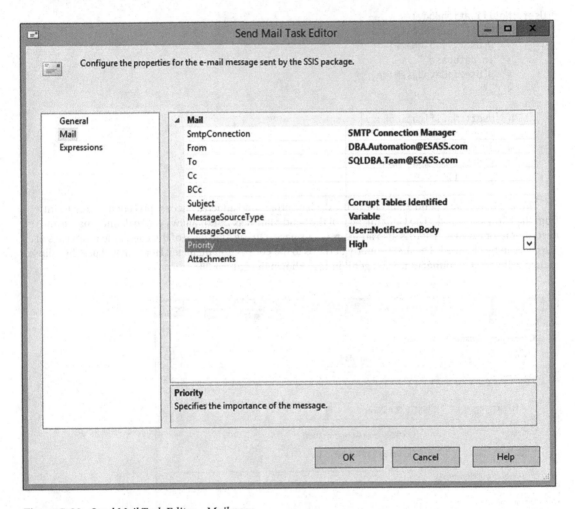

Figure 5-29. *Send Mail Task Editor—Mail page*

On this page, we will populate the From, To, Cc, BCc, and Subject fields with appropriate values. We will then have to define the source type of the e-mail body. This can be configured with the MessageSourceType property, which allows Direct Input, Variable, or File Connection to be specified. In our case, we will, of course, choose the Variable option. This will allow us to pick the correct variable from a drop-down list in the MessageSource field. Optionally, a file system path can be used to specify the location of an attachment.

■ **Tip**   If your package will build the attachment file and write it to the file system, you should set the
DelayValidation property of the Send Mail Task to true. This will stop the package from failing in the
validation phase.

We will now create another variable, called SQLText. This variable will be used to store the DBCC
statements that the package will use to attempt to repair the corrupt databases. This is the final variable that
we will require for the event handler, and the complete set of variables is displayed in Figure 5-30.

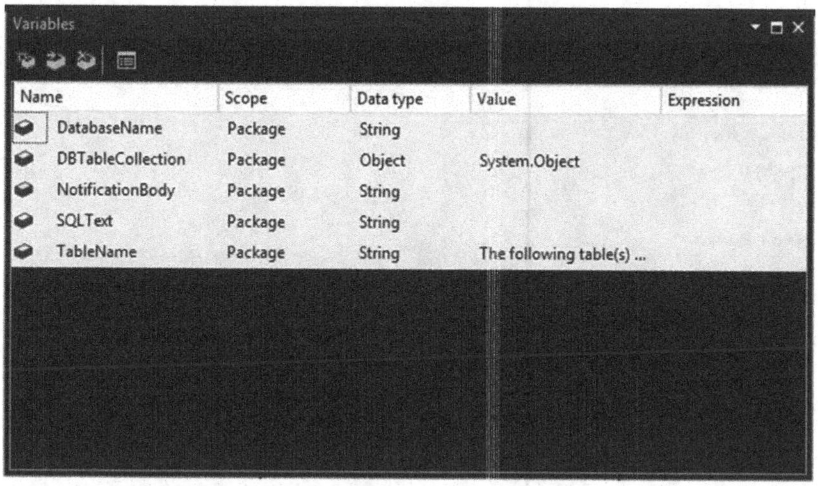

Figure 5-30. Variables window

We will now add another Foreach Loop Container to the design surface. This loop will enumerate
through each database name and build an SQL statement to execute. Therefore, we will configure the
Foreach Loop Container to enumerate through the rows in the DBTableCollection variable.

Inside the Foreach Loop Container, we will place an Expression Task and an Execute SQL Task. The
Expression Task will be configured to run first, followed by the Execute SQL Task, using a Success constraint.
The Expression Task will build the SQL statement, by using the expression in Listing 5-4.

Listing 5-4. Build SQL Statement Expression

```
@[User::SQLText] =
    "ALTER DATABASE " + @[User:DatabaseName] + " SET SINGLE_USER WITH ROLLBACK IMMEDIATE;
    DBCC CHECKDB (" + @[User:DatabaseName] + ",REPAIR_REBUILD);
    ALTER DATABASE " + @[User:DatabaseName] + " SET MULTI_USER;"
```

This expression will populate the SQLText variable with the appropriate command to attempt to repair
the database. This means that we can now configure our Execute SQL Task to run the command contained
within this variable. We will do this by setting the SQLSourceType as Variable and then selecting SQLText
from the drop-down list in the SourceVariable field.

We should also consider giving each of our tasks friendlier names. This is especially pertinent, because
we have used the same task types on more than one occasion. Tasks can be renamed on the General page of
their editor, or by clicking their name in the flow. The final event handler is illustrated in Figure 5-31.

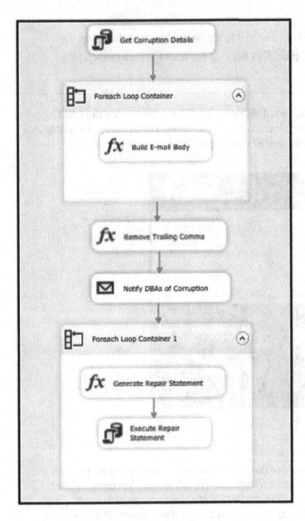

Figure 5-31. *Completed event handler*

Run Against Each Server in the Enterprise

We could, of course, use SQL Server Agent to run our package on all servers in our environment, but for SSIS packages, this has the limitation of requiring SSIS to be installed on each server. Therefore, a more strategic approach is to run a single package from our management server and build in the logic, to enumerate through each server in the environment.

Normally, we would pull the details of our servers from an inventory database, and this is discussed in Chapter 6. For now, however, we will simulate this approach, by using an Execute SQL Task at the start of our package, to create a temporary table, which will hold the server details.

To create this Execute SQL Task, we will have to create a new ADO.NET connection manager that connects to the ESASSMGMT1 server. We will perform this task by right-clicking in the Connection Manager window, selecting New ADO.NET connection. This will cause the Configure ADO.NET Connection Manager dialog box to be invoked. We will use the New button within this window, to cause the Connection Manager dialog box to be displayed. This dialog box is shown in Figure 5-32. Here, we have specified the name of the server and selected TempDB as the landing database. The All page can be used to configure advanced connection settings, but these are rarely required for administrative purposes and are therefore outside the scope of this book.

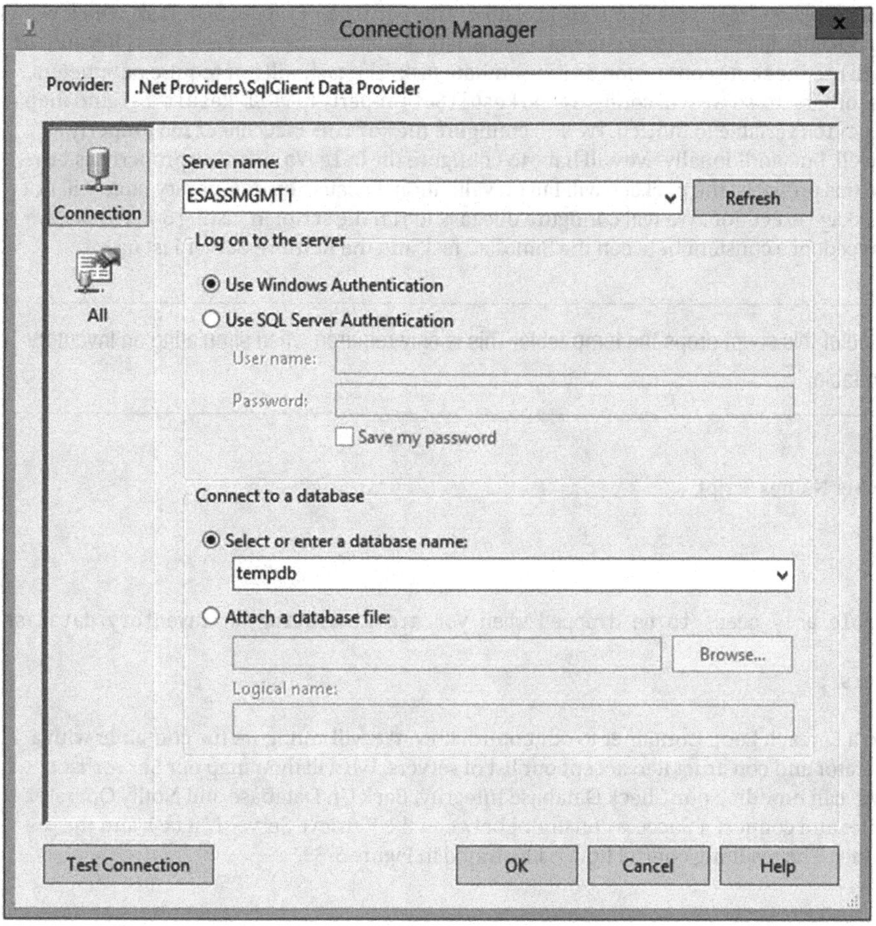

Figure 5-32. *Connection Manager dialog box*

Our next task will be to create two new variables. We will name one of these variable ServerNameCollection. This will be defined with the object data type and store the server names that we will enumerate through. The second will be called ServerName. This variable will be a string, which stores each server name in turn.

We will now create an Execute SQL Task that uses this connection manager and name it Simulation. The query that this task will run can be found in Listing 5-5. The task will not require parameters or return a result set. Because we are using a temporary table, we will have to keep the connection open. To do this, we must change the RetainSameConnection property of the connection manager to true. This will keep the connection open and prevent the temp table from being dropped.

Listing 5-5. Simulate Inventory Database Script

```
CREATE TABLE ##Servers
(
 ServerName      NVARCHAR(128)
) ;

INSERT INTO ##Servers
VALUES ('ESPROD1'), ('ESPROD2') ;
```

We will now create the first "real" task in our control flow. This will be an Execute SQL Task, which will read the results from our simulated inventory database. We will name it Retrieve Server List. Because of the temp table, we will use the same connection as the Simulate task. The task will not require parameters, but it will return a list of servers, so we will configure the ResultSet property to Full Result Set and map our ServerNameCollection variable to index 0. We will configure the RetainSameConnection property as true for this task as well, but, additionally, we will have to configure the DelayValidation property as true. If we fail to configure this property, the package will fail on validation, because the temporary table will not exist at the start of package execution. We will configure this task to run the script in Listing 5-6. Finally, we will add a Success precedence constant between the Simulate task and the Retrieve Server List task.

■ **Note**   The final line of this script drops the temp table. This is only required when simulating an inventory database with a temp table.

Listing 5-6. Find Server Names Script

```
SELECT ServerName
FROM ##Servers ;

--The temporary table only needs to be dropped when you are simulating an inventory database

DROP TABLE ##Servers ;
```

We will now add a Foreach Loop Container to our control flow. We will configure the container with a Foreach ADO enumerator and construct it to accept our list of servers. We will then map our ServerName variable to index 0. We can now drag our Check Database Integrity, Back Up Database and Notify Operator tasks into the container and connect a Success constraint between the Retrieve Server List task and the Foreach Loop Container. The resulting control flow is illustrated in Figure 5-33.

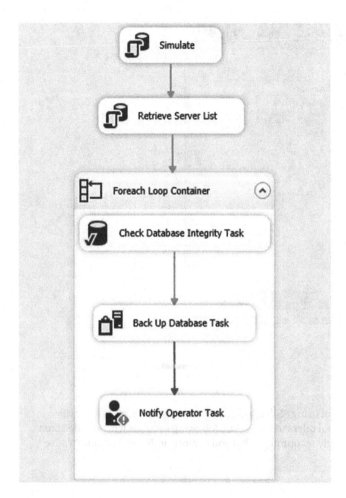

Figure 5-33. *Final control flow*

Even though our control flow is complete, there are other configuration changes that we have to make to our data source dynamic, so that the package will work as designed. The first and most significant of these is to change the connection manager so that the server connection is dynamic, based on the ServerName variable. To do this, we will highlight the connection manager and enter the Expression Editor, via the Expression ellipse, in the properties window. This is illustrated in Figure 5-34. We will also rename the connection manager to DynamicConnection, as the name of ESPROD1 no longer makes sense.

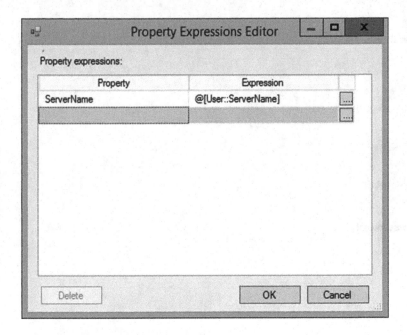

Figure 5-34. *Property Expressions Editor*

Automation Recipes

Now that you have learned the fundamentals of using SSIS to automate administrative tasks, you will appreciate the power and flexibility that the tool offers to DBAs. The following sections will provide some recipes for automaton techniques, but I strongly recommend that you explore additional administrative scenarios with SSIS.

Verifying Backups

There is an old adage that warns: "You do not have a backup until you have restored it." Therefore, a best practice DR strategy will include periodically restoring backups. SQL Server offers a less intensive compromise, however, in the form of the VERIFYONLY restore option. This option will fully check that the back is complete and that all volumes are readable. It will also check some (but not all) of the page metadata, and if the backup was taken with a CHECKSUM, it will verify that CHECKSUM. Of course, the only way to be 100% confident that there are no issues whatsoever with a backup is to restore it and then run DBCC CHECKDB against it, but this is usually not practical for time and resource reasons. Therefore, the majority of organizations accept RESTORE WITH VERIFYONLY as the best approach to testing backup validity.

The requirement to test backups can be automated using SSIS. We will create an SSIS package that enumerates around each database within an instance. The package will follow the process flow that is illustrated in Figure 5-35.

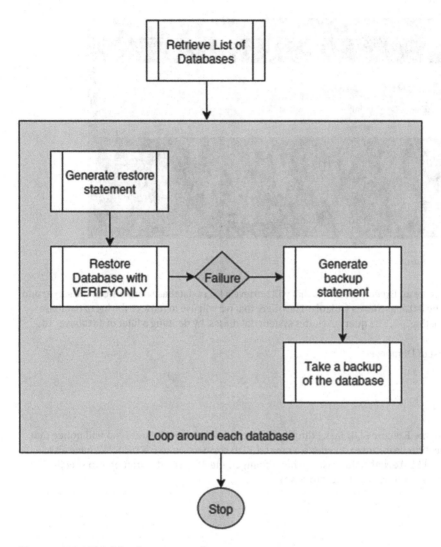

Figure 5-35. *Check backups process flow*

■ **Note** The demonstrations in this section will make several assumptions, which you may have to tailor to your individual requirements. It is assumed that you take backups to the default backup location. It is also assumed that your backup naming convention is databasename.bak. In addition, the demonstration only takes databases in SIMPLE recovery model into account. You will need to add additional steps to handle log backups if your database is in FULL recovery model.

We will use SSDT to create an Integration Services project named VerifyBackups. Within our new package, we will create three variables. A variable of the object data type named DatabaseNames will store the list of databases. A variable called Name will be defined as a data type string and used to store each database name in turn as the enumeration progresses. The third variable, called SQLText, will be defined as a string and store the RESTORE and BACKUP statements to run. The Variables window, showing the newly created variables, can be found in Figure 5-36.

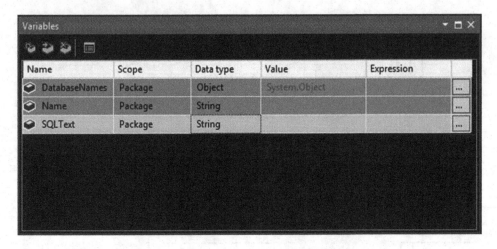

Figure 5-36. *Variables window*

Our next step is to create an Execute SQL Task that will retrieve a list of database names from the server and use this list to populate the DatabaseNames variable. The query that we will use to retrieve the list of database names can be found in Listing 5-7. The query excludes system databases, by defining a filter of database_id.

Listing 5-7. Retrieve List of Databases

```
SELECT name
FROM sys.databases
WHERE database_id > 4 ;
```

The General page of the Execute SQL Task Editor is displayed in Figure 5-37. Here, you will notice that we have used the Connection drop-down, to create a new OLEDB connection to ESPROD1. We have also added our query to the SQLStatement field. Last, we have changed the ResultSet parameter to specify that we are expecting the query to return a Full result set.

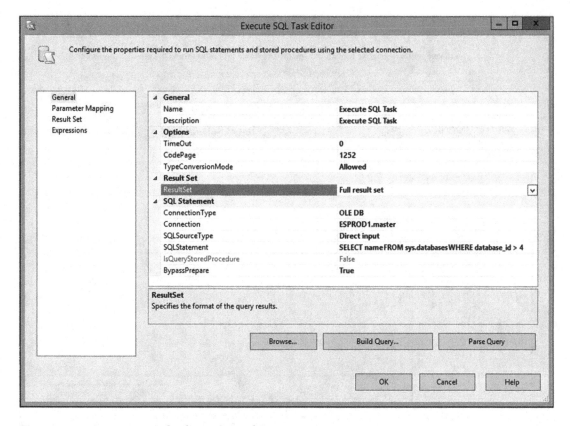

Figure 5-37. *Execute SQL Task Editor—General page*

On the Result Set page of the Execute SQL Task Editor, we will configure our DatabaseNames variable to accept the output from the task. This is illustrated in Figure 5-38.

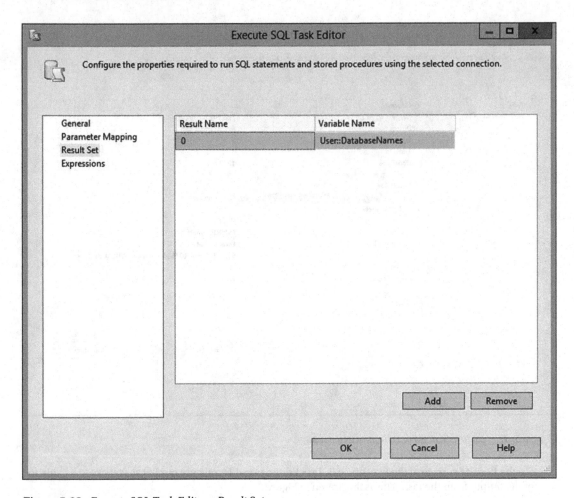

Figure 5-38. *Execute SQL Task Editor—Result Set page*

We will now create a Foreach Loop Container and connect our Execute SQL Task to this container, using a Success constraint. We will configure the container to iterate through the rows in our DatabaseNames variable and map the Name variable to index 0 of the collection, so that it receives a database name in each iteration of the loop. The configuration of the Foreach Loop Container can be seen in Figure 5-39 and Figure 5-40.

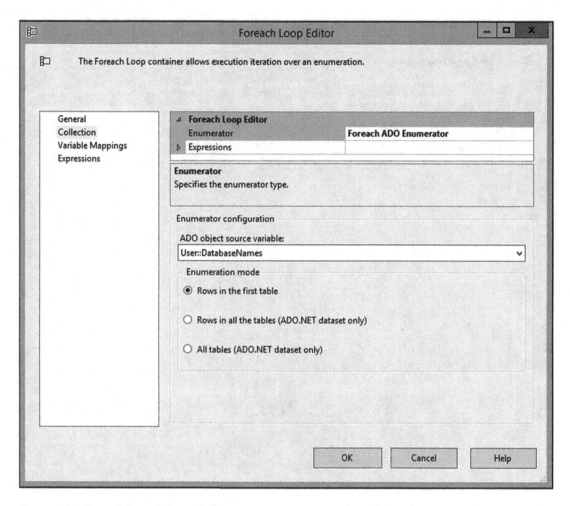

Figure 5-39. Foreach Loop Editor—Collection page

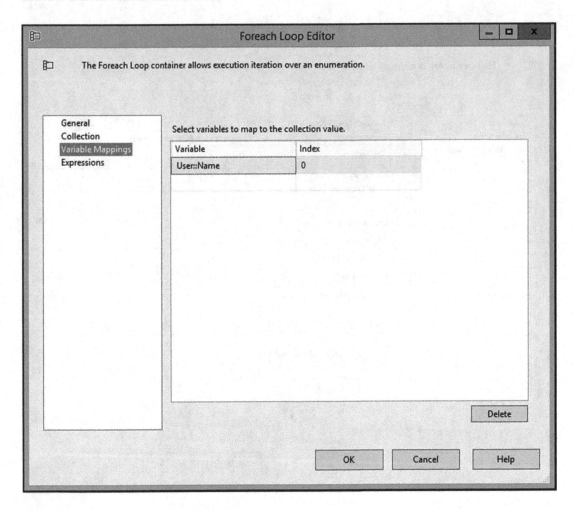

Figure 5-40. *Foreach Loop Editor—Variable Mappings page*

We will now add an Expression Task to the Foreach Loop Container. We will use this task to build the RESTORE command and populate the SQLText variable with the command. The expression to achieve this can be found in Listing 5-8.

Listing 5-8. Build RESTORE Statement

```
@[User::SQLText] = "RESTORE VERIFYONLY FROM DISK = '" + @[User::Name] + ".bak'"
```

This will be the first task to run within the Foreach Loop Container. Therefore, it does not require an upstream precedence constraint. We will name the task BuildRestoreStatement, to avoid confusion with other Expression Tasks within the package.

We will then execute the RESTORE statement with an Execute SQL Task. We will configure the Execute SQL Task to run the command stored in the SQLText variable, against the same connection as the first Execute SQL Task in the package. This can be seen in Figure 5-41. We will name the task TestRestore, to avoid confusion with other Execute SQL Tasks within the package.

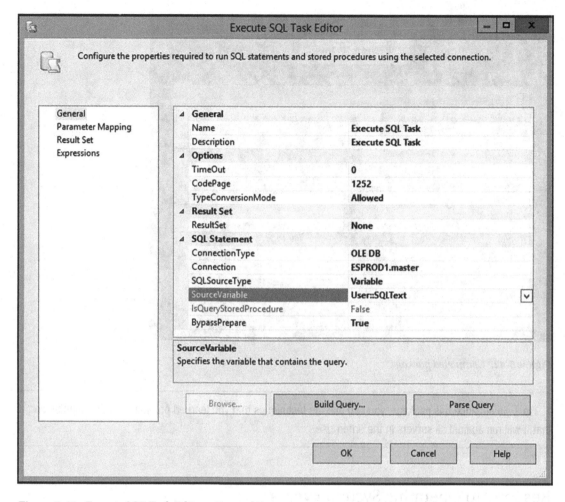

Figure 5-41. *Execute SQL Task Editor—General Page*

We will now have to add another Expression Task to the Foreach Loop Container. We will name it BuildBackupStatement, and it will be connected to the TestRestore task, using a Failure constraint, meaning that it (and downstream tasks) will only be executed in the event of the TestRestore task failing. The BuildBackupStatement task will be configured with the expression listed in Listing 5-9.

Listing 5-9. Build Backup Statement

```
@[User::SQLText] = "BACKUP DATABASE " + @[User::Name] + " TO DISK = '" + @[User::Name] + "'"
```

Our final Execute SQL Task will be called BackupDatabase and will be configured to execute the BACKUP statement that is now contained within the BuildBackupStatement variable. This will ensure that we have a valid backup, in the case of a disaster. Our completed package is displayed in Figure 5-42.

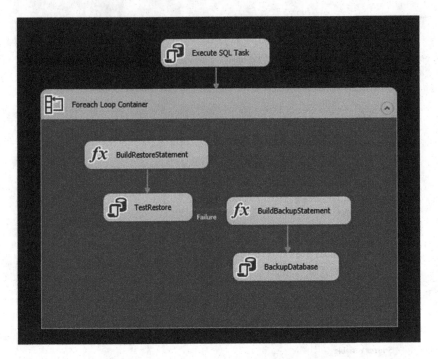

Figure 5-42. *Completed package*

■ **Tip**   To enhance this package, you can use the techniques that you learned previously in this chapter, so that it will run against all servers in the enterprise.

Respond to Operating System Events

Imagine a scenario in which you have purchased STaaS (Storage as a Service) and have a policy to take all backups to Windows Azure, as opposed to local shares. If you have a large or outsourced DBA team, it may be tricky to stop people "sneaking" backups, such as copy-only backups, onto the local SAN. You can mitigate this by using an SSIS package to watch for .bak files being created in the default backup directory of the instance and immediately delete them. An SSIS package to implement this logic would follow the logical flow detailed in Figure 5-43.

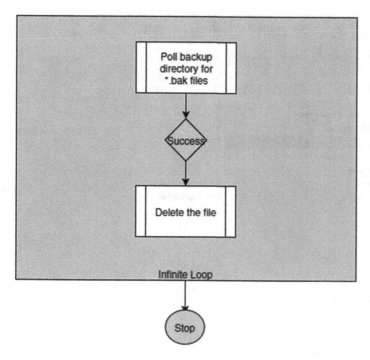

Figure 5-43. *Prevent local backups process flow*

We will begin by creating an Integration Service project named `PreventLocalBackups`. Inside the default package, we will add a ForLoop Container to the control flow. There are three key properties involved when configuring a ForLoop Container: `InitExpression`, `EvalExpression`, and `AssignExpression`.

The `InitExpression` is used to initialize a variable that will be used to control the loop, for example, `i = 1`. The `EvalExpression` is the only mandatory property, and this will specify the exit criterial of the loop, for example, `i > 10`. The `AssignExpression` is used to increment the variable that controls the loop, for example, `i = i + 1`.

Because we want to create an infinite loop, the only property that we will configure is `EvalExpression`. Because the condition will cause the loop to break when it evaluates to `false`, we will use constants to ensure that it always evaluates to `true`. The standard approach to this is to use `1==1`. In fact, an infinite loop is sometimes referred to as a 1=1 loop. This configuration is illustrated in Figure 5-44.

■ **Tip** Because SSIS is based on .NET, when evaluating an expression for equality, you must use double equals (==). Single equals (=) denote that you are assigning a value, as opposed to evaluating.

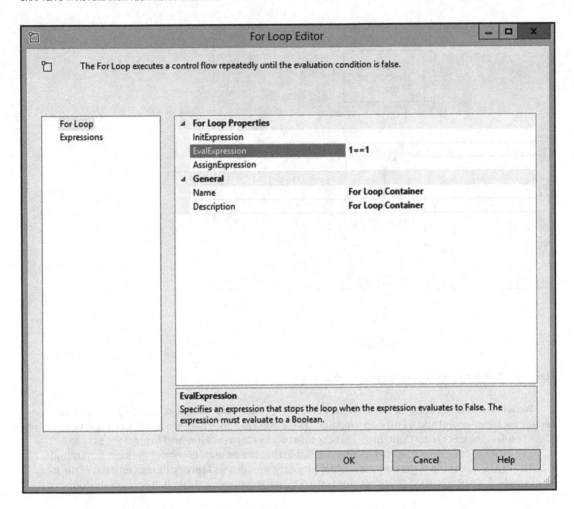

Figure 5-44. *For Loop Editor—For Loop Properties page*

We can now drag a WMI Event Watcher Task into the ForLoop Container. This type of task can be used to watch for the occurrence of a WMI (Windows Management Instrumentation) event. A WMI event can range from a performance condition, such as CPU spiking at 75%, through a file being created in a folder.

On the WMI Options page of the WMI Event Watcher Task Editor, we will use the drop-down against the WMIConnection property to invoke the WMI Connection Manager Editor, from which we will create a new connection manager. In this dialog box, which is shown in Figure 5-45, we will change the Server name property to point the connection manager at our ESPROD1 sever and check the box to specify Use Windows Authentication. Assuming that the package is scheduled to run with SQL Server Agent, this means that authentication will be made using either the SQL Server Agent service account or the Proxy that has been configured to run the job step. The Namespace will remain as \root\cimv2, which is the default value.

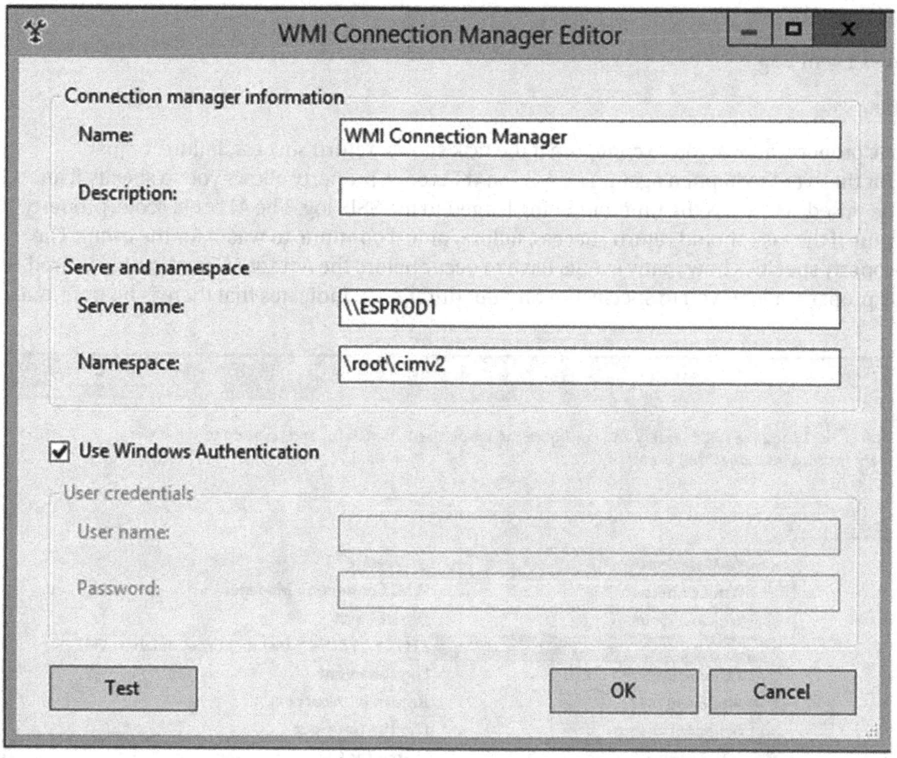

Figure 5-45. *WMI Connection Manager Editor*

Back on the WMI Options page of the WMI Event Watcher Task Editor, we will configure the WqlQuerySourceType as Direct input. (In line with SQL query source types, other options are Variable or Fie connection.) In the WmiQuerySource field, we will add the WQL (Windows Query Language) query to be used by our task. This task can be found in Listing 5-10.

■ **Tip**   WQL is semantically similar to ANSI SQL; however, a full discussion of writing queries in WQL is beyond the scope of this book. A full reference can be found at https://msdn.microsoft.com/en-us/library/windows/desktop/aa394606(v=vs.85).aspx.

Listing 5-10. WMI Query to Check for File Creation

```
SELECT * FROM __InstanceCreationEvent WITHIN 10
WHERE TargetInstance ISA "CIM_DirectoryContainsFile"
AND TargetInstance.GroupComponent= "Win32_Directory.Name=\"C:\\\\Program Files\\\\Microsoft
SQL Server\\\\MSSQL13.MSSQLSERVER\\\\MSSQL\\\\Backup\""
```

The WMI Options page is displayed in Figure 5-46. The ActionAtEvent property allows you to specify if an SSIS event should be raised, as well as the event being logged to the SSIS log, which supports the following log providers:

- Profiler

- Text file

151

- SQL Server

- Windows Event Log

- XML file

The AfterEvent property allows you to configure if the task should return success, failure, or just continue to watch for the event to happen again. The ActionAtTimeout property allows you to specify if an SSIS event should be raised, as well as the time-out being logged to the SSIS log. The AfterTimeout property allows you to configure if the task should return success, failure, or just continue to watch for the event. The NumberOfEvents property specifies how many events have to occur before the ActionAtEvent action is fired. Finally, the Timeout property allows you to specify the timeout duration. 0 indicates that there is no time-out.

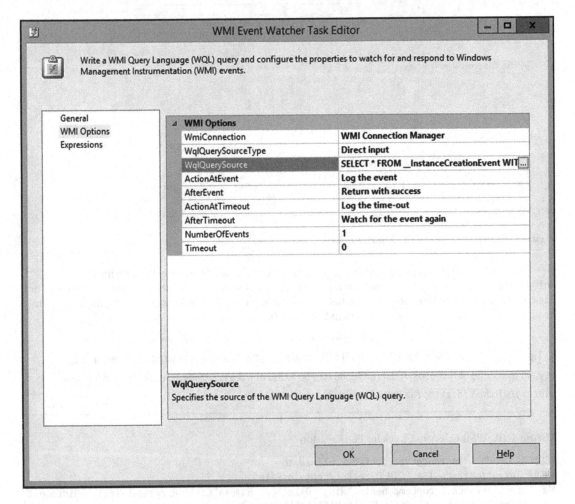

Figure 5-46. *WMI Event Watcher Task Editor—WMI Options page*

We will then add a File System Task to our ForLoop Container and connect it to the WMI Event Watcher Task using a Success constraint. Before we can go any further, we must ensure that the default backup location on ESPROD1 has been shared and map a network drive to this share on ESASSMGMT1. For this demonstration, we have mapped the share to drive B:.

Back in our package, we can now begin the configure the File System Task. On the General page of the File System Task Editor, we will set the Operation property to Delete directory content (Figure 5-47). This will allow us to delete the file(s) that have just been written. Other possible operations are as follows:

- Copy directory

- Copy file

- Create directory

- Delete directory

- Delete file

- Move directory

- Move file

- Rename file

- Set Attributes

■ **Tip**   On selecting the operation, the properties exposed on the General page will update dynamically, to display only properties that are relevant to the selected operation.

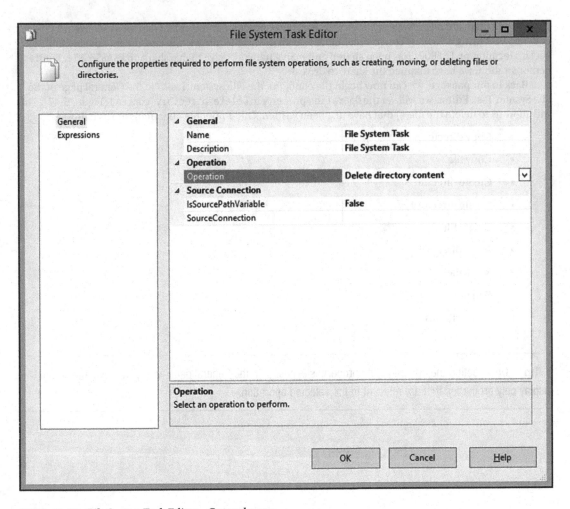

Figure 5-47. *File System Task Editor—General page*

We will now use the drop-down in the SourceConnection property to invoke the File Connection Manager Editor, on which we can create our connection to the ESPROD1 file system. As illustrated in Figure 5-48, we will configure the folder to point to our mapped network drive and configure the Usage type as Existing folder. Other possible usage types are

- Create file
- Create folder
- Existing file

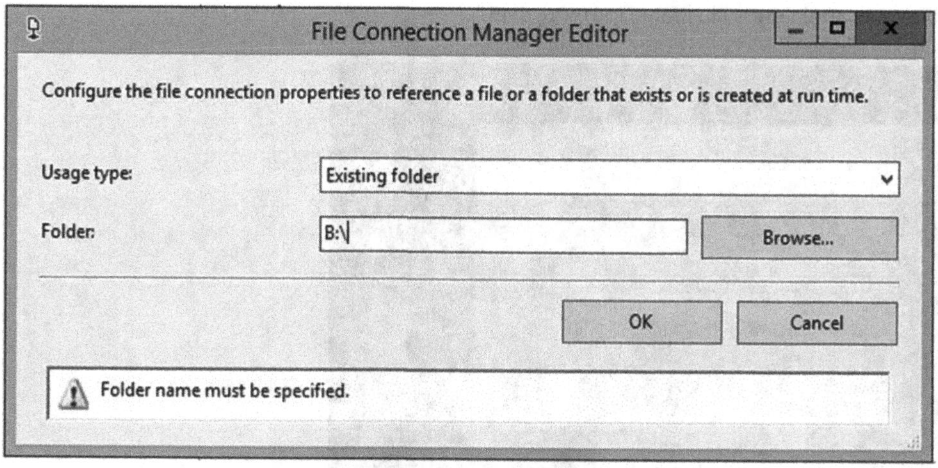

Figure 5-48. *File Connection Manager Editor*

■ **Tip** The WMI Event Watcher Task does not have an EOF (End of File) marker. This means that if large files are being written to the folder, the file system task may attempt to delete them before they have finished being written. This will result in a failure, because the file will be locked by the process that is writing the file. If you experience this issue, I recommend using the open source Konesans File Watcher Task, which can be downloaded from www.konesans.com/products/file-watcher-task. This task has extended functionality, including an EOF marker, ensuring that the flow will not continue until the file write has completed.

The completed control flow is illustrated in Figure 5-49.

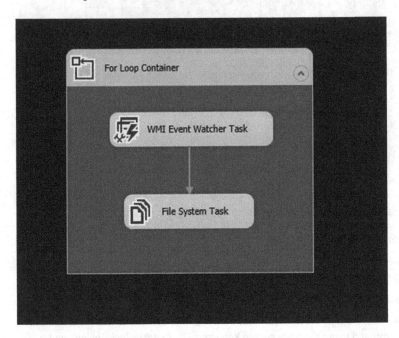

Figure 5-49. *Completed control flow*

Summary

SQL Server Integration Services provides a flexible framework with an intuitive GUI that allows DBAs to automate administrative work flows and reduce manual effort. The control flow within SSIS is used to orchestrate the required tasks. Tasks can sit directly within a control flow, or they can be nested in containers. Containers can be used to loop for a specific number of times or to enumerate through a set of objects.

Tasks can be joined to one another by using precedence constraints. Precedence constraints control which tasks are executed, based on the success, failure, or completion of preceding tasks. Constraints can also be configured to control execution flow, based on Boolean expressions.

Event handlers can be used as a way of orchestrating responses to errors, without complicating the control flow and allowing you to create reusable modules. Event handlers offer far more power than just responding to errors, however. In fact, event handlers can respond to virtually any event that can occur in your package, including pre-execute events, post-execute events, and variable values changing.

CHAPTER 6

∎ ∎ ∎

Building an Inventory Database

An inventory database is critical to the success of your automation strategy. Despite being a relatively small and simple database, an inventory database will act as your hub for orchestrating your automation efforts throughout the enterprise.

Even if your company has a fully fledged CMDB, which includes databases, the astute DBA will still have his or her own inventory system. This is because a DBA will have more control over his or her own database, limiting the chances of the data becoming stale or dirty.

Having full control over the system also means that you can easily extend and enhance it, so that you can also easily grow and extend your automation solution.

Your automated build will keep the database up-to-date, by inserting the details of every new SQL Server instance that is built in your enterprise. The database can then feed automated maintenance routines that you create, using multiserver jobs or SSIS packages.

Inventory Database Platform Design

Before designing the inventory database itself, you should first consider the platform requirements of the database, such as availability. For example, imagine that your organization has four data centers, dispersed across EMEA and NTAM, as depicted in Figure 6-1. You have decided to place the inventory database on a management instance in EMEA. What will happen in the event of the EMEA1 data center loosing connectivity to the rest of the network? The SQL Server instances in EMEA1 will continue to see the inventory database, but instances in the other three data centers will not. If your inventory database is used as a hub to control automation, this scenario could pose real issues. If you have all hands on deck, firefighting a data center outage and potentially invoking DR strategies for dozens of data-tier applications, the last thing that you probably want to be worrying about is users complaining of performance issues across the rest of the enterprise because their maintenance jobs have not been able to run.

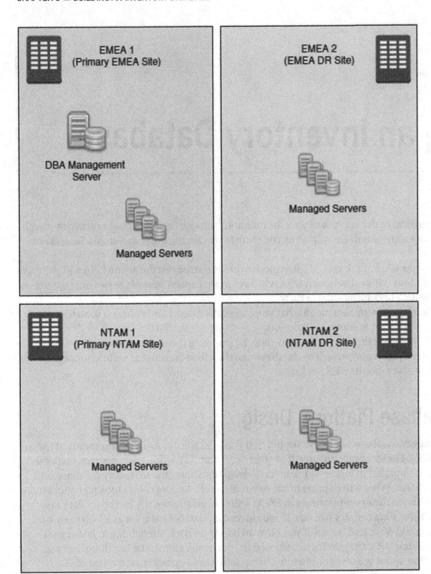

Figure 6-1. Data center topology

There are two potential resolutions to this issue. You could either keep the inventory database synchronized between two data centers, or you could host the inventory database in a separate location. A few years ago, my advice would have been to keep the inventory database synchronized between two data centers. The primary reason for this was because a holistic automation strategy should have a single centralized hub, and it is unlikely that your organization has a data center with no SQL Server instances, wherein you could spin up a server to host the inventory database. Therefore, placing the database in any data center would likely be susceptible to the isolation issue described previously.

With the rise of cloud computing, however, my advice is now different. An inventory database is a perfect candidate for Windows Azure SQL Database. An inventory database will be small enough to fit comfortably in Azure. There will also be a relatively low throughput, meaning that the database will be cost-effective to host in the cloud. Hosting in the cloud also has the additional benefit of providing out-of-the-box high availability and disaster recovery, which will be managed for you as part of Microsoft's DaaS (Database as a Service) offering, and as the database will reside in the cloud, as opposed to an on-premise data center, the isolation issue cannot occur.

■ **Tip**   To provide even more continuity for your supported servers, you could (and should) consider expanding on this concept and using a Windows Azure VM, running SQL Server to host an entire management instance, which includes your SQL Server Agent Master Server and management routines exposed as SSIS packages. For this to work, Windows Azure should be integrated with your on-premise AD infrastructure. This will help prevent issues with multiserver jobs and packages alike. For the purpose of this book, we will reduce complexity by hosting both the inventory database and the management instance on-premise.

If your inventory database is implemented in Windows Azure SQL Database and your management instance remains on-premise, your management topology would look similar to that illustrated in Figure 6-2. You will notice that although the inventory database is stored in Azure, there is still a DR instance, which will provide resilience for the SQL Server Agent Master Server and SSIS packages.

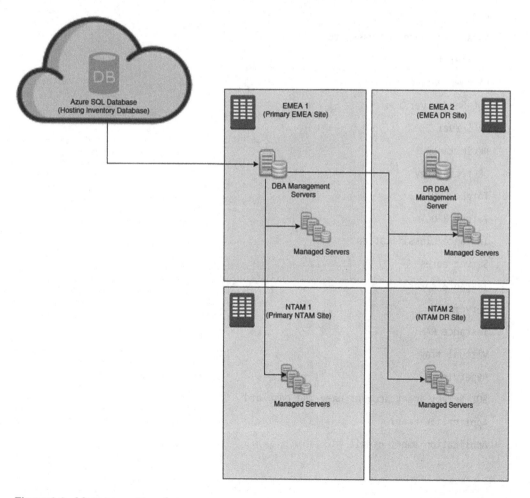

Figure 6-2. Management topology

Inventory Database Logical Design

When designing any database, the first task should be to determine what data you need to store. Do not think about table design yet, just the data that you will need—in a flat list. For database developers, this involves conversations with business analysts or business stakeholders to determine requirements. For an application developer, this task will usually be handled by his/her chosen framework, such as LINQ. The DBA who wishes to create an inventory database, however, will play the role of both the developer and business stakeholder. Below is a list of attributes that you may wish to record. Of course, this list should be tailored to your individual requirements.

Server name

Instance name

Port

IP Address

Service account name and password

Authentication mode

sa account name and password

Cluster flag

Windows version

SQL Server version

DR Server

DR instance

DR technology

Target RPO

Target RTO

Instance classification

Server cores

Instance cores

Server RAM

Instance RAM

Virtual flag

Hypervisor

SQL Server Agent account name and password

Application owner

Application owner e-mail

Normalization

Now that we have identified the data (known as attributes) that we need to store, we have to group these attributes together into related groups. Each of these groups is called an entity, and the attributes are, in fact, attributes of the resulting entities.

The process for modeling the entities is known as *normalization*. This is a process that was invented by Edgar J Codd in 1970 and has endured the test of time, although additional normal forms were added over the subsequent decade.

There are eight normal forms in total, which are listed following:

- 1NF (first normal form)

- 2NF (second normal form)

- 3NF (third normal form. This is the last of the original normal forms, as defined by Edgar Codd.)

- BCNF (Boyce-Codd normal form, also known as 3.5 normal form)

- 4NF (fourth normal form)

- 5NF (fifth normal form)

- 6NF (sixth normal form)

- DKNF (domain key normal form)

The normal forms BCNF to DKNF deal with special circumstances, and the majority of the time, if a database is in 3NF, it will also be in DKNF. For this reason, the following sections will discuss the first three normal forms only.

The reason for modeling a database with normalization is to reduce data redundancy, meaning that every piece of data should be stored only once, with the exception of a unique key, which is used to identify the data. This is less about saving storage space (although this has obvious cost and performance benefits) and more about avoiding database anomalies that may be caused by having to update data in more than one place. It also avoids the complexities and overheads associated with avoiding these anomalies.

■ **Tip**   Normalization is only suitable for OLTP (On-line Transactional Processing) databases. Data Warehouses and Data Marts should be de-normalized. Therefore, they should be modeled using techniques such as Kimball methodology. An ODS (Operational Data Store) will also have to be modeled differently, usually based on the heterogeneous sources that it unites.

The objectives of modeling data in 1NF are to ensure that values are atomic, that repeating groups of attributes are moved to separate entities, and that all attributes are dependent on a key (also known as prime) attribute. The objective of modeling data into 2NF is to ensure that all non-prime attributes are dependent on all prime attributes within the entity. The objective of modeling data into 3NF is to ensure that no non-prime attributes are dependent on any other non-prime attributes. I like to remember this by using the phrase "first, second, and third normal forms ensure that all attributes are dependent on the key, the whole key, and nothing but the key."

1NF

The first step in our normalization journey is to move the required attributes into first normal form (1NF). To do this, we must ensure that each attribute is atomic (holds only one piece of information) and that each attribute is dependent upon a key. In this phase, we will also break out repeating groups to new entities. So, first, let's break out the repeating groups. We will do this by starting with the first attribute (Server name) and then asking the following question about each other attribute: "Can we have more than one per server?" Table 6-1 answers this question for each attribute.

Table 6-1. *Can There Be More Than One per Server Name?*

Attribute	More Than One Per Server?
Instance name	Yes
Port	Yes
IP Address	Yes
Service account name and password	Yes
Authentication mode	Yes
sa account name and password	Yes
Cluster flag	No
Windows version	No
SQL Server version	No (Technically possible, but against most corporate policies)
DR Server	Yes
DR instance	Yes
DR technology	Yes
Target RPO	Yes
Target RTO	Yes
Instance classification	Yes
Server cores	No
Instance cores	Yes
Server RAM	No
Instance RAM	Yes
Virtual flag	No
Hypervisor	No
SQL Server Agent account name and password	Yes
Application owner	No
Application owner e-mail	No

Any attribute for which the answer to the question is no will remain within the same entity as Server name in this phase of normalization. Therefore, we know that our first entity will contain the following attributes:

> Server name
>
> Cluster flag
>
> Windows version
>
> SQL Server version
>
> Server cores
>
> Virtual flag
>
> Hypervisor
>
> Application owner
>
> Application owner e-mail

We should give this entity a meaningful name, so we will call it Server. We should now ensure that each attribute in the Server entity is dependent on a key. A key should uniquely identify any row, and Server name will fulfill this requirement. Therefore, we will make Server name the key (prime) attribute. We can see that each attribute contains only a single value, meaning that we are also fulfilling the requirement to be autonomous.

If we look at the remaining attributes, we can see that they naturally fall together into two groups: Instance and DR Server. Therefore, we will break the rest of the attributes out to new entities that align with these repeating groups.

First, let's look at the Instance entity, which will contain the following attributes:

> Instance name
>
> Port
>
> IP Address
>
> Service account name and password
>
> Authentication mode
>
> sa account name and password
>
> Instance classification
>
> Instance cores
>
> Instance RAM
>
> SQL Server Agent account name and password

We will have to add the Server name attribute to the Instance entity, so that we can link the entities together. In this entity, we can also easily identify three attributes that do not contain atomic values: sa account name and password, Service account name and password, and SQL Server Agent account name and password. Each of these attributes contains two values: the account name and the password. Therefore, the columns should be broken up, giving the following set of attributes:

> Instance name
>
> Server name
>
> Port

    IP Address

    Service account name

    Service account password

    Authentication mode

    sa account name

    sa password

    Instance classification

    Instance cores

    Instance RAM

    Additional services

    SQL Server Agent account name

    SQL Server Agent account password

In regards to a key, all attributes can be uniquely identified by the Instance name. Therefore, an instance name will become the key of the entity.

■ **Tip**　I have seen some environments in which instances always follow the naming convention SQL001, SQL002, etc. This pattern is then repeated on every server. In this scenario, the instance name will not be unique and cannot be used as a key. Therefore, either IP address would have to be used, or you would have to create a composite key consisting of Server name and Instance name.

The DR entity will consist of the following attributes:

    DR Server

    DR instance

    DR technology

    Target RPO

    Target RTO

All of the values are atomic, so there is no need for us to split out any attributes. In this entity, there is no single attribute that can uniquely identify all other attributes. We will, therefore, have to construct a composite key for this entity. This key will consist of DR Server and DR instance. Again, we move the key of the Server entity to the DR Server entity, so that we can link the entities together. Figure 6-3 illustrates our completed 1NF entity model.

Server	Instance	DR Server
Server Name Clustered Flag Windows Version SQL Server Version Server Cores Server RAM Virtual Flag Hypervisor Application Owner Application Owner E-Mail	Instance Name Server Name Port IP Address Service Account Name Service Account Password Authentication Mode sa Account Name sa Account Password Instance Classification Instance Cores Instance RAM SQL Server Agent Account Name SQL Server Agent Account Password	DR Server Name Server Name DR Instance DR Technology Target RPO Target RTO

Figure 6-3. *1NF entities*

2NF

The next step in the normalization process will move our entities into second normal form (2NF). To be in 2NF, the entities must already be in 1NF, and you must also ensure that no non-key attribute (also known as a non-prime attribute) is dependent on only part of the entity's key. If it is, you must split the attribute(s) out to an additional entity.

As the Server and Instance entities all have a single attribute key, we know that these entities are already in second normal form. We do, however, have to review the DR Server entity, as this entity has a composite key. We should look at each non-prime attribute in turn, and identify if the attribute is dependent on the whole of the composite key or just a subset of the key. Table 6-2 shows this analysis.

Table 6-2. *Key Dependencies*

Non-Prime Attribute	Key Dependencies	2NF Compliant?
DR technology	DR Instance name	No
Target RPO	DR Instance name	No
Target RTO	DR Instance name	No

As you can see, all three of the non-prime attributes can be identified without knowing the name of the DR server. This means that these columns should all be moved to a separate entity, which we will call DR Instance.

The only attributes that will remain in the DR Server entity are the key attributes. This may seem a little odd, but it has happened to avoid a many-to-many relationship between the Server entity and the DR Instance entity and is perfectly valid design.

3NF

The final stage of normalization that I will cover in this book is how to move entities into third normal form (3NF). In order to be in 3NF, the entity should already be in 2NF, and no non-prime attributes of an entity should be dependent on any other non-prime attributes. If we find an attribute that is dependent on a non-prime attribute, this is known as a transitive dependency, and the attribute should be moved to a separate entity.

In the Server, DR Server, and DR Instance entities, there are no transitive dependencies. In the Instance entity, however, there are three attributes that are dependent on non-prime attributes. These are listed in Table 6-3.

Table 6-3. *Transitive Dependencies*

Attribute	Dependency
sa password	sa account name
Service account password	Service account name
SQL Server agent account	SQL Server agent account password

Following the rules of normalization, we should move each of these attributes to its own entity. Using our understanding of the business rules, however, we know that in some cases, the same service account may be used for both the database engine service account and the SQL Server agent service account. Therefore, we will move the service account attributes to a single entity, which we will call Service Account. We can then link the Service Account entity back to the DR Instance entity twice: once for the Service Account Name and again for the SQL Server Agent Service Account Name.

The sa account details do not fit with the service account details, as the sa account can never be shared between instances. Therefore, we will move the sa account details to a separate entity, called sa Account. We will move the primary key of both the Service Account and sa Account entities back up to the Instance entity, so that they can be linked together. Figure 6-4 shows how the Instance, sa Account, and Service Account entities have been modeled.

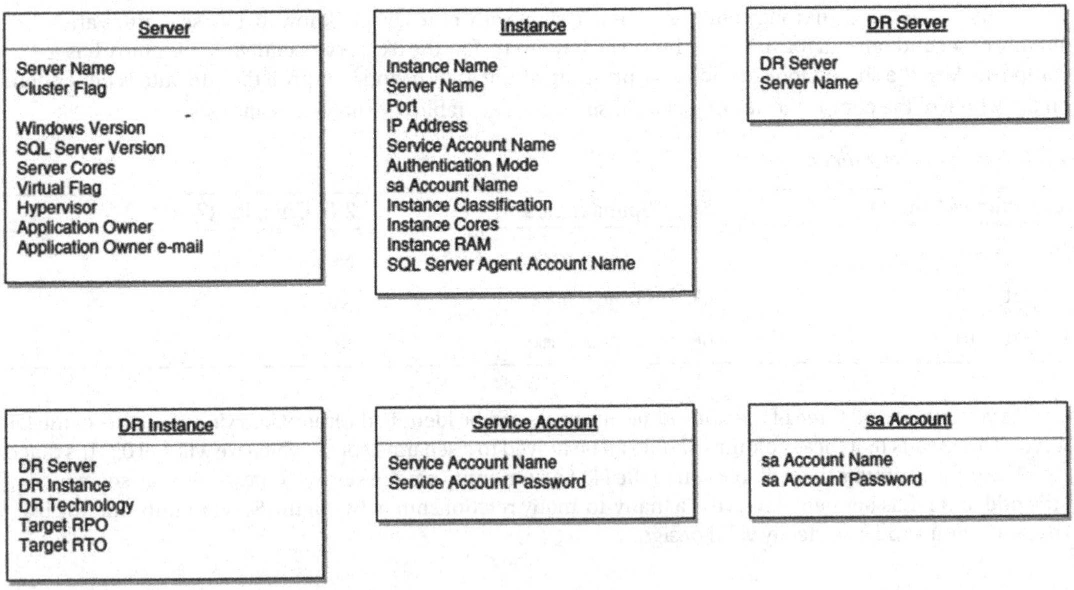

Server

Server Name
Cluster Flag

Windows Version
SQL Server Version
Server Cores
Virtual Flag
Hypervisor
Application Owner
Application Owner e-mail

Instance

Instance Name
Server Name
Port
IP Address
Service Account Name
Authentication Mode
sa Account Name
Instance Classification
Instance Cores
Instance RAM
SQL Server Agent Account Name

DR Server

DR Server
Server Name

DR Instance

DR Server
DR Instance
DR Technology
Target RPO
Target RTO

Service Account

Service Account Name
Service Account Password

sa Account

sa Account Name
sa Account Password

Figure 6-4. *Transitive dependencies*

Testing Normalization

We can test whether our normalization process has worked by creating a simple ERD (Entity Relationship Diagram). This diagram will graphically depict the entities, along with the keys that join them. Where a key is unique, the line that connects the entity will be attached with a standard end. Where repeating key values can occur, the line will attach with a crow's foot.

When we examine the completed ERD, we want to see every line that joins entities depicted as a standard line on one end and a crow's foot on the other. This is known as a one-to-many relationship and will map directly to the Primary and Foreign Key constraints in your physical database tables.

If we discover many-to-many relationships, the likelihood is that we have missed an entity and will have to add an additional entity to our design that will work in the same way as our DR Server entity to resolve the many-to-many relationship into two one-to-many relationships.

On the other hand, if we discover a one-to-one relationship, we have almost certainly normalized the entities to a point that will add query complexity, without adding any value. In this case, we should de-normalize our entities back to a point where all entities are joined together using a one-to-many relationship. An ERD for our normalized Inventory database can be found in Figure 6-5.

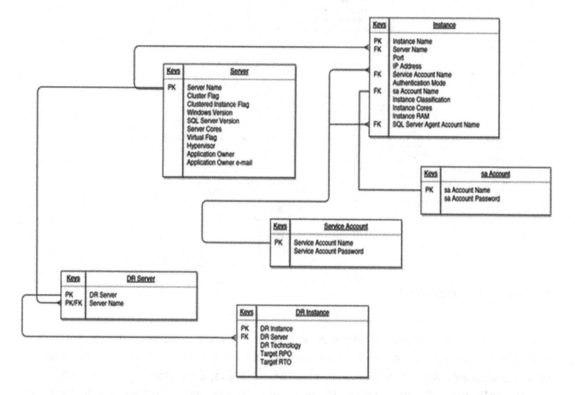

Figure 6-5. *Entity relationship diagram*

You will notice that the ERD has identified an issue with our modeling. The sa Account entity is joined to the Instance entity with a one-to-one relationship. This means that we should de-normalize the sa Account entity back into the Instance entity. The resulting ERD is displayed in Figure 6-6.

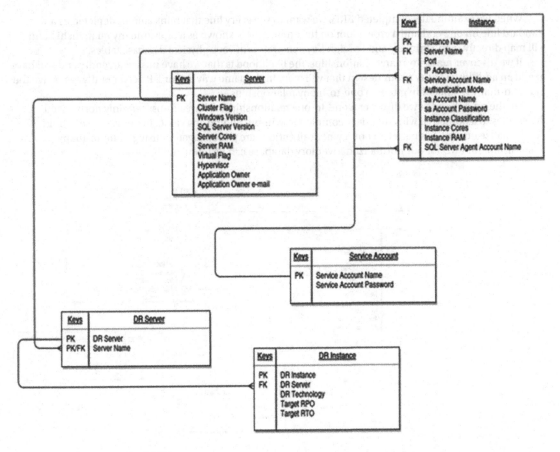

Figure 6-6. *De-normalized ERD*

■ **Tip**   The preceding examples have demonstrated how to model a simple inventory database. When creating an inventory database to support your production environment, you may also wish to store details relating to HA technologies, such as AlwaysOn failover clusters or AlwaysOn availability groups. You may also wish to model Servers, DR Servers, and (potentially) HA Servers as supertype and subtypes. Further details of supertypes and subtypes can be found at https://msdn.microsoft.com/en-us/library/cc505839.aspx.

Inventory Database Physical Design

Now that we have a logical model for our database, we have to consider a physical design. The first consideration may be our attribute and entity names and how they will map to SQL Server–friendly object identifiers, which will not have to be encapsulated in square brackets. An object identifier will have to be encapsulated in square brackets when being referenced in code, if any of the following rules are broken:

1. Identifiers may not contain spaces.

2. Identifiers may not contain the following special characters:

~	'
-	&
!	.
{	(
%	\
}	)
^	`

3. Identifiers may not be the same as a T-SQL keyword.

If identifiers do not meet these rules, they are known as delimited identifiers. Our Server and Instance entities conform to these rules, but our DR Server entity will become DRServer; our DR Instance entity will become DRInstance; and our Service Account Entity will become ServiceAccount. Table 6-4 details the mapping of attribute names to column names.

Table 6-4. *Removing Delimited Identifiers*

Attribute Name	Column Name
Server name	ServerName
Instance name	InstanceName
Port	Port
IP Address	IPAddress
Service account name	ServiceAccountName
Service account password	ServiceAccountPassword
Authentication mode	AuthenticationMode
sa account name	saAccount
sa account password	saPassword
Cluster flag	ClusterFlag
Windows version	WindowsVersion
SQL Server version	SQLVersion
DR Server	DRServerName
DR instance	DRInstanceName
DR technology	DRTechnology
Target RPO	TargetRPO
Target RTO	TargetRTO
Instance classification	InstanceClassification
Server cores	ServerCores
Instance cores	InstanceCores
Server RAM	ServerRAM
Instance RAM	InstanceRAM
Virtual flag	VirtualFlag
Hypervisor	Hypervisor
SQL Server Agent account name	SQLServerAgentAccountName
SQL Server Agent account password	SQLServerAgentAccountPassword
Application owner	ApplicationOwner
Application owner e-mail	ApplicationOwnerEMail

A data type is the only constraint that a column will always have, and care should be given when implementing this constraint. If the data type is too restrictive, some data will not fit into the column, and you will find yourself having to fix the issue by changing the column's data type or length specification. If the data type is larger than it need be, however, you will find yourself using more server resources to satisfy disk and RAM requirements.

Table 6-5 lists each column in our Inventory database and recommends a suitable data type. Where applicable, an explanation is given of the rationale behind the choice.

Table 6-5. *Data Types*

Column	Data Type	Explanation
Server name	NVARCHAR(128)	SQL Server uses an internal data type called sysname for storing object identifiers. The sysname data type is essentially a synonym for NVARCHAR(128) NOT NULL. Therefore, we will use NVARCHAR(128) as the data type for any object identifier, in order to keep consistency.
Instance name	NVARCHAR(128)	
Port	NVARCHAR(8)	Stored as a character string, to include the protocol
IP Address	NVARCHAR(15)	
Service account name	NVARCHAR(128)	
Service account password	NVARCHAR(64)	
Authentication mode	BIT	0 indicates Windows Authentication 1 indicates Mixed Mode Authentication
sa account name	NVARCHAR(128)	
sa account password	NVARCHAR(64)	
Cluster flag	BIT	
Windows version	NVARCHAR(64)	The version of Windows installed on the server, for example, "Windows Server 2012 R2 Enterprise SP1 CU1"
SQL Server version	NVARCHAR(64)	The version of SQL Server installed on the server, for example, "SQL Server 2016 Enterprise Core RTM CU2"
DR Server	NVARCHAR(128)	
DR instance	NVARCHAR(128)	
DR technology	NVARCHAR(128)	
TargetRPO	TINYINT	
TargetRTO	TINYINT	
Instance classification	TINYINT	1 indicates OLTP 2 indicates Data warehouse 3 indicates Mixed workload 4 indicates ETL
Server cores	TINYINT	
Instance cores	TINYINT	
Server RAM	SMALLINT	
Instance RAM	SMALLINT	
Virtual flag	BIT	0 indicates physical server 1 indicates virtual machine

(continued)

Table 6-5. (*continued*)

Column	Data Type	Explanation
Hypervisor	BIT	0 indicates VMWare 1 indicates Hyper-V
SQL Server Agent account name	NVARCHAR(128)	
SQL Server Agent account password	NVARCHAR(64)	
Application owner	NVARCHAR(256)	
Application owner e-mail	NVARCHAR(512)	

We should now consider the design of our Primary Keys for each table. Are the logical "natural" keys that we have already identified sufficient, or should we create artificial keys, which are usually implemented through an IDENTITY column?

We can see that each of our Primary Key columns has the data type NVARCHAR(128). Although these columns will uniquely identify each row in their respective tables, they are wide columns that will consume up to 256 bytes for each row.

The Primary Key will be replicated in each Foreign Key, and because the Primary Key is usually the column(s) that the table's clustered index is built on, it is also likely to be replicated in all non-clustered indexes. Therefore, we want the Primary Key value to be as narrow as possible. If we add an artificial Primary Key to each table using the INT data type, each key value will only consume 4 bytes, as opposed to a possible 256.

■ **Tip**   Because we are taking the approach of using an artificial key, it is likely that each natural key will require a unique constraint.

Creating the Database

The physical design of our Inventory database is now complete, and all that remains is to create the database. We could create the database using our familiar DBA tool: SQL Server Management Studio. We will gain a much richer development environment, however, if we use SSDT (SQL Server Data Tools), as shown in Figure 6-7. SSDT allows us to perform actions such as refactoring identifiers and comparing the T-SQL in two versions of the database.

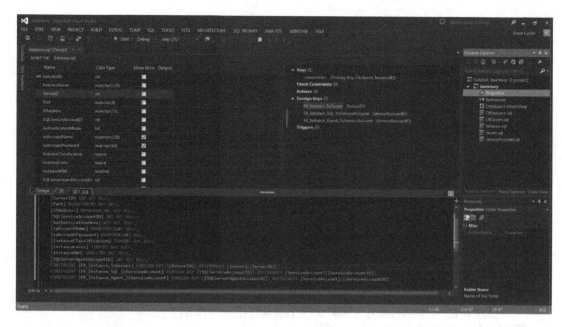

Figure 6-7. *Creating the database*

Listing 6-1 provides the T-SQL scripts for creating the entire Inventory database.

Listing 6-1. Create Inventory Database

```sql
CREATE DATABASE Inventory
GO

USE Inventory
GO

--Create the ServiceAccount table

CREATE TABLE [dbo].[ServiceAccount]
(
    [ServiceAccountID] INT NOT NULL IDENTITY PRIMARY KEY,
    [ServiceAccountName] NVARCHAR(128) NOT NULL UNIQUE,

) ;

GO

--Create the Server table

CREATE TABLE [dbo].[Server]
(
    [ServerID] INT NOT NULL IDENTITY PRIMARY KEY,
    [ServerName] NVARCHAR(128) NOT NULL UNIQUE,
    [ClusterFlag] BIT NOT NULL,
```

```
    [WindowsVersion] NVARCHAR(64) NOT NULL,
    [SQLVersion] NVARCHAR(64) NOT NULL,
    [ServerCores] TINYINT NOT NULL,
    [ServerRAM] BIGINT NOT NULL,
    [VirtualFlag] BIT NOT NULL,
    [Hypervisor] BIT NULL,
    [ApplicationOwner] NVARCHAR(256) NULL,
    [ApplicationOwnerEMail] NVARCHAR(512) NULL

) ;

GO

--Create the DRServer table

CREATE TABLE [dbo].[DRServer]
(
    [DRServerID] INT NOT NULL IDENTITY ,
    [ServerID] INT NOT NULL,
    CONSTRAINT [FK_DRServer_ToServer]
        FOREIGN KEY ([ServerID]) REFERENCES [Server]([ServerID]),
    PRIMARY KEY ([DRServerID], [ServerID])
) ;

GO
--Create the DRInstance table

CREATE TABLE [dbo].[DRInstance]
(
    [DRInstanceID] INT NOT NULL IDENTITY PRIMARY KEY,
    [DRInstanceName] NVARCHAR(128) NOT NULL UNIQUE,
    [DRServerID] INT NOT NULL,
        [ServerID] INT NOT NULL,
    [DRTechnology] NVARCHAR(128) NOT NULL,
    [TargetRPO] TINYINT NOT NULL,
    [TargetPTO] TINYINT NOT NULL,
    CONSTRAINT [FK_DRInstance_ToDRServer]
        FOREIGN KEY ([DRServerID], [ServerID]) REFERENCES [DRServer]
([DRServerID],[ServerID])
) ;

GO
--Create the Instance table

CREATE TABLE [dbo].[Instance]
(
    [InstanceID] INT NOT NULL IDENTITY  PRIMARY KEY,
    [InstanceName] NVARCHAR(128) NOT NULL UNIQUE,
    [ServerID] INT NOT NULL,
    [Port] NVARCHAR(8) NOT NULL,
    [IPAddress] NVARCHAR(15) NOT NULL,
```

```
    [SQLServiceAccountID] INT NOT NULL,
    [AuthenticationMode] BIT NOT NULL,
    [saAccountName] NVARCHAR(128) NULL,
    [saAccountPassword] NVARCHAR(64) NULL,
    [InstanceClassification] TINYINT NOT NULL,
    [InstanceCores] TINYINT NOT NULL,
    [InstanceRAM] BIGINT NOT NULL,
    [SQLServerAgentAccountID] INT NOT NULL,
    CONSTRAINT [FK_Instance_ToServer]
        FOREIGN KEY ([ServerID]) REFERENCES [Server]([ServerID]),
    CONSTRAINT [FK_Instance_SQL_ToServiceAccount]
        FOREIGN KEY ([SQLServiceAccountID]) REFERENCES [ServiceAccount]([ServiceAccountID]),
    CONSTRAINT [FK_Instance_Agent_ToServiceAccount]
        FOREIGN KEY ([SQLServerAgentAccountID]) REFERENCES [ServiceAccount]
([ServiceAccountID])
) ;
GO
```

Summary

A well-designed inventory database can assist DBAs in their automation effort by providing an automatically maintained, central repository of information that can in turn drive automated maintenance routines.

When designing the inventory database, you will have to consider both platform requirements and also the logical and physical design of the database tables. When designing the platform requirements of the database, you should consider HA/DR strategies and also placement of the inventory database, to avoid data center isolation issues. Ideally, you will host the inventory database, and other elements of the DBAs automation toolset, outside of the data centers that you are monitoring and maintaining, such as in the cloud.

When performing the logical design of the database, you should model the data using normalization, which is a process invented in 1970 for the elimination of data duplication. You can then test your model by using an entity relationship diagram, to ensure that all entities are joined with one-to-many relationships.

The physical design of the database will involve designing the physical tables that will store the data. This involves ensuring that there are no delimited identifiers, choosing appropriate data types, and defining any artificial keys that may be required.

■ ■ ■

## CHAPTER 7

Automating Instance Builds

Automating an instance build not only reduces DBA effort and time to market for a new data-tier application, it also reduces operational overhead, as it provides a consistent platform for all new data-tier applications across the enterprise.

A fully automated build will consist of far more than just running setup.exe from the command line. After designing and producing automated builds for three different FTSE 100 companies, I have realized the importance of using the build process to ensure that the instance is installed using an organization's most current patching level, the instance is configured to the DBA team's standard, and the inventory database (and any other supporting applications) is updated to reflect the build.

This chapter will discuss how to automate each of these activities, before finally pulling them together into a single PowerShell orchestration.

Building the Instance

We can install an instance of SQL Server from PowerShell by calling the setup.exe program from the SQL Server installation media. When calling setup.exe, there are switches and parameters that can be passed to let setup know what type of installation you require and how to configure the instance. Many of these are optional and can be omitted, depending on the features that you are choosing to install, but there are some that must always be specified when installing the database engine. Table 7-1 details the parameters that must always be specified when installing the SQL Server 2016 Database Engine.

Table 7-1. *Required Parameters*

Parameter	Description
/ACTION	Specifies the action that you wish to perform, such as install or repair. A complete list of actions is detailed in Table 7-2.
/IACCEPTSQLSERVERLICENSETERMS	Confirms that you accept the SQL Server license terms
/FEATURES	Specifies the features that you wish to install. This parameter is only required if /ROLE is not specified. A complete list of features is detailed in Table 7-3.
/ROLE	Specifies which pre-configured SQL Server role you would like to install. This parameter is only required if /FEATURES is not specified. A complete list of roles can be found in Table 7-4.
/INSTANCENAME	Specifies a name for the instance
/AGTSVCACCOUNT	Specifies the account that will run the SQL Server Agent service

(continued)

Table 7-1. (*continued*)

Parameter	Description
/AGTSVCPASSWORD	Specifies the password of the account that will run the SQL Server Agent service
/SQLSVCACCOUNT	Specifies the account that will run the SQL Server Database Engine service
/SQLSVCPASSWORD	Specifies the password for the account that will run the SQL Server Database Engine service
/SQLSYSADMINACCOUNTS	Specifies the Windows security context(s) that will be given administrator permissions to the Database Engine
/q	Performs the installation in Quiet mode. While not technically a required parameter, it is required for automating an installation, to avoid interaction.

The /ACTION parameter specifies the action that setup will perform. When you are installing a stand-alone instance of SQL Server, the action will be install. Table 7-2 details the other acceptable values for the /ACTION parameter.

Table 7-2. *Acceptable Values for the* /ACTION *Parameter*

Value	Description
install	Installs a stand-alone instance
PrepareImage	Prepares a vanilla stand-alone image, with no account, computer, or network details specified
CompleteImage	Completes the installation of a prepared stand-alone image by configuring account-, computer-, and network-related settings
Upgrade	Upgrades an instance from SQL Server 2008, 2012, or 2014
EditionUpgrade	Upgrades a SQL Server 2014 from a lower edition, such as Developer Edition to Enterprise Edition, or Enterprise Edition to Enterprise Core
Repair	Repairs a corrupt instance
RebuildDatabase	Rebuilds corrupted system databases
Uninstall	Uninstalls a stand-alone instance
InstallFailoverCluster	Installs a failover clustered instance
PrepareFailoverCluster	Prepares a vanilla clustered image, with no account, computer, or network details specified
CompleteFailoverCluster	Completes the installation of a prepared clustered image by configuring account-, computer-, and network-related settings
AddNode	Adds a node to a failover cluster
RemoveNode	Removes a node from a failover cluster

The /FEATURES parameter is used to specify which components of SQL Server you wish to install. This parameter also acts as the driver for deciding which optional parameters are required. For example, if you are not installing SSIS, there is no need to pass parameters specifying the service account and service account password to use for the Integration Services service.

The features that can be selected for install are detailed in Table 7-3, along with the parameter value that should be passed. Parameter values should be comma-separated.

Table 7-3. *Acceptable Values for the /FEATURES Parameter*

Parameter Value	Feature Installed
SQL	The Database Engine, including Full Test, Replication, and PolyBase components
SQLEngine	The Database Engine, without its related components
FullText	Full test components
Replication	Replication components
PolyBase	PolyBase components
AdvancedAnalytics	R Services
DQ	The components required to perform install Data Quality Server
AS	Analysis Services
RS	Reporting Services
DQC	Data Quality Client
IS	Integration Services
MDS	Master Data Services
SQL_SHARED_MR	Microsoft R Server
Tools	All client tools and Books Online
BC	Backward compatibility components
BOL	Books Online component
Conn	Connectivity components
SSMS	SQL Server Management Studio, SQLCMD, and the SQL Server PowerShell provider
Adv_SSMS	SSMS support for AS, RS, and IS; Profiler; Database Engine Tuning Advisor; and Utility management
DREPLAY_CTLR	Distributed Replay Controller
DREPLAY_CLT	Distributed Replay Client
SNAC_SDK	SDK for SQL Server Native Client
SDK	Client tools SDK

The /ROLE parameter that can be used as an alternative to the /FEATURES parameter, to install pre-configured roles, which can be used to install SQL Server, are detailed in Table 7-4.

Table 7-4. SQL Server Setup Roles

Role	Description
SPI_AS_ExistingFarm	Installs SSAS in PowerPivot mode into an existing SharePoint farm
SPI_AS_NewFarm	Installs SSAS in PowerPivot mode into a new SharePoint farm and configures the farm
AllFeatures_WithDefaults	Installs a Database Engine instance with all available features, including SSAS, SSRS, and SSIS, but excluding the PolyBase Query Service and the SSRS add-in for SharePoint Products

Performing a Simple Installation

Table 7-5 details the syntax for using parameters when running setup.exe from PowerShell.

Table 7-5. Syntax for Parameters

Parameter Type	Syntax
Simple switch	/SWITCH
True/False	/PARAMETER=true/false
Boolean	/PARAMETER=0/1
Text	/PARAMETER="Value"
Multi-valued text	/PARAMETER="Value1" "Value2"

The exception to these rules is the /FEATURES parameter, which is comma-separated, with the syntax /FEATURES=Feature1,Feature2.

■ **Tip** Technically, you only have to use quotation marks when a parameter value contains spaces; however, I generally recommend always including the quotation marks, for consistency and readability.

If you are calling setup.exe, or any other executable, from the folder wherein the executable resides, you should prefix the call with .\, to indicate that the executable resides in the same location. Therefore, assuming that PowerShell is scoped to the root of the SQL Server installation media, we could install a named instance, called ESPROD3, with default values for all optional parameters, by using the command in Listing 7-1.

■ **Tip** Change the service account details to match your own configuration, before executing the script.

Listing 7-1. Simple Installation of the Database Engine

```
.\SETUP.EXE /IACCEPTSQLSERVERLICENSETERMS /ACTION="Install" /FEATURES=SQLEngine,Replication,Conn
/INSTANCENAME="ESPROD3" /SQLSYSADMINACCOUNTS="ESASS\SQLAdmin"
/AGTSVCACCOUNT="ESASS\SQLServiceAccount" /AGTSVCPASSWORD="Pa££w0rd"
/SQLSVCACCOUNT="ESASS\SQLServiceAccount" /SQLSVCPASSWORD="Pa££w0rd" /q
```

This command will install the Database Engine, Replication components, and connectivity components. The Database Engine service and SQL Server Agent service will both run under the context of the domain account SQLServerService, and the SQLAdmin domain account will be added to the sysadmin fixed server role. The /q switch will ensure that no interaction is required.

Depending on the features that you choose to install, there are a variety of parameters that can be configured. Table 7-6 details each of the optional parameters that can be configured when installing the Database Engine and Integration Services.

■ **Note** Parameters used for the installation of Analysis Services and Reporting Services are beyond the scope of this book.

Table 7-6. *Optional Parameters*

Parameter	Description
/ENU	Dictates that the English version of SQL Server will be used. Use this switch if you are installing the English version of SQL Server on a server with localized settings and the media contains language packs for both English and the localized operating system.
/UPDATEENABLED	Specifies if Product Update functionality will be used. Pass a value of 0 to disable or 1 to enable.
/MICROSOFTUPDATE	Specifies that Microsoft Update will be used to check for updates
/UpdateSource	Specifies a location for Product Update to search for updates. A value of MU will search Windows Update, but you can also pass a file share or UNC.
/CONFIGURATIONFILE	Specifies the path to a configuration file, which contains a list of switches and parameters, so that they do not have to be specified inline when running setup.
/ERRORREPORTING	Determines if error reporting will be sent to Microsoft. Set to 0 for off or 1 for on.
/INDICATEPROGRESS	When this switch is used, the setup log is piped to the screen during installation.
/INSTALLSHAREDDIR	Specifies a folder location for 64-bit components that are shared between instances
/INSTALLSHAREDWOWDIR	Specifies a folder location for 32-bit components that are shared between instances. This location cannot be the same as the location for 64-bit shared components.
/INSTANCEDIR	Specifies a folder location for the instance
/INSTANCEID	Specifies an ID for the instance. It is considered bad practice to use this parameter.
/PID	Specifies the PID for SQL Server. Unless the media is pre-pidded, failure to specify this parameter will cause Evaluation edition to be installed.
/qs	Runs the installation in Quiet Simple mode, to avoid the need for interaction. Cannot be specified when the /qs parameter is specified
/UIMODE	Specifies if only the minimum amount of dialog boxes should be displayed. Cannot be used in conjunction with either /q or /qs

(continued)

Table 7-6. (*continued*)

Parameter	Description
/SQMREPORTING	Specifies if SQL Reporting will be enabled. Use a value of 0 to disable or 1 to enable.
/HIDECONSOLE	Specifies that the console window should be hidden
/AGTSVCSTARTUPTYPE	Specifies the startup mode of the SQL Agent Service. This can be set to Automatic, Manual, or Disabled.
/BROWSERSVCSTARTUPTYPE	Specifies the startup mode of the SQL Browser Service. This can be set to Automatic, Manual, or Disabled.
/INSTALLSQLDATADIR	Specifies the default folder location for instance data
/SAPWD	Specifies the password for the SA account. This parameter is used when /SECURITYMODE is used to configure the instance as mixed-mode authentication. This parameter becomes required if /SECURITYMODE is set to SQL.
/SECURITYMODE	Use this parameter, with a value of SQL, to specify mixed mode. If you do not use this parameter, Windows authentication will be used.
/SQLBACKUPDIR	Specifies the default location for SQL Server backups
/SQLCOLLATION	Specifies the collation the instance will use
/ADDCURRENTUSERASSQLADMIN	Adds the security context that is running setup.exe to the sysadmin server role. Cannot be specified if /SQLSYSADMINACCOUNTS is specified. I recommend using /SQLSYSADMINACCOUNTS for consistency.
/SQLSVCSTARTUPTYPE	Specifies the startup mode of the Database Engine Service. This can be set to Automatic, Manual, or Disabled.
/SQLTEMPDBDIR	Specifies a folder location for TempDB data files
/SQLTEMPDBLOGDIR	Specifies a folder location for TempDB log files
/SQLTEMPDBFILECOUNT	Specifies the number of TempDB data files that should be created. The maximum value for this parameter equates to the maximum number of cores in the server
/SQLTEMPDBFILESIZE	Specifies the initial size of the TempDB data files
/SQLTEMPDBFILEGROWTH	Specifies the growth increment for TempDB data files
/SQLTEMPDBLOGFILESIZE	Specifies the initial size of the TempDB transaction log
/SQLTEMPDBLOGFILEGROWTH	Specifies the growth increment for TempDB transaction log
/SQLUSERDBDIR	Specifies a default location for the data files or user databases
/SQLSVCINSTANTFILEINIT	Specifies that Instant File Initialization should be enabled for the instance
/SQLUSERDBLOGDIR	Specifies the default folder location for log files or user databases
/FILESTREAMLEVEL	Used to enable FILESTREAM and set the required level of access. This can be set to 0 to disable FILESTREAM, 1 to allow connections via SQL Server only, 2 to allow IO streaming, or 3 to allow remote streaming. The options from 1 to 3 build on each other, so by specifying level 3, you are implicitly specifying levels 1 and 2 as well.
/FILESTREAMSHARENAME	Specifies the name of the Windows file share in which FILESTREAM data will be stored. This parameter becomes required when /FILESTREAMLEVEL is set to a value of 2 or 3.

(*continued*)

Table 7-6. (*continued*)

Parameter	Description
/FTSVCACCOUNT	Specifies the service account that will be used to run the Full Text service
/FTSVCPASSWORD	Specifies the password of the service account that will be used to run the Full Text service
/ISSVCACCOUNT	Specifies the service account that will be used to run the Integration Services service
/ISSVCPASSWORD	Specifies the password of the service account that will be used to run the Integration Services service
/ISSVCStartupType	Specifies the startup mode of the Integration Services service. This can be set to Automatic, Manual, or Disabled.
/NPENABLED	Specifies if Named Pipes should be enabled. This can be set to 0 for disabled or 1 for enabled.
/TCPENABLED	Specifies if TCP will be enabled. Use a value of 0 to disable or 1 to enable.
/PBENGSVCACCOUNT	Specifies the password of the service account that will be used to run the PolyBase service
/PBDMSSVCPASSWORD	Specifies the service account that will be used to run the PolyBase service
/PBENGSVCSTARTUPTYPE	Specifies the startup mode of the PolyBase service. This can be set to Automatic, Manual, or Disabled.
/PBPORTRANGE	Specifies a port range, of at least six ports, to be used by the PolyBase service
/PBSCALEOUT	Specifies if the instance will be part of a PolyBase scale-out group

Using a Configuration File

If you have to configure many parameters for your build, it is cumbersome to create a script that passes the value for every parameter, every time you call it. To resolve this, you can use a configuration file, which will store the values for any parameters that are consistent across every build. Parameters that will be specific to each individual build, such as instance name, or service account should still be passed from the script.

Every time you install an instance from the GUI, a configuration file is automatically generated and placed in C:\Program Files\Microsoft SQL Server\130\Setup Bootstrap\Log\YYYYMMDD_HHMMSS. This path assumes that you installed SQL Server in the default location. The timestamp relates to the time that the installation began.

■ **Tip** For older versions of SQL Server, replace the folder 130 with the appropriate version number. For example, SQL Server 2014 would be 120, and SQL Server 2012 would be 110.

Listing 7-2 shows the configuration file that was created when the ESPROD3 instance was installed. Lines that are prefixed with a semicolon are comments and are ignored by the installer.

■ **Tip** You will notice that the following parameters are specified: MATRIXCMBRICKCOMMPORT, MATRIXCMSERVERNAME, MATRIXNAME, COMMFABRICENCRYPTION, COMMFABRICNETWORKLEVEL, and COMMFABRICPORT. These parameters are intended for internal use by Microsoft only and should be ignored.

Listing 7-2. ESPROD3 Configuration File

```
;SQL Server 2016 Configuration File
[OPTIONS]

; Specifies a Setup work flow, like INSTALL, UNINSTALL, or UPGRADE. This is a required
parameter.

ACTION="Install"

; Use the /ENU parameter to install the English version of SQL Server on your localized
Windows operating system.

ENU="True"

; Parameter that controls the user interface behavior. Valid values are Normal for the full
UI,AutoAdvance for a simplied UI, and EnableUIOnServerCore for bypassing Server Core setup
GUI block.

UIMODE="Normal"

; Setup will not display any user interface.

QUIET="True"

; Setup will display progress only, without any user interaction.

QUIETSIMPLE="False"

; Specify whether SQL Server Setup should discover and include product updates. The valid
values are True and False or 1 and 0. By default SQL Server Setup will include updates that
are found.

UpdateEnabled="True"

; Specify if errors can be reported to Microsoft to improve future SQL Server releases.
Specify 1 or True to enable and 0 or False to disable this feature.

ERRORREPORTING="True"

; If this parameter is provided, then this computer will use Microsoft Update to check for
updates.

USEMICROSOFTUPDATE="False"

; Specifies features to install, uninstall, or upgrade. The list of top-level features
include SQL, AS, RS, IS, MDS, and Tools. The SQL feature will install the Database Engine,
Replication, Full-Text, and Data Quality Services (DQS) server. The Tools feature will
install Management Tools, Books online components, SQL Server Data Tools, and other shared
components.

FEATURES=SQLENGINE,REPLICATION
```

; Specify the location where SQL Server Setup will obtain product updates. The valid values are "MU" to search Microsoft Update, a valid folder path, a relative path such as .\MyUpdates or a UNC share. By default SQL Server Setup will search Microsoft Update or a Windows Update service through the Window Server Update Services.

UpdateSource="MU"

; Displays the command line parameters usage

HELP="False"

; Specifies that the detailed Setup log should be piped to the console.

INDICATEPROGRESS="False"

; Specifies that Setup should install into WOW64. This command line argument is not supported on an IA64 or a 32-bit system.

X86="False"

; Specify the root installation directory for shared components. This directory remains unchanged after shared components are already installed.

INSTALLSHAREDDIR="C:\Program Files\Microsoft SQL Server"

; Specify the root installation directory for the WOW64 shared components. This directory remains unchanged after WOW64 shared components are already installed.

INSTALLSHAREDWOWDIR="C:\Program Files (x86)\Microsoft SQL Server"

; Specify a default or named instance. MSSQLSERVER is the default instance for non-Express editions and SQLExpress for Express editions. This parameter is required when installing the SQL Server Database Engine (SQL), Analysis Services (AS), or Reporting Services (RS).

INSTANCENAME="ESPROD3"

; Specify that SQL Server feature usage data can be collected and sent to Microsoft. Specify 1 or True to enable and 0 or False to disable this feature.

SQMREPORTING="True"

; Specify the Instance ID for the SQL Server features you have specified. SQL Server directory structure, registry structure, and service names will incorporate the instance ID of the SQL Server instance.

INSTANCEID="ESPROD3"

; Specify the installation directory.

INSTANCEDIR="C:\Program Files\Microsoft SQL Server"

; Agent account name

AGTSVCACCOUNT="SQLServiceAccount"

; Auto-start service after installation.

AGTSVCSTARTUPTYPE="Manual"

; CM brick TCP communication port

COMMFABRICPORT="0"

; How matrix will use private networks

COMMFABRICNETWORKLEVEL="0"

; How inter brick communication will be protected

COMMFABRICENCRYPTION="0"

; TCP port used by the CM brick

MATRIXCMBRICKCOMMPORT="0"

; Startup type for the SQL Server service.

SQLSVCSTARTUPTYPE="Automatic"

; Level to enable FILESTREAM feature at (0, 1, 2 or 3).

FILESTREAMLEVEL="0"

; Set to "1" to enable RANU for SQL Server Express.

ENABLERANU="False"

; Specifies a Windows collation or an SQL collation to use for the Database Engine.

SQLCOLLATION="SQL_Latin1_General_CP1_CI_AS"

; Account for SQL Server service: Domain\User or system account.

SQLSVCACCOUNT="SQLServiceAccount"

; Set to "True" to enable instant file initialization for SQL Server service. If enabled, Setup will grant Perform Volume Maintenance Task privilege to the Database Engine Service SID. This may lead to information disclosure as it could allow deleted content to be accessed by an unauthorized principal.

SQLSVCINSTANTFILEINIT="False"

186

```
; Windows account(s) to provision as SQL Server system administrators.

SQLSYSADMINACCOUNTS="SQLAdmin"

; The number of Database Engine TempDB files.

SQLTEMPDBFILECOUNT="2"

; Specifies the initial size of a Database Engine TempDB data file in MB.

SQLTEMPDBFILESIZE="8"

; Specifies the automatic growth increment of each Database Engine TempDB data file in MB.

SQLTEMPDBFILEGROWTH="64"

; Specifies the initial size of the Database Engine TempDB log file in MB.

SQLTEMPDBLOGFILESIZE="8"

; Specifies the automatic growth increment of the Database Engine TempDB log file in MB.

SQLTEMPDBLOGFILEGROWTH="64"

; Provision current user as a Database Engine system administrator for %SQL_PRODUCT_SHORT_
NAME% Express.

ADDCURRENTUSERASSQLADMIN="False"

; Specify 0 to disable or 1 to enable the TCP/IP protocol.

TCPENABLED="1"

; Specify 0 to disable or 1 to enable the Named Pipes protocol.

NPENABLED="0"

; Startup type for Browser Service.

BROWSERSVCSTARTUPTYPE="Automatic"
```

Because every build of SQL Server generates a configuration file, an easy way to generate a configuration is to run through the installation steps using the GUI. At the end of the process, you will be provided a link to the configuration file, without actually installing the instance. This configuration file can then be used as a template for your automated build.

Let's install another instance of SQL Server 2016, this time using a configuration file. We have determined the parameters that we want to configure, and these are detailed in Table 7-7. All parameters not listed will use default values.

Table 7-7. *Required Instance Configuration*

Parameter	Required Value	Static
/FEATURES	SQLEngine,Replication,Conn, IS,Adv_SSMS	Yes
/INSTANCENAME	As required	No
/AGTSVCACCOUNT	As required	No
/AGTSVCPASSWORD	As required	No
/SQLSVCACCOUNT	As required	No
/SQLSVCPASSWORD	As required	No
/SQLSYSADMINACCOUNTS	As required	No
/q	TRUE	Yes
/NPENABLED	1	Yes
/ISSVCACCOUNT	As required	No
/ISSVCPASSWORD	As required	No
/ISSVCStartupType	As required	No
/SQLSVCINSTANTFILEINIT	TRUE	Yes

The parameters that will be static across all builds, we will specify in the configuration file. Parameters which change for every build, we will specify in our PowerShell script. Listing 7-3 shows the configuration file for our new build.

Listing 7-3. New Configuration File

```
;SQL Server 2016 Configuration File
[OPTIONS]

; Accept the SQL Server license terms

IACCEPTSQLSERVERLICENSETERMS="True"

; Specifies a Setup work flow, like INSTALL, UNINSTALL, or UPGRADE. This is a required parameter.

ACTION="Install"

; Use the /ENU parameter to install the English version of SQL Server on your localized
Windows operating system.

ENU="True"

; Setup will not display any user interface.

QUIET="True"

; Setup will display progress only, without any user interaction.

QUIETSIMPLE="False"
```

; Specify whether SQL Server Setup should discover and include product updates. The valid values are True and False or 1 and 0. By default SQL Server Setup will include updates that are found.

UpdateEnabled="True"

; Specify if errors can be reported to Microsoft to improve future SQL Server releases. Specify 1 or True to enable and 0 or False to disable this feature.

ERRORREPORTING="True"

; If this parameter is provided, then this computer will use Microsoft Update to check for updates.

USEMICROSOFTUPDATE="False"

; Specifies features to install, uninstall, or upgrade. The list of top-level features include SQL, AS, RS, IS, MDS, and Tools. The SQL feature will install the Database Engine, Replication, Full-Text, and Data Quality Services (DQS) server. The Tools feature will install Management Tools, Books online components, SQL Server Data Tools, and other shared components.

FEATURES=SQLENGINE,REPLICATION,IS

; Specify the location where SQL Server Setup will obtain product updates. The valid values are "MU" to search Microsoft Update, a valid folder path, a relative path such as .\MyUpdates or a UNC share. By default SQL Server Setup will search Microsoft Update or a Windows Update service through the Window Server Update Services.

UpdateSource="E:\SQLServer2016\Patches"

; Displays the command line parameters usage

HELP="False"

; Specifies that the detailed Setup log should be piped to the console.

INDICATEPROGRESS="False"

; Specifies that Setup should install into WOW64. This command line argument is not supported on an IA64 or a 32-bit system.

X86="False"

; Specify the root installation directory for shared components. This directory remains unchanged after shared components are already installed.

INSTALLSHAREDDIR="C:\Program Files\Microsoft SQL Server"

; Specify the root installation directory for the WOW64 shared components. This directory remains unchanged after WOW64 shared components are already installed.

INSTALLSHAREDWOWDIR="C:\Program Files (x86)\Microsoft SQL Server"

; Specify that SQL Server feature usage data can be collected and sent to Microsoft. Specify 1 or True to enable and 0 or False to disable this feature.

SQMREPORTING="True"

INSTANCEDIR="C:\Program Files\Microsoft SQL Server"

; Auto-start service after installation.

AGTSVCSTARTUPTYPE="Manual"

; CM brick TCP communication port

COMMFABRICPORT="0"

; How matrix will use private networks

COMMFABRICNETWORKLEVEL="0"

; How inter brick communication will be protected

COMMFABRICENCRYPTION="0"

; TCP port used by the CM brick

MATRIXCMBRICKCOMMPORT="0"

; Startup type for the SQL Server service.

SQLSVCSTARTUPTYPE="Automatic"

; Level to enable FILESTREAM feature at (0, 1, 2 or 3).

FILESTREAMLEVEL="0"

; Set to "1" to enable RANU for SQL Server Express.

ENABLERANU="False"

; Specifies a Windows collation or an SQL collation to use for the Database Engine.

SQLCOLLATION="SQL_Latin1_General_CP1_CI_AS"

; Account for SQL Server service: Domain\User or system account.

SQLSVCACCOUNT="SQLServiceAccount"

; Set to "True" to enable instant file initialization for SQL Server service. If enabled, Setup will grant Perform Volume Maintenance Task privilege to the Database Engine Service SID. This may lead to information disclosure as it could allow deleted content to be accessed by an unauthorized principal.

```
SQLSVCINSTANTFILEINIT="True"
```

```
; The number of Database Engine TempDB files.
```

```
SQLTEMPDBFILECOUNT="2"
```

```
; Specifies the initial size of a Database Engine TempDB data file in MB.
```

```
SQLTEMPDBFILESIZE="8"
```

```
; Specifies the automatic growth increment of each Database Engine TempDB data file in MB.
```

```
SQLTEMPDBFILEGROWTH="64"
```

```
; Specifies the initial size of the Database Engine TempDB log file in MB.
```

```
SQLTEMPDBLOGFILESIZE="8"
```

```
; Specifies the automatic growth increment of the Database Engine TempDB log file in MB.
```

```
SQLTEMPDBLOGFILEGROWTH="64"
```

```
; Provision current user as a Database Engine system administrator for %SQL_PRODUCT_SHORT_
NAME% Express.
```

```
ADDCURRENTUSERASSQLADMIN="False"
```

```
; Specify 0 to disable or 1 to enable the TCP/IP protocol.
```

```
TCPENABLED="1"
```

```
; Specify 0 to disable or 1 to enable the Named Pipes protocol.
```

```
NPENABLED="0"
```

```
; Startup type for Browser Service.
```

```
BROWSERSVCSTARTUPTYPE="Automatic"
```

You may notice that we have left UpdateEnabled configured as "True", but we have changed the UpdateSource parameter to point to a local folder, as opposed to "MU". This means that we can drop into a folder on a network share all SQL Server updates that we wish to apply. We can then ensure that all new database servers have a network drive mapped to this location, as part of the Windows build.

With the use of the UpdateEnabled and UpdateSource parameters, we can now ensure that all new builds are patched to our latest tested version. We can also drop multiple updates into the folder location. So, for example, we could drop SP1 and CU3. The instance will then patch the instance to SP1, CU3 during the installation. This reduces the overhead of applying the patches manually post-installation.

■ **Tip** The update files will have to be unzipped, in order to be applied by the setup utility.

Assuming that we save the configuration file in the root of the SQL Server installation media and name it ConfigurationFile.ini (the default name), the command in Listing 7-4 demonstrates the command that we would use to install an instance named ESPROD4.

▪ **Tip**   Change the service account details to match your own configuration, before running the script.

Listing 7-4. Install an Instance with a Configuration File

```
.\setup.exe /INSTANCENAME="ESPROD4" /SQLSYSADMINACCOUNTS="ESASS\SQLAdmin"
/AGTSVCACCOUNT="ESASS\SQLServiceAccount" /AGTSVCPASSWORD="Pa££w0rd"
/SQLSVCACCOUNT="ESASS\SQLServiceAccount" /SQLSVCPASSWORD="Pa££w0rd"
/CONFIGURATIONFILE=".\ConfigurationFile.ini"
```

Parameterizing the Script

To maximize the potential of using PowerShell to automate our SQL Server build, we will have to parameterize the script. This means that instead of having to modify the script with appropriate parameter values every time we install a new instance, we will simply be able to pass those parameter values into the script when we call it.

The additional benefit of this approach is that when we create an orchestration script (which is discussed in the "Orchestrating the Build" section of this chapter), we can pass parameter values into the orchestration script, and common parameters can then be passed into our scripts to install the instance, configure the instance, and update the Inventory database. This saves the DBA time and reduces the risk of human error causing delays.

In order to parameterize the script, we will have to add a param block at the beginning of the script. We will then replace the parameter values that we are passing into setup.exe with the parameters declared in the param block, as demonstrated in Listing 7-5.

Listing 7-5. Parameterizing the Script

```
param(
[string] $InstanceName,
[string] $SQLServiceAccount,
[string] $SQLServiceAccountPassword,
[string] $AgentServiceAccount,
[string] $AgentServiceAccountPassword,
[string] $Administrators
)

.\SETUP.EXE /INSTANCENAME=$InstanceName /SQLSYSADMINACCOUNTS=$Administrators
/SQLSVCACCOUNT=$SQLServiceAccount /SQLSVCPASSWORD=$SQLServiceAccountPassword
/AGTSVCACCOUNT=$AgentServiceAccount /AGTSVCPASSWORD=$AgentService AccountPassword
/CONFIGURATIONFILE="./ConfigurationFile.ini"
```

If we now save the script as AutoBuild.ps1 in the root folder of the SQL Server installation media, we can run the script to create ESPROD5, by using the command in Listing 7-6.

Listing 7-6. Call the AutoBuild.ps1 Script

```
# To specify multiple members of the sysadmin server role,
# pass a comma seperate list to the -Administrators parameter
./AutoBuild.ps1 -InstanceName 'ESPROD5' -SQLServiceAccount 'SQLServiceAccount'
-SQLServiceAccountPassword 'Pa££w0rd' -AgentServiceAccount 'SQLServiceAccount'
-AgentServiceAccountPassword 'Pa££w0rd' -Administrators 'SQLAdmin'
```

Configuring the Instance

There is a vast amount of configuration changes that may be appropriate for the SQL build in your specific environment. This section attempts to cover some of the most common configuration changes, but any SQL Server configuration can be scripted, so I encourage you to explore other scripted configurations that are appropriate for your enterprise.

Configure Database Scoped Configurations

Microsoft has simplified the task of configuring an instance in SQL Server 2016 by adding the ability to configure the number of TempDB files required and if the instance should use Instant File Initialization during the installation. There are also more sensible file size settings, with data and log files defaulting to 8MB instead of 1MB, and file growth defaulting to 64MB. In my opinion, these settings should still be configured based on your capacity planning, but if you do forget to configure them, your log fragmentation will not be quite as bad as in previous versions.

Microsoft has also simplified instance configuration by bringing the functionality of some common trace flags to the database scope, as opposed to the server scope, through fully supported ALTER DATABASE statements. Additionally, some instance-level configurations, such as MAXDOP and parameter sniffing, have also been implemented at the database level.

Table 7-8 details our required configurations for instances supporting Data Warehouse workloads and OLTP workloads.

Table 7-8. Instance Configurations

Configuration	OLTP Workloads	Data Warehouse Workloads	Notes
MAXDOP	8	8	MAXDOP can now be configured at the database level, as well as the instance and query levels
LEGACY_CARDINALITY_ ESTIMATION	OFF	ON	When joining many tables together, as with some complex data warehouses that break data down into separate tables for month or year, instead of implementing partitioning, the new cardinality optimizer can take a very long time (sometimes hours) to complete. In SQL Server 2014, the new cardinality estimator could be configured with T9482. In SQL Server 2016, it can be toggled on or off with this ALTER DATABASE SET option.

(continued)

Table 7-8. (*continued*)

Configuration	OLTP Workloads	Data Warehouse Workloads	Notes
AUTOGROW_ALL_FILES	OFF	ON	This configuration is a filegroup scoped implementation of T1117, which causes all files within a filegroup to grow, if any file within the filegroup grows.
MIXED_PAGE_ALLOCATION	ON	OFF	A database level implementation of T1118, this specifies if mixed page allocations should take place before a table reaches 64KB of used space. Unlike previous versions, this behavior is turned off by default.

We can create a PowerShell script, which will accept a parameter detailing the type of instance and then conditionally configure these settings, by using the invoke-sqlcmd cmdlet, to modify the Model database. Once the Model database has been configured, all user databases that are created will inherit its properties, unless specifically overridden. For properties that are not permitted to be configured in Model, we will conditionally create a DDL trigger, which will fire on new database creation. This is demonstrated in Listing 7-7.

■ **Tip** If you are following the examples in this chapter, you should save this configuration file for later use. You should also change the Owner_Login_Name to match your own configuration, before executing this script.

Listing 7-7. Conditionally Configure Instance

```
param(
[string] $InstanceName,
[string] $InstanceWorkload #The expected workload of the instance
)

$ServerInstance = $env:COMPUTERNAME + "\" + $InstanceName

IF ($InstanceWorkload -eq "Data Warehouse")
{
    Invoke-Sqlcmd -Server $ServerInstance -Query "--Configure Model
USE Model
GO

ALTER DATABASE SCOPED CONFIGURATION SET LEGACY_CARDINALITY_ESTIMATION = ON;
GO

ALTER DATABASE SCOPED CONFIGURATION SET MAXDOP = 8

USE [msdb]
```

```
GO

EXEC  msdb.dbo.sp_add_job @job_name='ConfigureNewDatabase',
                @enabled=1,
                @notify_level_eventlog=0,
                @notify_level_email=2,
                @notify_level_netsend=2,
                @notify_level_page=2,
                @delete_level=0,
                @category_name='[Uncategorized (Local)]',
                @owner_login_name='ESPROD3\SQLAdmin'

GO

EXEC msdb.dbo.sp_add_jobstep @job_name='ConfigureNewDatabase', @step_
name='ConfigureDatabase',
                @step_id=1,
                @cmdexec_success_code=0,
                @on_success_action=1,
                @on_fail_action=2,
                @retry_attempts=0,
                @retry_interval=0,
                @os_run_priority=0, @subsystem='TSQL',
                @command='DECLARE @DatabaseName AS NVARCHAR(128)
DECLARE @SQL AS NVARCHAR(MAX)
SET @DatabaseName = (
        SELECT TOP 1 name
        FROM sys.databases
        ORDER BY create_date DESC
        )

IF @DatabaseName IS NOT NULL
BEGIN
    SELECT @sql = ''ALTER DATABASE '' + @DatabaseName + '' MODIFY FILEGROUP [PRIMARY]
AUTOGROW_ALL_FILES''
    EXEC(@SQL)
END',
                @database_name='master',
                @flags=0
GO

EXEC msdb.dbo.sp_add_jobserver @job_name='ConfigureNewDatabase', @server_name = @@SERVERNAME
GO

--Create the trigger

CREATE TRIGGER ConfigureNewDatabase
ON ALL SERVER
FOR CREATE_DATABASE
AS
    EXEC msdb..sp_start_job 'ConfigureNewDatabase'
GO"
```

195

```
}

IF ($InstanceWorkload -eq "OLTP")
{
     Invoke-Sqlcmd -Server $ServerInstance -Query "--Configure Model

USE Model
GO

ALTER DATABASE SCOPED CONFIGURATION SET MAXDOP = 8

USE [msdb]
GO

EXEC  msdb.dbo.sp_add_job @job_name='ConfigureNewDatabase',
                @enabled=1,
                @notify_level_eventlog=0,
                @notify_level_email=2,
                @notify_level_netsend=2,
                @notify_level_page=2,
                @delete_level=0,
                @category_name='[Uncategorized (Local)]',
                @owner_login_name='ESPROD3\SQLAdmin'

GO

EXEC msdb.dbo.sp_add_jobstep @job_name='ConfigureNewDatabase', @step_
name='ConfigureDatabase',
                @step_id=1,
                @cmdexec_success_code=0,
                @on_success_action=1,
                @on_fail_action=2,
                @retry_attempts=0,
                @retry_interval=0,
                @os_run_priority=0, @subsystem='TSQL',
                @command='DECLARE @DatabaseName AS NVARCHAR(128)
DECLARE @SQL AS NVARCHAR(MAX)
SET @DatabaseName = (
        SELECT TOP 1 name
        FROM sys.databases
        ORDER BY create_date DESC
        )

IF @DatabaseName IS NOT NULL
BEGIN
    SELECT @sql = ''ALTER DATABASE '' + @DatabaseName + '' SET MIXED_PAGE_ALLOCATION ON''
    EXEC(@SQL)
END',
                @database_name='master',
                @flags=0
GO
```

```
EXEC msdb.dbo.sp_add_jobserver @job_name='ConfigureNewDatabase', @server_name = @@SERVERNAME
GO

--Create the trigger

CREATE TRIGGER ConfigureNewDatabase
ON ALL SERVER
FOR CREATE_DATABASE
AS
    EXEC msdb..sp_start_job 'ConfigureNewDatabase'
GO"
}
```

■ **Tip**   The script will only configure the PRIMARY filegroup of a new database to autogrow all files. You can use the skills that you have learned in this book so far, to extend the script to loop around all filegroups of the new database.

Configure the Port Number

If you install a named instance of SQL Server, the installer will configure the instance to use dynamic ports. When dynamic ports are configured, every time the instance starts, it will request a port number from Windows. Windows will then assign it a random available port from the dynamic range, which is from 49152 to 65535, assuming that you are running on Windows Server 2008 or later versions. For earlier versions of Windows, the dynamic port range was from 1024 to 5000, but Microsoft changed this in Windows Vista and Windows Server 2008, to comply with the IANA (Internet Assigned Numbers Authority).

If your instance is configured to use dynamic ports, configuring firewalls can be challenging. At the Windows Firewall level, it is possible to configure a specific service to communicate on any port, but this can be hard to replicate at the corporate firewall level. Instead of this approach, you have to keep the full dynamic port range open bidirectionally. This is an obvious security hole, so I recommend that the instance is configured to use a specific port.

■ **Tip**   In environments where security is the overriding priority, you may also choose to change the port number of the default instance, so that there is not a well-known port number for hackers to attack.

You can create a PowerShell script that will be called off as part of your automated build, which will assume the responsibility of changing the port number. This is achieved through SMO, as demonstrated in Listing 7-8.

Listing 7-8. Configure the Port Number

```
Param(
[string] $InstanceName,
[string] $Port
)

# Load SMO Wmi.ManagedComputer assembly
```

```
[System.Reflection.Assembly]::LoadWithPartialName("Microsoft.SqlServer.SqlWmiManagement") |
out-null

# Create a new smo object

$m = New-Object ('Microsoft.SqlServer.Management.Smo.Wmi.ManagedComputer')

#Disable dynamic ports

$m.ServerInstances[$Instance].ServerProtocols['Tcp'].IPAddresses['IPAll'].IPAddressPropertie
s['TcpDynamicPorts'].Value = ""

# Set static port

$m.ServerInstances[$Instance].ServerProtocols['Tcp'].IPAddresses['IPAll'].
IPAddressProperties['TcpPort'].Value = "$Port"

# Reconfigure TCP

$m.ServerInstances[$Instance].ServerProtocols['Tcp'].Alter()
```

Updating the Inventory Database

In order to drive automation, one key aspect of the automated build will be to update the Inventory database that we created in Chapter 6. We will also have to update the list of target servers used by the SQL Server Agent Master Server. The script in Listing 7-9 will insert the details of the new instance into the Inventory database. This is a standalone server, with no DR instance. Therefore, the only tables to be populated will be ServiceAccount, Server, and Instance. Finally, it will enlist the new instance as a Target Server of our MSX Server.

Listing 7-9. Insert into Inventory Database

```
param(
[string] $InstanceName,
[string] $SQLServiceAccount,
[string] $InstanceType,
[string] $VMFlag,
[string] $Hypervisor,
[string] $ApplicationOwner,
[string] $ApplicationOwnerEmail,
[string] $saAccount,
[string] $saAccountPassword
)

import-module sqlps

#Get Windows Version
[string]$WindowsVersion = Get-CimInstance Win32_OperatingSystem | Select-Object  caption
$WindowsVersion = $WindowsVersion.substring(10,$WindowsVersion.Length-11)

#Get ServerName
```

```
$ServerName = $env:COMPUTERNAME

#Get SQL Version, LoginMode, InstanceCores, InstanceRAM, PortNumber

$ServerInstance = $env:COMPUTERNAME #+ "\" + $ServerInstance

$SQLVersion = invoke-sqlcmd -ServerInstance $ServerInstance -Query "SELECT SUBSTRING(@@
VERSION,1,CHARINDEX(')',@@VERSION)) AS Version" | Select-Object -expand Version

$LoginMode = Invoke-Sqlcmd -ServerInstance $ServerInstance -Database "Master" -Query "CREATE
TABLE #LoginMode
(
Value        NVARCHAR(128),
Data         TINYINT
)
INSERT INTO #LoginMode
EXEC xp_instance_regread N'HKEY_LOCAL_MACHINE', N'Software\Microsoft\MSSQLServer\
MSSQLServer', N'LoginMode'
GO

SELECT Data
FROM #LoginMode" | Select-Object -expand Data

$InstanceCores = Invoke-Sqlcmd -ServerInstance $ServerInstance -Query "SELECT  COUNT(*) AS
Cores
FROM sys.dm_os_schedulers
WHERE status = 'VISIBLE ONLINE'" | Select-Object -expand Cores

$InstanceRAM = Invoke-Sqlcmd -ServerInstance $ServerInstance -Query "SELECT value
FROM sys.configurations
where name = 'max server memory (MB)'" | Select-Object -expand Value

$PortNumber = Invoke-Sqlcmd -ServerInstance $ServerInstance -Query "
DECLARE        @Port   NVARCHAR(8)

CREATE TABLE #PortNumber
(
PortNumber        NVARCHAR(8)
)

EXEC    xp_instance_regread
@rootkey      = 'HKEY_LOCAL_MACHINE'
,@key         = 'Software\Microsoft\Microsoft SQL Server\MSSQLServer\SuperSocketNetLib\Tcp\
IpAll'
,@value_name = 'TcpPort'
,@value       = @Port OUTPUT

INSERT INTO #PortNumber
SELECT @Port

EXEC    xp_instance_regread
```

```
@rootkey      = 'HKEY_LOCAL_MACHINE'
,@key         = 'Software\Microsoft\Microsoft SQL Server\MSSQLServer\SuperSocketNetLib\Tcp\
IpAll'
,@value_name = 'TcpDynamicPorts'
,@value       = @Port OUTPUT

INSERT INTO #PortNumber
SELECT @Port

SELECT PortNumber
FROM #PortNumber
WHERE PortNumber IS NOT NULL

DROP TABLE #PortNumber" | Select-Object -expand PortNumber

foreach ($Version in $SQLVersion)
{
[string]$SQLVersionShred = $SQLVersion.Version
}


foreach ($Mode in $LoginMode)
{
$LoginModeShred = $LoginMode.Data
}


foreach ($Core in $InstanceCores)
{
[string]$InstanceCoresShred = $InstanceCores.Cores
}


foreach ($RAM in $InstanceRAM)
{
[string]$InstanceRAMShred = $InstanceRAM.Value
}


foreach ($Port in $PortNumber)
{
[string]$PortNumberShred = $PortNumber.PortNumber
}

#Get Server Cores
[string]$NoOfCores = Get-WmiObject –class Win32_processor | SELECT NumberOfCores
$ServerCores = $NoOfCores.Substring($NoOfCores.IndexOf("=") + 1,$NoOfCores.Length-
$NoOfCores.IndexOf("=")-2)

#Get Server RAM
$ServerRAMarray = Get-WmiObject -class Win32_physicalmemory | SELECT capacity

$ServerRAM = ($ServerRAMarray.capacity | Measure-Object -Sum).sum

#Get IP Address
```

```
[string]$IPAddress = Get-NetIPAddress -InterfaceAlias "Ethernet" -AddressFamily "IPv4" |
SELECT IPAddress
$IPAddress = $IPAddress.Substring(12,$IPAddress.Length-13)

#Insert into Inventory database
Invoke-Sqlcmd -ServerInstance "ESASSMGMT1" -Database "Inventory" -Query "BEGIN TRANSACTION
    BEGIN TRY
            DECLARE @ServerIdentityTbl TABLE(ID INT)
            DECLARE @ServiceAccountIdentityTbl TABLE(ID INT)

        DECLARE @ServiceAccountIdentity INT
        DECLARE @ServerIdentity INT

            MERGE ServiceAccount AS Target
        USING(SELECT '$($SQLServiceAccount)' AS SQLServiceAccount) AS Source
            ON (Target.ServiceAccountName = Source.SQLServiceAccount)
        WHEN NOT MATCHED BY TARGET THEN
            INSERT (ServiceAccountName)
            VALUES (Source.SQLServiceAccount)
        OUTPUT inserted.ServiceAccountID INTO @ServiceAccountIdentityTbl(ID);

        SET @ServiceAccountIdentity = (SELECT ID FROM @ServiceAccountIdentityTbl)

        IF @ServiceAccountIdentity IS NULL
        BEGIN
            SET @ServiceAccountIdentity = (SELECT ServiceAccountID FROM ServiceAccount WHERE
            ServiceAccountName = '$($SQLServiceAccount)')
        END

        MERGE dbo.Server AS Target
        USING (SELECT '$($ServerName)' AS ServerName) AS Source
            ON (Target.ServerName = Source.ServerName)
        WHEN NOT MATCHED BY TARGET THEN
            INSERT (ServerName, ClusterFlag, WindowsVersion, SQLVersion, ServerCores,
            ServerRAM, VirtualFlag, Hypervisor, ApplicationOwner, ApplicationOwnerEmail)
            VALUES('$($ServerName)',0,'$($WindowsVersion)','$($SQLVersion)',
            '$($ServerCores)','$($ServerRAM)','$($VirtualFlag)','$($Hypervisor)',
            '$($ApplicationOwner)','$($ApplicationOwnerEmail)')
        OUTPUT inserted.ServerID INTO @ServerIdentityTbl(ID);

            SET @ServerIdentity = (SELECT ID FROM @ServerIdentityTbl)

        IF @ServerIdentity IS NULL
        BEGIN
            SET @ServerIdentity = (SELECT ServerID FROM dbo.Server WHERE ServerName =
            '$($ServerName)')
        END

            INSERT INTO dbo.Instance(InstanceName, ServerID, Port, IPAddress,
            SQLServiceAccountID, AuthenticationMode, saAccountName, saAccountPassword,
            InstanceClassification, InstanceCores, InstanceRAM, SQLServerAgentAccountID)
```

```
        VALUES('$($InstanceName)',@ServerIdentity,'$($Port)','$($IPAddress)',
        @ServiceAccountIdentity,'$($LoginMode)','$($saAccount)','$($saAccountPassword)',
        '$($InstanceType)','$($InstanceCores)','$($InstanceRAMShred)',
        @ServiceAccountIdentity)

    COMMIT
END TRY
BEGIN CATCH
    THROW
    ROLLBACK
END CATCH"

#EnlistMSX Server
Invoke-Sqlcmd -ServerInstance $ServerInstance -Database "MSDB" -Query "sp_msx_enlist
    @msx_server_name = 'ESASSMGMT1'
  , @location = 'NTAM - PROD network block' ;"
```

The script uses PowerShell and T-SQL (via the Invoke-Sqlcmd cmdlet), as appropriate, to identify each of the required properties of the build, before inserting the values into the Inventory database, on our Management instance (ESASSMGMT1). Invoke-Sqlcmd will use value substitution of the scripting variables, meaning that we do not need to create a variables list.

Assuming that we save the script as InsertInventory.ps1, we can run the script from an orchestration, using the command in Listing 7-10.

■ **Tip**   Change the sa account's password, to match your own configuration, before running this script.

Listing 7-10. Run the Inventory Update Script

```
.\InsertInventory.ps1 -InstanceName 'testInstance' -SQLServiceAccount 'ESASS\
SQLSVCACCOUNT' -InstanceType '1' -VMFlag '0' -Hypervisor '' -ApplicationOwner 'MyOwner'
-ApplicationOwnerEmail 'MyOwnerEmail' -saAccount 'SA' -saAccountPassword 'SAPassword'
```

■ **Tip**   For an explanation of each of the columns into which we are adding an insert, please refer to Chapter 6.

Orchestrating the Build

Now that we have all of the scripts that will be required to install and configure an instance of SQL Server, we should create a final script, which will be used to orchestrate the build. This is important, as it means that we only have to pass variables once, even though they will be used by multiple scripts.

Across all of our scripts, we will require values for the following parameters:

        $InstanceName,

        $SQLServiceAccount,

        $SQLServiceAccountPassword,

      $AgentServiceAccount,

      $AgentServiceAccountPassword,

      $Administrators

      $InstanceWorkload

      $InstanceType (This will be derived from $InstanceWorkload)

      $VMFlag

      $Hypervisor

      $ApplicationOwner

      $ApplicationOwnerEmail

      $saAccount

      $saAccountPassword

      $Port

We will use the Read-Host PowerShell cmdlet to prompt the user to enter a value for each parameter. We will store this input in variables and pass the variables to each script, as required. This is demonstrated in Listing 7-11.

Listing 7-11. Create the Orchestration

```
#Prompt for parameter values
$InsanceName = Read-Host -Prompt "Please enter the name of the Instance: "
$SQLServiceAccount = Read-Host -Prompt "Please enter the SQL Server service account: "
$SQLServiceAccountPassword = read-host -Prompt "Please enter the SQL Server service account
password: "
$AgentServiceAccount = Read-Host -Prompt "Please enter the SQL Server Agent service account:
"
$AgentServiceAccountPassword = Read-Host -Prompt "Please enter the SQL Server Agent service
account password: "
$Administrators = Read-Host -Prompt "Please enter the account that should be given SQL
Administrative permissions: "
$InstanceWorkload = Read-Host -Prompt "Please enter the expected instance workload (OLTP,
Data Warehouse or Mixed): "
$Port = Read-Host -Prompt "Please enter the name of the TCP Port that the instance should
listen on: "

IF ($InstanceWorkload = "OLTP")
{
    $InstanceType = 1
}
ELSEIF ($InstanceWorkload = "Data Warehouse")
{
    $InstanceType = 2
}
ELSEIF ($InstanceType = "Mixed")
{
    $InstanceType = 3
}
```

```
$VMFlag = Read-Host -Prompt "Please indicate if the server is a VM (0 for physical, 1 for
virtual): "

IF ($VMFlag = 1)
{
    $Hypervisor = read-host -Prompt "Please enter the name of the Hypervisor: "
}

$ApplicationOwner = read-host -prompt "Please enter the application owner: "
$ApplicationOwnerEmail = read-host -Prompt "Please enter the application owner's e-mail
address: "
$saAccount = Read-Host -Prompt "Please enter the name of the sa account: "
$saAccountPassword = read-host -Prompt "Please enter the password of the sa account: "

#Install the Instance
./AutoBuild.ps1 -InstanceName $InstanceName -SQLServiceAccount $SQLServiceAccount
-SQLServiceAccountPassword $SQLServiceAccountPassword -AgentServiceAccount
$AgentServiceAccount -AgentServiceAccountPassword $AgentServiceAccountPassword
-Administrators $Administrators

#Configure the Instance
./ConfigureInstance.ps1 -InstanceName $InstanceName -InstanceWorkload $InstanceWorkload

#Configure the Port
./ConfigurePort.ps1 -InstanceName $InstanceName -Port $Port

#Insert into the Inventory database
.\InsertInventory.ps1 -InstanceName $InstanceName -SQLServiceAccount $SQLServiceAccount
-InstanceType $InstanceType -VMFlag $VMFlag -Hypervisor $Hypervisor -ApplicationOwner
$ApplicationOwner -ApplicationOwnerEmail $ApplicationOwnerEmail -saAccount $saAccount
-saAccountPassword $saAccountPassword
```

Summary

Automating the build of SQL Server instances will reduce administrative effort and time to market of a new instance request. It will also help you to ensure consistency across your environment. It will also act as a driver for automation, by updating the Inventory database, which will act as the hub that drives automation.

There is more to automating an SQL build than simply running setup.exe You should also consider the configuration of the instance. In some cases, you may also have to configure aspects of the operating system, if your organization's Windows Gold Build is not optimized for database servers. After installing and configuring SQL Server, be sure to update the Inventory database.

The final step of build automation is to create an orchestration. This orchestration will allow users to type parameter values only once, rather than for every script that is called. This reduces effort and minimizes the risk of human error.

CHAPTER 8

■ ■ ■

Driving Automation Through Monitoring

Working with Data Collection and the Management Data Warehouse

Monitoring is key to producing sophisticated automation. It allows you to respond to performance conditions by running appropriate routines to resolve an issue. SQL Server provides DBAs with extensible data collection, which is capable of collecting any data, not just performance data. The data is then stored in the MDW (Management Data Warehouse), which provides a single repository for data that has been collected throughout the enterprise.

Understanding Data Collection

Data Collection provides an extensible method of capturing data throughout the enterprise. On the top level, it can be accessed through SQL Server Management Studio, wherein there is a wizard for configuring the Management Data Warehouse and a set of reports that can be viewed against a set of standard collector items that are configured automatically.

At the level below, Data Collection provides an API and a set of system-stored procedures for creating and managing collector items and collector sets. At the lowest level, Data Collector uses SQL Server Integration Services packages to collect the data and SQL Server Agent to schedule the collection, as well as the upload to the Management Data Warehouse.

When working with Data Collection, you will become familiar with the terminology that is detailed in Table 8-1.

© Peter A. Carter 2016
P. A. Carter, *Expert Scripting and Automation for SQL Server DBAs*, DOI 10.1007/978-1-4842-1943-0_8

Table 8-1. *Data Collection Terminology*

Term	Meaning
Collector item	An instance of a collector type that has been configured and scheduled
Collection mode	Specifies if the data collected will be cached before being sent to the MDW*
Collector set	A group of collected items
Collector type	<ul><li>A class of collector. Valid collector types are as follows:</li><li>Generic T-SQL Query Collector Type</li><li>Generic SQL Trace Collector Type</li><li>Query Activity Collector Type</li><li>Performance Counters Collector Type</li></ul>
Data provider	A data source specific to the target type
Management Data Warehouse	A data warehouse that is used as a central repository for collected data
Target	An instance of SQL Server from which data is collected
Target root	A defined target within the target hierarchy, this can be a computer, an SQL Server instance, or a database.
Target set	A set of targets that are defined by applying a filter to the target root
Target type	The type of target root within the target hierarchy, for example, an SQL Server instance or a database

Caching will be discussed in the next section.

Data Caching

Data Collectors can be configured either to send the results directly to the Management Data Warehouse or to cache the results on the target of the collection first, before uploading it to the Management Data Warehouse. If the Data Collector is configured to cache the results, it is possible to configure the Data Collector to collect data constantly or on a scheduled basis. If the Data Collector is configured in non-cached mode, however, continuous collection is not supported. If caching is used, the same SQL Server Agent schedule will be used for both collection and upload.

If caching is configured, it is also possible to configure a caching window. This defines if the process will retry the upload of data to the Management Data Warehouse, in the event of failure.

It is also possible to configure the folder on the target machine in which the data will be cached. If this is not configured, the Data Collector will attempt to use the TEMP directory stored, either in the %TEMP% or %TMP% environmental variables. If neither of these is available, the process will fail.

Data Collector Security

Data Collection uses role-based permissions to implement security. There are two separate sets of database roles that users can be added into. One set of roles is for administering the Management Data Warehouse, and the other set is for administering Data Collection itself. The following sections will discuss each of these sets of roles.

Data Collection Roles

Data Collection roles are stored in the MSDB database. By default, they have no members, and while members of the sysadmin server role will have access to Data Collection views and SQL Server Agent objects, they should still be explicitly added to the Data Collection roles.

Table 8-2 defines each of the Data Collector roles.

Table 8-2. *Data Collector Roles*

Role	Description	Inherited Permissions
dc_proxy	Members are able to view the configuration of collector sets and log collection set runtime events. Additionally, they are able to view encrypted information stored in SQL Server internal tables.	db_ssisltduser db_ssisoperator
dc_operator	Members are able to view detailed configuration information and start or stop collection sets. They can also change the frequency of data collection and uploads.	db_ssisltduser db_ssisoperator
dc_admin	In addition to being able to perform any task carried out by a member of the dc_operator role, members can also add new collection sets, install new collector types, and set properties of collectors.	SQLAgentUserRole dc_operator

Management Data Warehouse Roles

In addition to the data collection roles, there are also a set of roles that provide the security mechanism for administering the Management Data Warehouse. These roles, which are located within the Management Data Warehouse database, are detailed in Table 8-3.

Table 8-3. *Management Data Warehouse Roles*

Role	Description
mdw_reader	Provides read-only access to data captured by the Data Collector
mdw_writer	Data Collectors are made members of this role, as it provides the ability to write and upload data to the Management Data Warehouse
mdw_admin	Provides the ability to run maintenance jobs against the Management Data Warehouse and also make schema changes in the database. This is required in scenarios such as adding a new collector, as a new table will be required. It is important to note, that adding a new collector will also require the user to be a member of the dc_admin role.

Simple Implementation of Management Data Warehouse

Creating a basic implementation of the Management Data Warehouse to collect the predefined system Data collectors is a relatively straightforward task. The following sections will demonstrate how to create and configure a Management Data Warehouse, called MDW, on the ESASSMGMT1 instance. You will then learn how to configure the predefined system Data Collectors. Finally, I will discuss how to view the data after it has been collected.

Implementing the Data Warehouse

We will first launch the Configure Management Data Warehouse Wizard, by drilling through the Management node in Object Explorer and selecting Tasks ➤ Configure Management Data Warehouse from the context menu of Data Collection. After passing through the Welcome page of the wizard, you will be prompted either to select an existing database or create a new database that will act as the Management Data Warehouse. We will use the New button, to enter the Create Database dialog box, and create a database named MDW. We can now select the MDW database from the drop-down list, as illustrated in Figure 8-1.

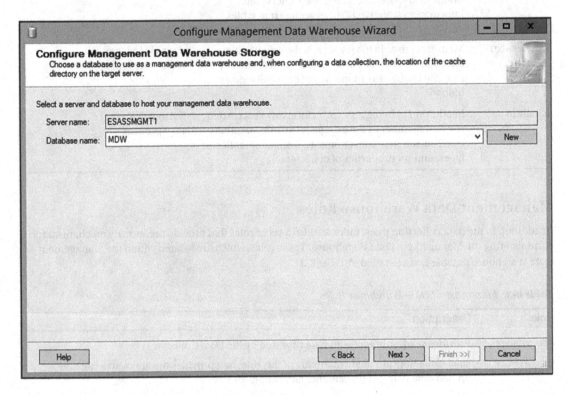

Figure 8-1. *Configure Management Data Warehouse Storage page*

On the Map Logins and Users page of the wizard, we will add the SQLAdmin login to the mdw_admin role. Because the mdw_admin role contains the mdw_reader and mdw_writer roles, these roles will be automatically selected for us as well. This is illustrated in Figure 8-2.

■ **Tip**   The wizard will create a user in the MDW database, which is mapped to the login specified. It is this database-level user that will be added to the role(s) specified. The name of the database user (displayed in the User column) will default to the same name as the login. While this can be changed, I recommend to always use the same name for database users, as thier associated logins, in order to avoid confusion.

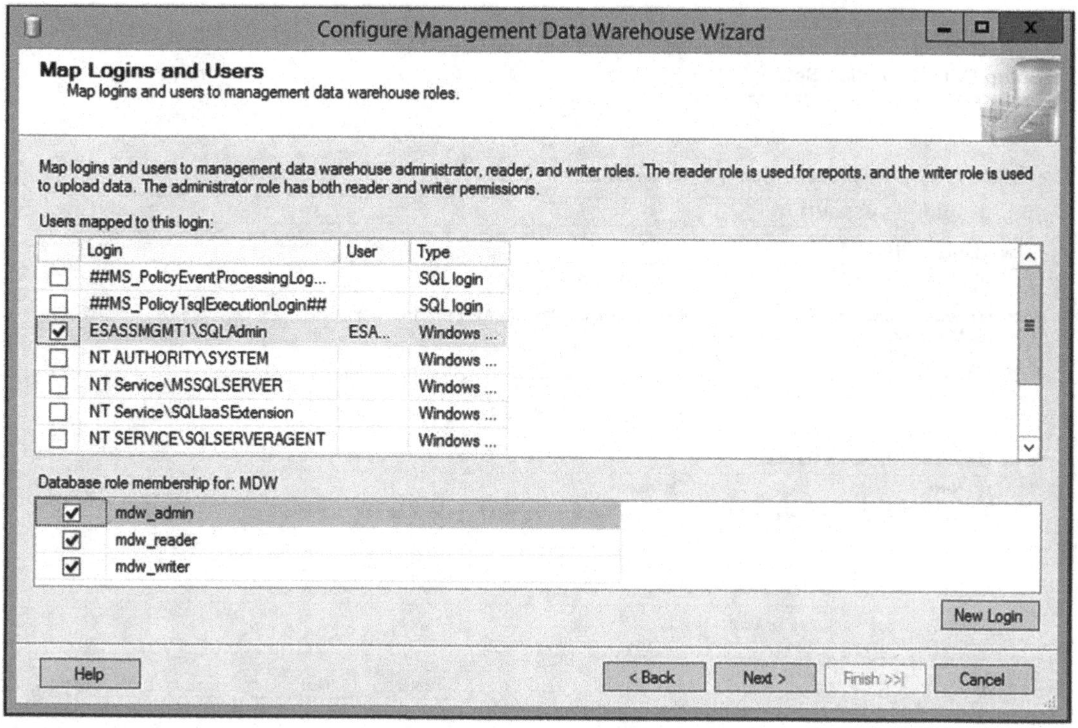

Figure 8-2. *Map Logins and Users page*

The Summary page of the wizard will now display the actions to be performed. Clicking the Finish button will cause the wizard to carry out the configuration. The results should be reviewed, on the completion page, before continuing.

Implementing the Predefined System Data Collectors

To implement the system data collectors, we will drill through the Management node in Object Explorer and then select Tasks ➤ Configure Data Collection from the context menu of Data Collection. This will cause the Configure Data Collection wizard to be invoked. After passing through the Welcome page of this wizard, you will be prompted to set up the data collection sets.

On this page of the wizard, illustrated in Figure 8-3, we will specify the instance that contains the Management Data Warehouse and the name of the Management Data Warehouse. We will leave the Cache Directory blank, so that the default folder will be used, and check the option of configuring the System Data Collector Sets. Because we are configuring the data collection on the same instance as the Management Data Warehouse, the option to use an SQL Server Agent Proxy for remote uploads is disabled.

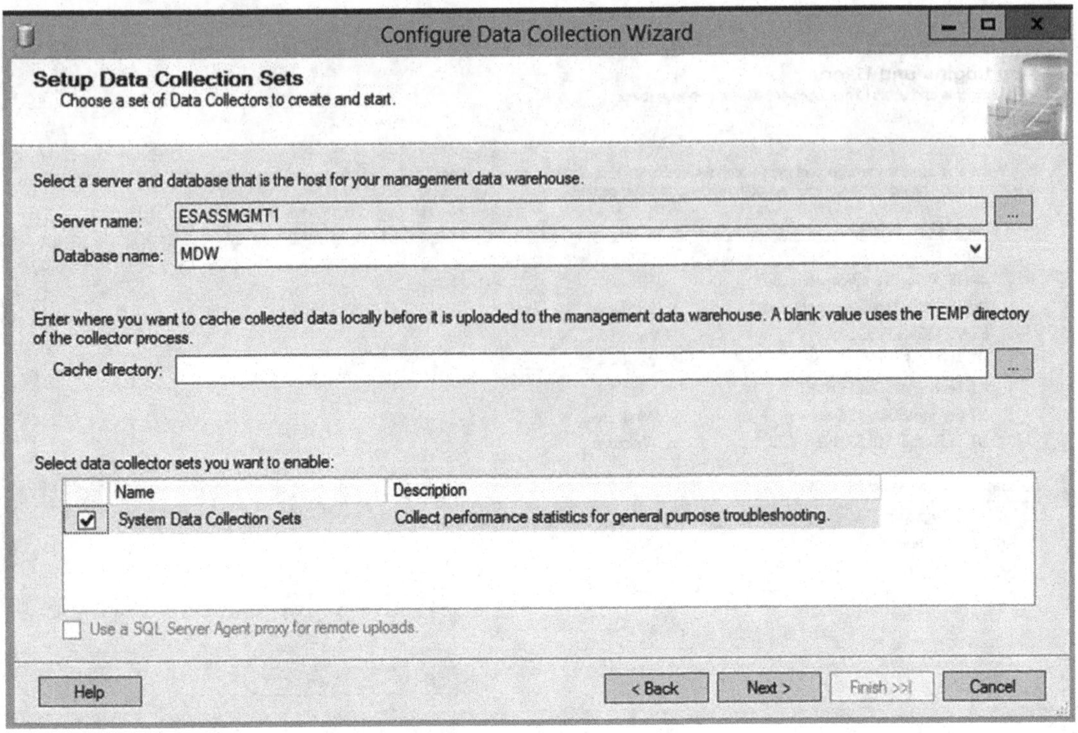

Figure 8-3. Setup Data Collection Sets page

■ **Tip** The SQL Server Agent Service must be running, in order to start the collection set. If the service is not running, the wizard will fail.

After clicking Finish on the Summary page, the wizard will implement the data collection sets. On the Completion page, you should ensure that there are no errors before continuing.

You should now repeat these steps on all servers from which you want to upload data to the Management Data Warehouse. On each instance, remember to change the instance of the Management Data Warehouse to ESASSMGMT1.

Viewing Collected Data

SQL Server Management Studio provides three pre-canned reports, which are based on the System Data Collector sets. These reports can be found by drilling through the Management node in Object Explorer and selecting Reports ➤ Management Data Warehouse ➤ [Name of Report] from the context menu of Data Collection.

The three available reports are

- Disk Usage Summary

- Server Activity History

- Query Statistics History

The Disk Usage Summary report provides a high-level summary of the amount of disk space used by each database, as illustrated in Figure 8-4.

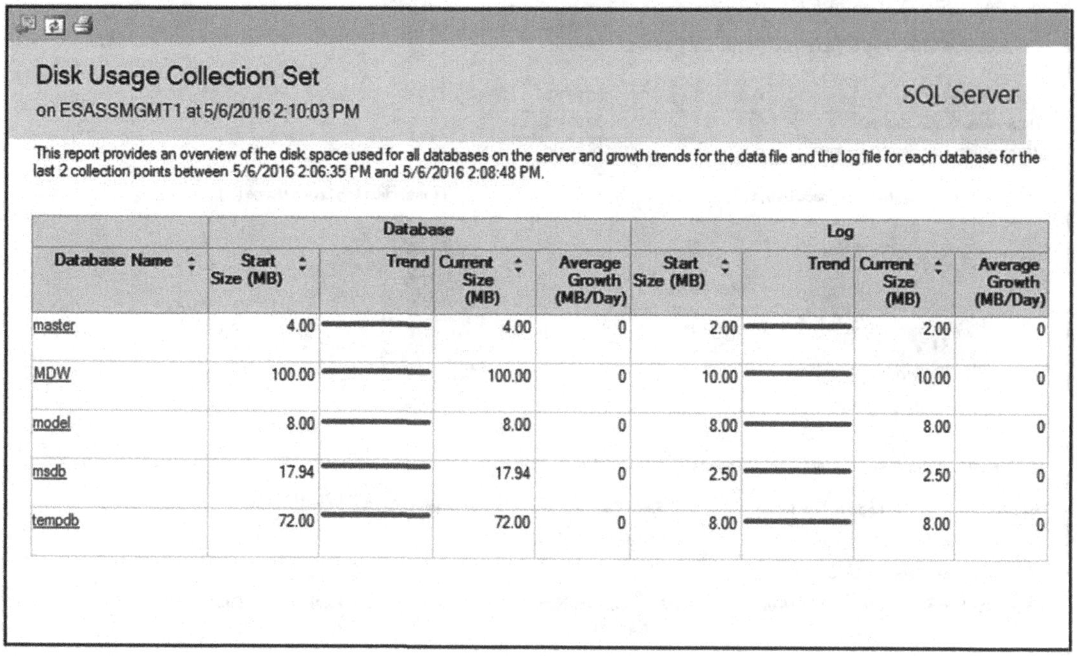

Disk Usage Collection Set
on ESASSMGMT1 at 5/6/2016 2:10:03 PM

SQL Server

This report provides an overview of the disk space used for all databases on the server and growth trends for the data file and the log file for each database for the last 2 collection points between 5/6/2016 2:06:35 PM and 5/6/2016 2:08:48 PM.

Database Name	Database				Log			
	Start Size (MB)	Trend	Current Size (MB)	Average Growth (MB/Day)	Start Size (MB)	Trend	Current Size (MB)	Average Growth (MB/Day)
master	4.00		4.00	0	2.00		2.00	0
MDW	100.00		100.00	0	10.00		10.00	0
model	8.00		8.00	0	8.00		8.00	0
msdb	17.94		17.94	0	2.50		2.50	0
tempdb	72.00		72.00	0	8.00		8.00	0

Figure 8-4. *Disk usage summary*

From this high-level summary, you are able to drill through a database name, to see more granular statistics for that specific database. Figure 8-5 illustrates this for the newly created MDW database.

Here, you will notice that we are presented with pie charts, detailing how the database space is allocated, alongside what percentage of the transaction log is being used. The Data/Log Files Autogrowth/Autoshrink Events section and Disk Space Used by Data Files section can also be expanded to reveal additional information.

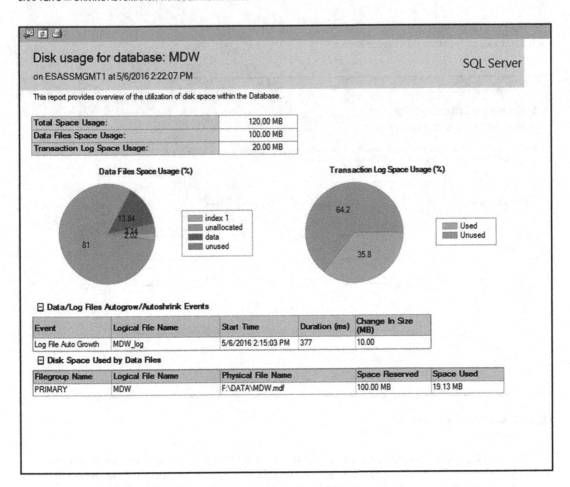

Figure 8-5. *Disk space usage history*

The Server Activity History report, illustrated in Figure 8-6, provides high-level information regarding resource consumption on the instance. Each section of the report offers drill-through functionality to further reports, offering more granular detail, in each area.

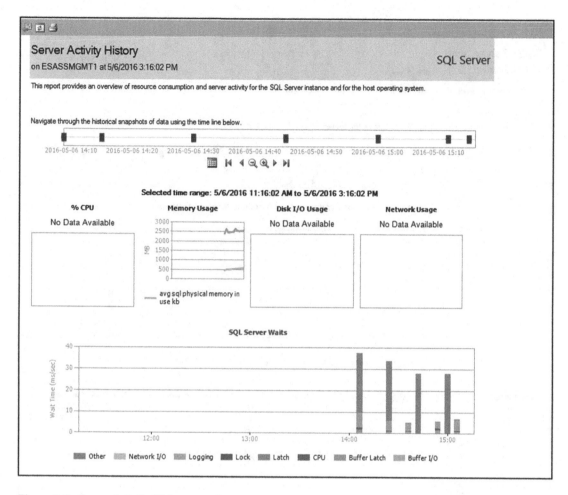

Figure 8-6. *Server Activity History report*

Figure 8-7 illustrates the granular SQL Server Waits report, which can be accessed by drilling through the SQL Server Waits area of the Server Activity History report. As you can see, this report offers a graphical illustration of wait statistics over time. The lower region of the report provides textual information, wherein each category can be expanded to show the wait statistics for each wait type within the category. Additionally, each wait type provides drill-through functionality to the Query Statistics History report, which allows you to order queries by CPU, Duration, Total IO, Physical Reads, and Logical Reads.

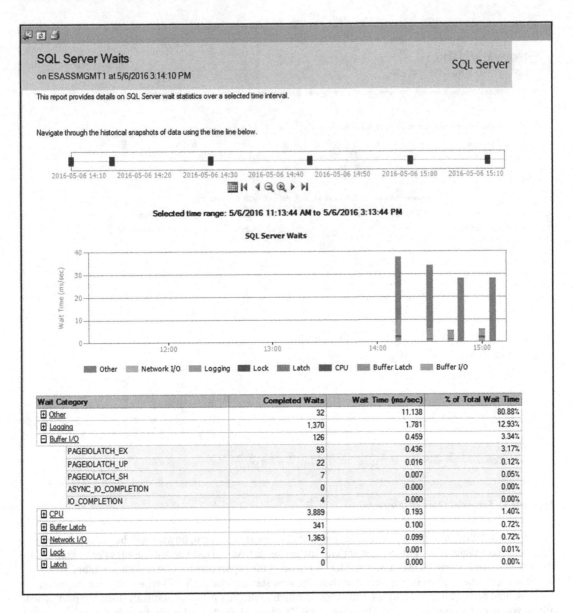

Figure 8-7. SQL Server Waits report

As previously mentioned, the Query Statistics History report, illustrated in Figure 8-8, allows you to order queries by CPU, Duration, Total IO, Physical Reads, and Logical Reads.

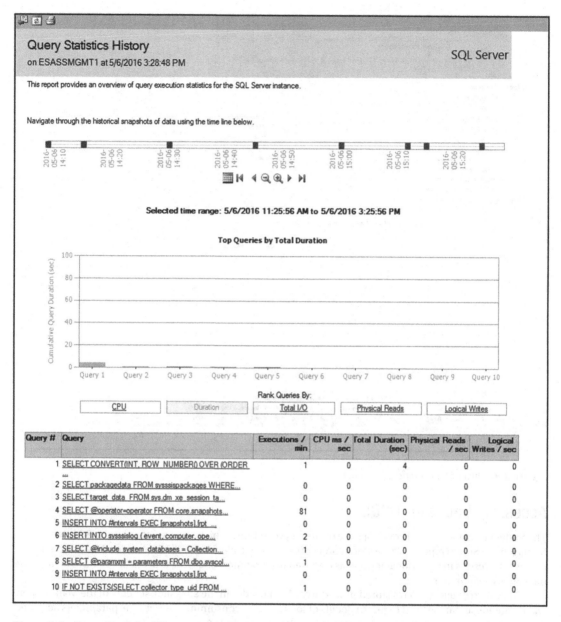

Figure 8-8. Query Statistics History report

Each query in the lower region of the report provides drill-through functionality to the Query Details report, which provides the query execution statistics for the query and displays the query's cost over time, including the ability to rank the query's top execution plans by cost. The report also displays the full text of the query and informs the DBA which object the query was executed within (where appropriate). This report is partially illustrated in Figure 8-9.

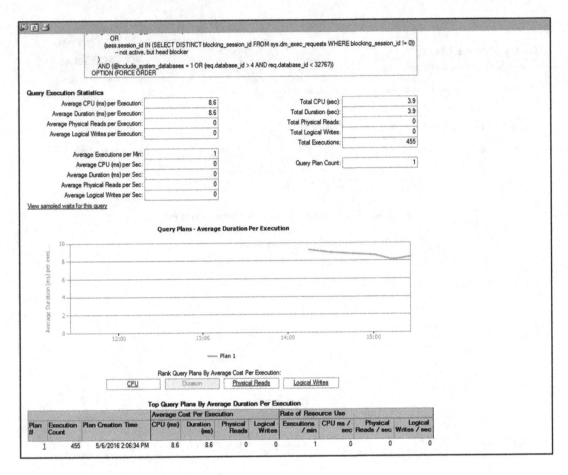

Figure 8-9. Query Details report (partial)

Accessing Data with T-SQL

The System Data Collectors provide a suite of stored procedures, which are used to drive the SQL Server Management Studio reports. These stored procedures can be called manually, however, allowing you to retrieve the results in a relational format, as opposed to a graphical one. This is useful if you have to mine the data, to discover trends.

The rpt_top_query_stats stored procedure, which resides in the snapshot schema of the Management Data Warehouse, can be used to return details of top resource-consuming queries. The parameters accepted by the rpt_top_query_stats stored procedure are detailed in Table 8-4.

Table 8-4. `rpt_top_query_stats` *Parameters*

Parameter	Description
@instance_name	Filters the results based on the name of an instance
@start_time	Specifies the earliest execution time of queries that should be included in the results
@end_time	Specifies the latest execution time of queries that should be included in the results
@time_window_size	If @start_time is NULL, can be used in conjunction with @time_interval_min to define the earliest execution time of queries that should be included in the results, using the formulae @start_time = DATEADD(minute, @time_window_size * @time_interval_min * -1.0, @end_time). Both @time_window_size and @time_interval_min must be passed, or neither will be used.
@time_interval_min	If @start_time is NULL, can be used in conjunction with @time_window_size_min to define the earliest execution time of queries that should be included in the results, using the formulae @start_time = DATEADD(minute, @time_window_size * @time_interval_min * -1.0, @end_time). Both @time_window_size and @time_interval_min must be passed, or neither will be used.
@order_by_criteria	The criteria used to order the results. Acceptable values are • CPU (the default value) • Duration • Physical Reads • Logical Reads • I/O
@database_name	Filters the results based on the name of the database that the queries were executed against. When NULL (the default value) is passed, no database filter will be applied.

The script in Listing 8-1 uses the `rpt_top_query_stats` stored procedure to generate query statistics for the top ten queries executed against the MDW database, ordered by CPU usage.

Listing 8-1. Using the `rpt_top_query_stats` Procedure

```
USE MDW
GO

EXEC snapshots.rpt_top_query_stats
      @instance_name = 'ESASSMGMT1'
      ,@order_by_criteria = 'CPU'
      ,@database_name = 'MDW' ;
```

■ **Caution** The `rpt_` procedures are not documented by Microsoft. This means that Microsoft will not offer support when you use them directly.

It is also possible to access the data directly from the underlying tables. This allows you to write your own custom queries, adding additional flexibility and extensibility.

The historically captured data is stored in tables in the snapshot schema of the Management Data Warehouse. Reference data, such as wait types and wait type categories, are stored in the core schema.

The query in Listing 8-2 can be used to determine how much the transaction log of the MDW database has grown over the course of the last month.

Listing 8-2. Report on Transaction Log Growth

```
USE MDW
GO

SELECT
(
        SELECT TOP 1 log_size_mb
        FROM snapshots.log_usage
        WHERE database_name = 'MDW'
        ORDER BY collection_time DESC
)
        -
(
        SELECT TOP 1 log_size_mb
        FROM snapshots.log_usage
        WHERE database_name = 'MDW'
                AND collection_time > DATEADD(MONTH,-1,GETDATE())
        ORDER BY collection_time ASC
) AS LogGrowthInLstMonthMB ;
```

Custom Implementation of Management Data Warehouse

Of course, if you were to implement the system data collectors only, Data Collection would prove rather limited. It is also possible to implement your own custom data collectors, which can then be used across the enterprise. The nice thing about implementing custom data collectors, as opposed to using many other monitoring tools, is that you can capture any metrics. You are not limited to performance counters. The following sections will demonstrate how to create a custom collector set and a custom collector item, using the Generic T-SQL collector type.

Create a Custom Collector Set

We can create custom data collector sets, using the sp_syscollector_create_collection_set system stored procedure, which can be found in the MSDB database. The parameters accepted by the sp_syscollector_create_collection_set procedure are detailed in Table 8-5.

Table 8-5. `sp_syscollector_create_collection_set` *Parameters*

Parameter	Description
@name	Specifies the name of the custom data collector
@target	Reserved for future use
@collection_mode	Specifies the collection mode • 0 indicates that data is collected and uploaded on different schedules • 1 indicates that data is collected and uploaded on the same schedule
@days_until_expiration	Specifies the retention period of collected data, in the Management Data Warehouse
@proxy_id	Specifies the ID of the Proxy to use for remote collection. If specified, @proxy_name must be NULL.
@proxy_name	Specifies the name of the Proxy to use for remote collection. If specified, @proxy_id must be NULL.
@schedule_uid	Specifies the GUID of the SQL Server Agent schedule that will be used for uploading data to the Management Data Warehouse. If passed, @schedule_name must be NULL. If @collection_mode is set to collect and upload on the same schedule, this parameter is ignored.
@schedule_name	Specifies the name of the SQL Server Agent schedule that will be used for uploading data to the Management Data Warehouse. If passed, @schedule_id must be NULL. If @collection_mode is set to collect and upload on the same schedule, this parameter is ignored.
@logging_level	Specifies the SSIS logging level to use • 0 indicates that starting and stopping collection sets, starting and stopping packages and error information will be logged • 1 indicates that execution statistics continuously running collection progress and SSIS warning will be logged, in addition to the events logged by level 0 • 2 indicates that verbose logging will be used
@description	Specifies a description for the Data Collector
@collection_set_id	An output parameter returning the ID of the collection set
@collection_set_uid	An output parameter returning the GUID of the collections set

The script in Listing 8-3 will use the `sp_syscollector_create_collection_set` system stored procedure to create a custom data collection set called `Chapter8CollectionSet`.

Listing 8-3. Create a Custom Data Collector Set

```
USE msdb;
GO

DECLARE @Collection_Set_ID INT
```

```
EXEC dbo.sp_syscollector_create_collection_set
    @name = 'Chapter8CollectionSet',
    @collection_mode = 0,
    @days_until_expiration = 90,
    @description = 'Collection set used for Chapter 8',
    @logging_level = 2,
    @schedule_name = 'CollectorSchedule_Every_30min' ,
    @collection_Set_ID = @collection_set_id OUTPUT ;
```

Create a Custom Collector Item

We can create custom data collector items using the sp_syscollector_create_collection_item system stored procedure. This procedure accepts the parameters detailed in Table 8-6.

Table 8-6. sp_syscollector_create_collection_item *Parameters*

Parameter	Description
@collection_set_id	Specifies the ID of the collection set to which this collection item will be bound
@collector_type_uid	Specifies the GUID of the collector type that will be used to create the collector item
@name	Specifies a name for the collector item
@frequency	Specifies how frequently, in seconds, data will be collected, with a default value of five seconds. This setting will be ignored if the collection set is using non-cached collection mode.
@parameters	Specifies the input parameters for the collection item. In the case of the generic T-SQL collection type, this parameter will be used to specify the query to run.
@collection_item_id	An output parameter returning the ID of the collector item

The @parameters argument has a data type of XML. While this adds complexity, it makes the argument generic for all collector types. Each collector type has its own XSD schema. The generic T-SQL query schema can be found in Listing 8-4.

Listing 8-4. Generic T-SQL Query Schema

```xml
<xs:schema xmlns:xs="http://www.w3.org/2001/XMLSchema" targetNamespace="DataCollectorType">
  <xs:element name="TSQLQueryCollector">
    <xs:complexType>
      <xs:sequence>
        <xs:element name="Query" minOccurs="1" maxOccurs="unbounded">
          <xs:complexType>
            <xs:sequence>
              <xs:element name="Value" type="xs:string" />
              <xs:element name="OutputTable" type="xs:string" />
            </xs:sequence>
          </xs:complexType>
        </xs:element>
        <xs:element name="Databases" minOccurs="0" maxOccurs="1">
          <xs:complexType>
            <xs:sequence>
              <xs:element name="Database" minOccurs="0" maxOccurs="unbounded"
              type="xs:string" />
```

```
            </xs:sequence>
            <xs:attribute name="UseSystemDatabases" type="xs:boolean" use="optional" />
            <xs:attribute name="UseUserDatabases" type="xs:boolean" use="optional" />
          </xs:complexType>
        </xs:element>
      </xs:sequence>
    </xs:complexType>
  </xs:element>
</xs:schema>
```

The schema for the generic SQL Trace collection type can be found in Listing 8-5.

Listing 8-5. Generic SQL Trace Schema

```
<xs:schema xmlns:xs="http://www.w3.org/2001/XMLSchema" targetNamespace="DataCollectorType">
  <xs:element name="SqlTraceCollector">
    <xs:complexType>
      <xs:sequence>
        <xs:element name="Events">
          <xs:complexType>
            <xs:sequence>
              <xs:element minOccurs="0" maxOccurs="unbounded" name="EventType">
                <xs:complexType>
                  <xs:sequence>
                    <xs:element maxOccurs="unbounded" name="Event">
                      <xs:complexType>
                        <xs:attribute name="id" type="xs:unsignedByte" use="required" />
                        <xs:attribute name="name" type="xs:string" use="required" />
                        <xs:attribute name="columnslist" type="xs:string" use="optional" />
                      </xs:complexType>
                    </xs:element>
                  </xs:sequence>
                  <xs:attribute name="id" type="xs:unsignedByte" use="optional" />
                  <xs:attribute name="name" type="xs:string" use="required" />
                </xs:complexType>
              </xs:element>
            </xs:sequence>
          </xs:complexType>
        </xs:element>
        <xs:element name="Filters">
          <xs:complexType>
            <xs:sequence>
              <xs:element name="Filter" minOccurs="0" maxOccurs="unbounded">
                <xs:complexType>
                  <xs:attribute name="columnid" type="xs:unsignedByte" use="required" />
                  <xs:attribute name="columnname" type="xs:string" use="required" />
                  <xs:attribute name="logical_operator" type="xs:string" use="required" />
                  <xs:attribute name="comparison_operator" type="xs:string" use="required" />
                  <xs:attribute name="value" type="xs:string" use="required" />
                </xs:complexType>
              </xs:element>
```

```
          </xs:sequence>
        </xs:complexType>
      </xs:element>
    </xs:sequence>
    <xs:attribute name="use_default" type="xs:boolean" />
  </xs:complexType>
  </xs:element>
</xs:schema>
```

The schema for the performance counters collector type can be found in Listing 8-6.

Listing 8-6. Performance Counters Collector Type Schema

```
<xs:schema xmlns:xs="http://www.w3.org/2001/XMLSchema" targetNamespace="DataCollectorType">
  <xs:element name="PerformanceCountersCollector">
    <xs:complexType>
      <xs:sequence>
        <xs:element minOccurs="0" maxOccurs="unbounded" name="PerformanceCounters">
          <xs:complexType>
            <xs:attribute name="Objects" type="xs:string" use="required" />
            <xs:attribute name="Counters" type="xs:string" use="required" />
            <xs:attribute name="Instances" type="xs:string" use="optional" />
          </xs:complexType>
        </xs:element>
      </xs:sequence>
      <xs:attribute name="StoreLocalizedCounterNames" type="xs:boolean" use="optional"
      default="false" />
    </xs:complexType>
  </xs:element>
</xs:schema>
```

Listing 8-7 demonstrates how to use the sp_syscollector_create_collection_item stored procedure to create a collector item that will collect details of infrequently used indexes. Because of the nature of the collector item, we will schedule the collection to occur only every six hours, which is the least frequent schedule that is created as standard by Data Collection. A complete list of standard schedules are as follows:

- CollectorSchedule_Every_5min

- CollectorSchedule_Every_10min

- CollectorSchedule_Every_15min

- CollectorSchedule_Every_30min

- CollectorSchedule_Every_60min

- CollectorSchedule_Every_6h

Listing 8-7. Create a Custom Collector Item

```
DECLARE @collection_set_id INT ;

SET @collection_set_id = (SELECT collection_set_id
                            FROM msdb..syscollector_collection_sets
```

```
                            WHERE Name = 'Chapter8CollectionSet') ;

DECLARE @collector_type_uid UNIQUEIDENTIFIER ;

SET @collector_type_uid = (SELECT collector_type_uid
                           FROM msdb..syscollector_collector_types
                           WHERE name = 'Generic T-SQL Query Collector Type') ;

DECLARE @collection_item_id INT ;

EXEC msdb..sp_syscollector_create_collection_item
    @name = 'Chapter8CollectorUnusedIndexes',
    @parameters='<ns:TSQLQueryCollector xmlns:ns="DataCollectorType">
        <Query>
            <Value>SELECT *
                    FROM sys.dm_db_index_usage_stats
                    WHERE   (
                                    (
                                    user_seeks &lt; 10
                                    AND user_scans &lt; 10
                                    AND user_lookups &lt; 10
                                    )
                            OR
                                    (
                                    last_user_seek &lt; GETDATE() - 30
                                    AND last_user_scan   &lt; GETDATE() - 30
                                    AND last_user_lookup  &lt; GETDATE() - 30
                                    )
                            )
                            AND database_id > 4
            </Value>
            <OutputTable>dm_db_index_usage_stats</OutputTable>
        </Query>
        </ns:TSQLQueryCollector>',
    @collection_item_id = @collection_item_id OUTPUT,
    @frequency=5,
    @collection_set_id = @collection_set_id,
    @collector_type_uid = @collector_type_uid ;
```

Here, you can see that we have used the <Query><Value> element to define the query that will be run for data collection and the <Query><OutputTable> element to specify the name of the table that the results will be uploaded to, within the Management Data Warehouse.

Drilling through Management ➤ Data Collection in Object Explorer will now reveal a data collector set called Chapter8CollectionSet. We can start the data collection set by choosing Start Data Collection Set, from the context menu of the newly created data collection set. Starting the collection set will cause a table to be created in the custom_snaphot schema of the Management Data Warehouse. This table will assume the name that was provided in the <Query><OutputTable> element of the XML document passed to the @ Parameters argument of the sp_syscollector_create_collection_item stored procedure.

■ **Tip** You may have to refresh the Data Collection node in Object Explorer, before the Collection Set becomes visible.

The table contains columns that map to the results of the data collection query. There will be additional columns to store the collection time and the snapshot ID of the snapshot that the row was uploaded from.

DBAs can now create stored procedures or write ad hoc SQL to retrieve data from the table. Custom reports can also be created, using SSRS, and added to the suite of SQL Server Management Studio reports.

Advanced Monitoring Techniques

Although it is very flexible and extensible, Data Collection still has limitations. For example, XML is not supported by the Generic T-SQL collection type. This makes recording data exposed by Extended Events impossible with the standard toolset.

To work around this, you must either use a custom collection type or your own custom collection routines. There is a custom collection type available on CodePlex, but this is designed specifically for use with Extended Events and may not meet every need. Therefore, the following sections will discuss how to create custom collection routines.

Architecting the Custom Collection Solution

When designing the custom collection routine, there are various factors that should be considered, namely:

1. How much standard data collection functionality will you reuse?

2. How will you store the collected data?

3. How will you collect the data?

The simple answer to the first question should always be "As much as possible." Following the principles of code reusability reduces time to market for new innovations and can save a significant amount of effort. In this case, we can create new tables, within the custom_snapshot schema of the MDW database. This reduces the complexity of additional databases, which we would otherwise have to manage. We can also use the standard CollectorSchedule schedules. This approach will make our solution easier to understand.

Before we can answer the second question, we must first define the requirement for the solution. In our scenario, we want to capture details of page splits coming from an Extended Events Session. We will create this Extended Events Session with the script in Listing 8-8.

■ **Tip** If you are following along with the demonstrations, you should ensure that you have created the folder structure and assigned the SQL Server service account permissions or changed the file name to match your own configuration, before running the script.

Listing 8-8. Create an Extended Events Session to Capture Page Splits

```
CREATE EVENT SESSION PageSplits
ON SERVER
--Add the module_start event
ADD EVENT sqlserver.module_start(SET collect_statement=(1)
--Add actions to the module_start event
ACTION(sqlserver.database_name, sqlserver.nt_username)),
--Add the page_split event
ADD EVENT sqlserver.page_split()
```

```
--Add the event_file target
ADD TARGET package0.event_file(SET FILENAME='c:\PageSplits\PageSplits',max_file_size=(512))
WITH (MAX_MEMORY=4096 KB,
                EVENT_RETENTION_MODE=ALLOW_SINGLE_EVENT_LOSS,
                MAX_DISPATCH_LATENCY=30 SECONDS,
                MAX_EVENT_SIZE=0 KB,
                MEMORY_PARTITION_MODE=NONE,
                TRACK_CAUSALITY=ON,
                STARTUP_STATE=ON) ;
GO

--Start the session
ALTER EVENT SESSION PageSplits
ON SERVER
STATE = STARTs;
```

■ **Tip**   Full details of working with Extended Events can be found in the book *Pro SQL Server Administration*, published by Apress. This book can be purchased at www.apress.com/9781484207116?gtmf=s.

Now that we know what our data will look like, we will have to create a table in the custom_snapshot schema of the MDW database, with the column definitions detailed in Table 8-7.

Table 8-7. *Page Split Monitoring Column Definitions*

Column	Data Type	Comments
ID	INT	Identity, Primary Key
database_name	NVARCHAR(128)	
object_name	NVARCHAR(128)	
statement	NVARCHAR(MAX)	
nt_username	NVARCHAR(128)	
collection_time	DATETIMEOFFSET(7)	We will populate this column from our SSIS package.

In answer to the third and final question, we will use SSIS to collect the data. SSIS will give us the flexibility to build an extensible framework for capturing data. SSIS is also the technology used by Data Collection.

■ **Tip**   Further details on SSIS can be found in Chapter 5.

Building the Solution

Now that we have an understanding of what we have to build, the next step is to move forward with developing the solution. The following sections will discuss how to create the database objects and the SSIS package. We will then deploy the package and schedule the custom data collection to run on an appropriate schedule.

Creating the Database Table

To create the custom_snapshots.page_splits table, you may incorrectly assume that the script in Listing 8-9 would do the job.

Listing 8-9. Creating the page_splits Table—Incorrect Code

```
USE MDW
GO

CREATE TABLE custom_snapshots.page_splits
(
ID                      INT             IDENTITY        PRIMARY KEY,
database_name           NVARCHAR(128),
object_name             NVARCHAR(128),
statement               NVARCHAR(MAX),
nt_username             NVARCHAR(128),
collection_time         DATETIMEOFFSET(7)
) ;
```

If you attempt to run this code, however, it will fail, with the error detailed in Listing 8-10.

Listing 8-10. Error Message

```
Msg 207, Level 16, State 1, Line 3
Invalid column name 'snapshot_id'.
```

This error is thrown because of a database level trigger in the MDW database, which references the snapshot_id column whenever a new table is created. Therefore, to proceed, we will have to perform two actions. The first action will be to add an addition row to the following tables:

> core.snapshot_timetable_internal
>
> core.snapshots_internal
>
> core.source_info_internal

These tables are used by a view named core.snapshots, and a foreign key constraint in our new table will reference the snapshot_id column in this view. Using these internal tables provides consistency with Data Collection and will allow us to easily identify the data that was captured by our custom solution.

■ **Tip** While we are configuring a static -1 value, it is also possible to configure your ETL process to populate these tables on every upload to the MDW. This allows you to integrate data collection functionality, such as retention periods, and also help you keep track of details such as the instance in which the collection happened and the security principle used to perform the upload.

The second task will be to alter the definition of our new table to include the snapsot_id column. We will use a DEFAULT constraint to assign a value of -1 to all rows. These two actions can be performed by using the script in Listing 8-11.

Listing 8-11. Creating the page_splits Table—Correct Code

```
USE MDW
GO

SET IDENTITY_INSERT core.source_info_internal ON

INSERT INTO core.source_info_internal (source_id, collection_set_uid,instance_name,days_
until_expiration,operator)
VALUES (-1, NEWID(), 'ESASSMGMT1', 30, 'CustomProcess') ;

SET IDENTITY_INSERT core.source_info_internal OFF

SET IDENTITY_INSERT core.snapshot_timetable_internal ON

INSERT INTO core.snapshot_timetable_internal (snapshot_time_id,snapshot_time)
VALUES (-1, SYSUTCDATETIME()) ;

SET IDENTITY_INSERT core.snapshot_timetable_internal OFF

SET IDENTITY_INSERT core.snapshots_internal ON

INSERT INTO core.snapshots_internal (snapshot_id,snapshot_time_id,source_id,log_id)
VALUES (-1,-1, -1, -1) ;

SET IDENTITY_INSERT core.snapshots_internal OFF

CREATE TABLE custom_snapshots.page_splits
(
ID                      INT             IDENTITY        PRIMARY KEY,
database_name           NVARCHAR(128),
object_name             NVARCHAR(128),
statement               NVARCHAR(128),
nt_username             NVARCHAR(MAX),
collectionTime          DATETIMEOFFSET(7),
snapshot_id             INT DEFAULT (-1)
) ;
```

Creating the SSIS Package

Now that our table structure is in place, we can create the SSIS package that will collect the data and upload it to the Management Data Warehouse. We will create the package using SQL Server Data Tools (SSDT). Please refer to Chapter 6, for further detailed information of SQL Server Integration Services.

Our package will be relatively simple, consisting of a single data flow and some basic error handling. (We will configure the Data Flow to ignore failed or truncated rows.) After creating a new Integration Services project called PageSplitsCustomCollector in SSDT, we will drag a Data Flow Task to the Control Flow. Inside the Data Flow, we will use the Source Assistant, to create a new SQL Server connection, as illustrated in Figure 8-10.

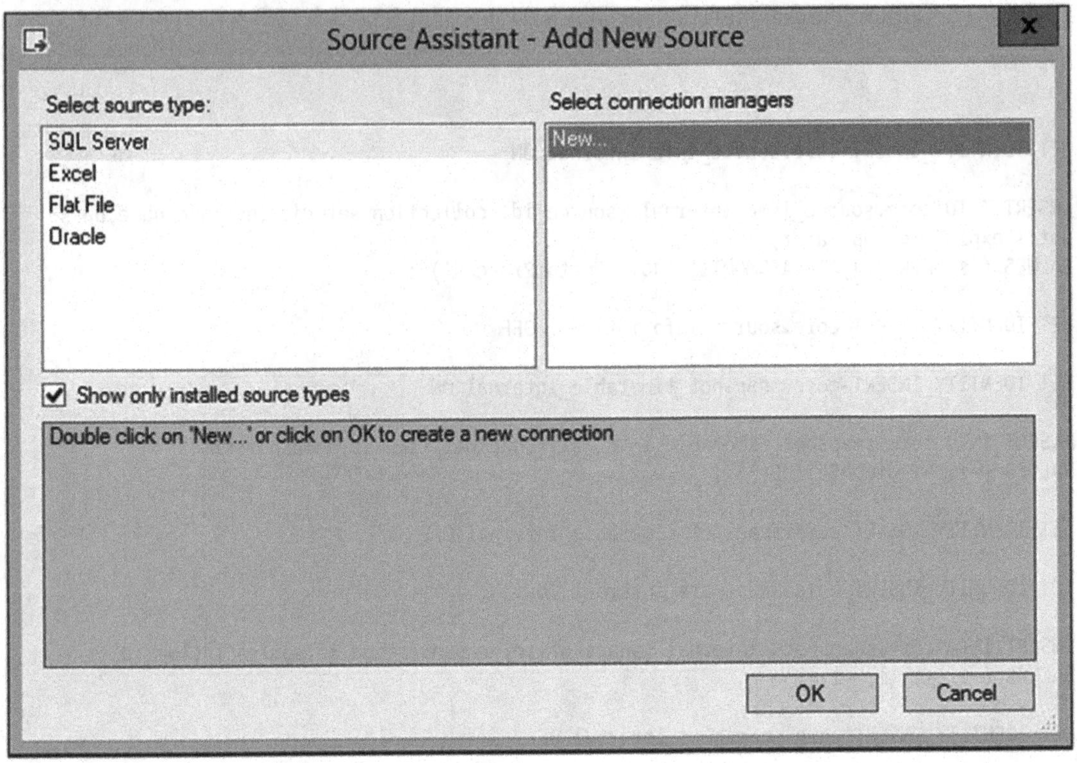

Figure 8-10. Creating a new SQL Server connection

In the Connection Manager dialog box, we will now specify the connection details for the ESASSMGMT1 instance. Later, we will parameterize this, so that we can run the package against multiple servers, each uploading to the same Management Data Warehouse. This replicates the functionality of Data Collection. The Connection Manager dialog box is illustrated in Figure 8-11.

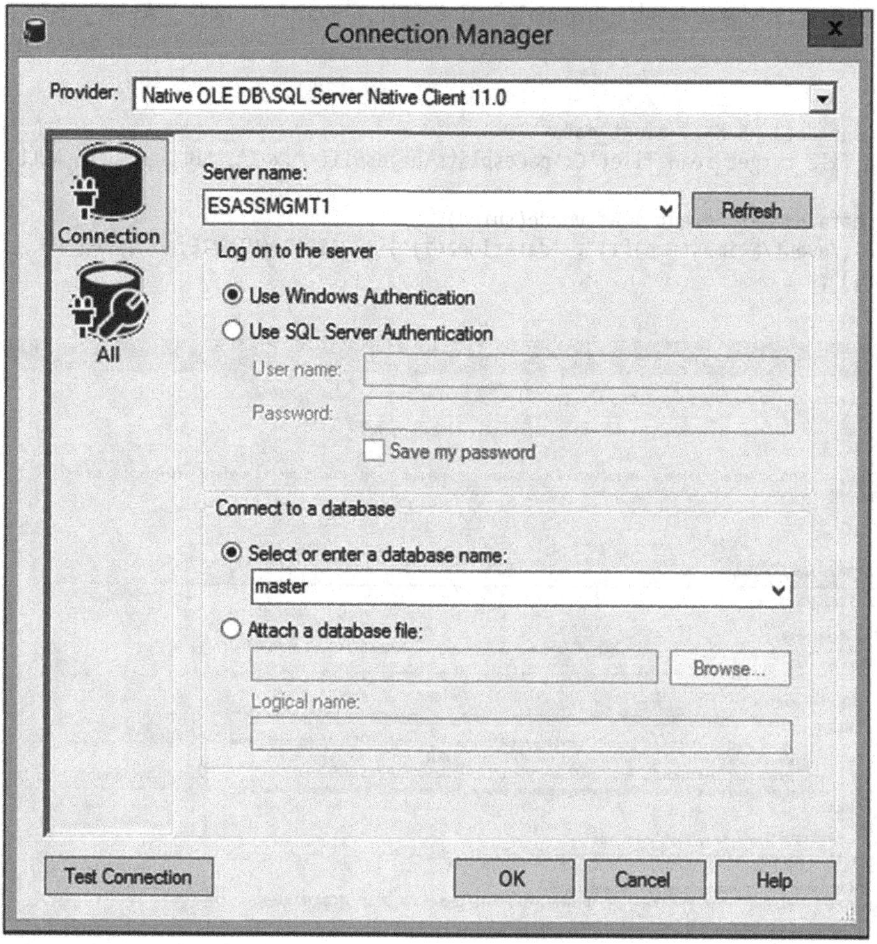

Figure 8-11. *Connection Manager dialog box*

An OLE DB Data Source will now be created in our Data Flow. We will use the Configuration Manager page of the dialog box, illustrated in Figure 8-12, to configure this Data Source to use the SQL Command data access mode and instruct it to run the command in Listing 8-12.

■ **Tip** Before running the script, you should ensure that the file path specified in the sys.fn_xe_file_ target_read_file function matches your configuration.

Listing 8-12. Command to Capture Page Splits

```
SELECT
shred.value('(/event/action[@name="database_name"]/value)[1]', 'nvarchar(128)')  AS
database_name
,shred.value('(/event/data[@name="object_name"]/value)[1]', 'nvarchar(128)') AS [object_name]
,shred.value('(/event/data[@name="statement"]/value)[1]', 'nvarchar(max)') AS [statement]
```

```
,shred.value('(/event/action[@name="nt_username"]/value)[1]', 'nvarchar(128)') AS nt_
username
FROM
(
    SELECT CAST(event_data AS XML) event_data
    FROM sys.fn_xe_file_target_read_file('C:\pagesplits\pagesplits*.xel', NULL , NULL, NULL)
) base
CROSS APPLY event_data.nodes('/event') as vnode(shred)
WHERE shred.value('(/event/@timestamp)[1]', 'datetime2(7)') > DATEADD(MINUTE,-
30,SYSUTCDATETIME()) ;
```

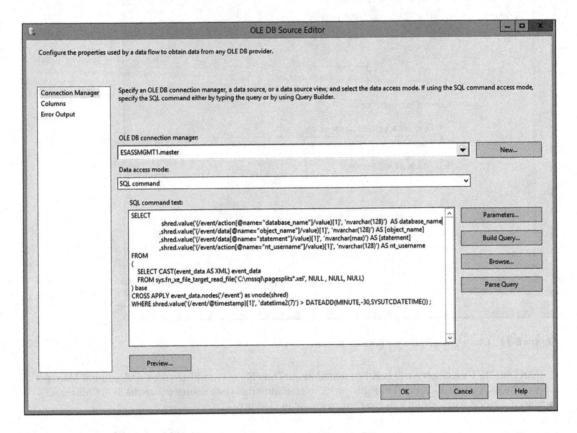

Figure 8-12. *Configuration Manager page*

If we navigate to the Columns page of the dialog box, the columns in our result set will be mapped to output columns of the Data Source, as illustrated in Figure 8-13.

230

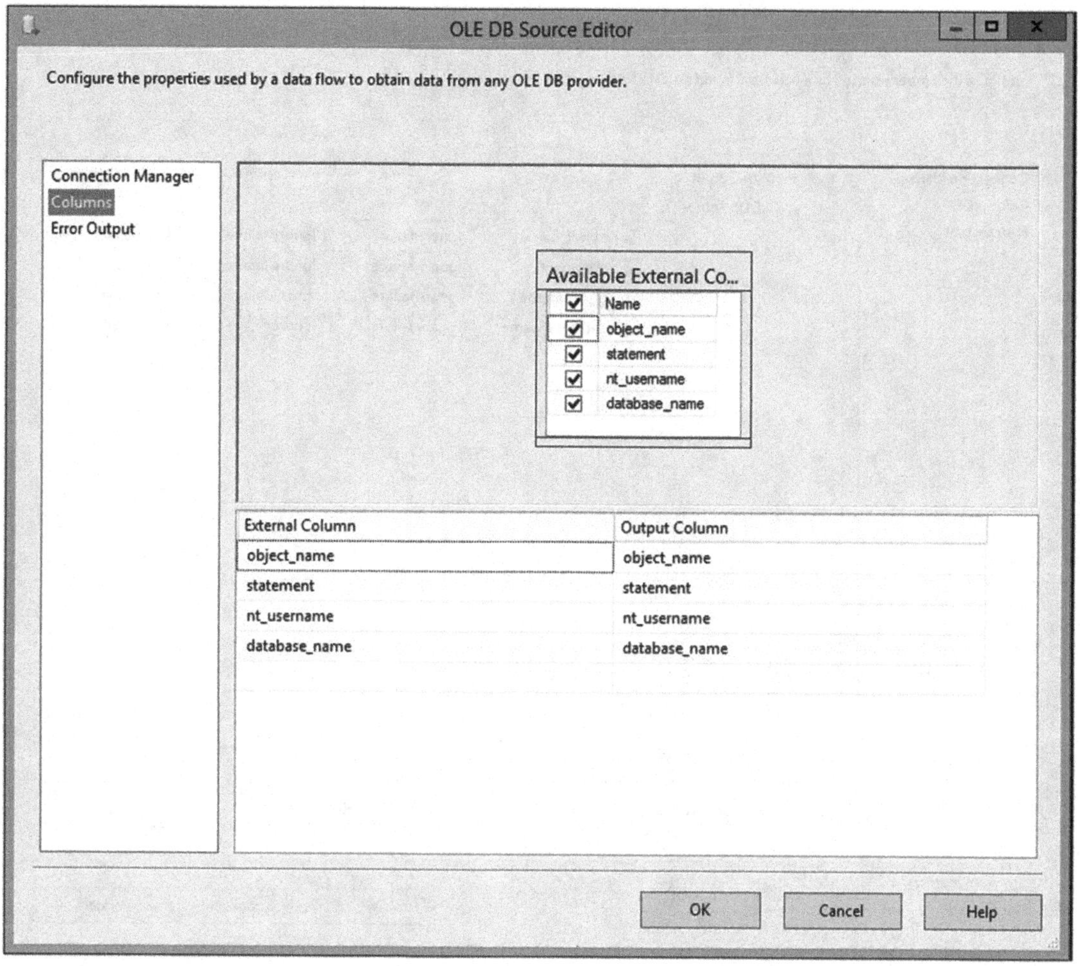

Figure 8-13. *Columns page*

Finally, we will navigate to the Error Output page of the dialog box and configure errors and truncations to be ignored, as opposed to failing the component. This is because we do not want all possible rows to be loaded, even if there is an issue with a single or small number of rows. This is depicted in Figure 8-14.

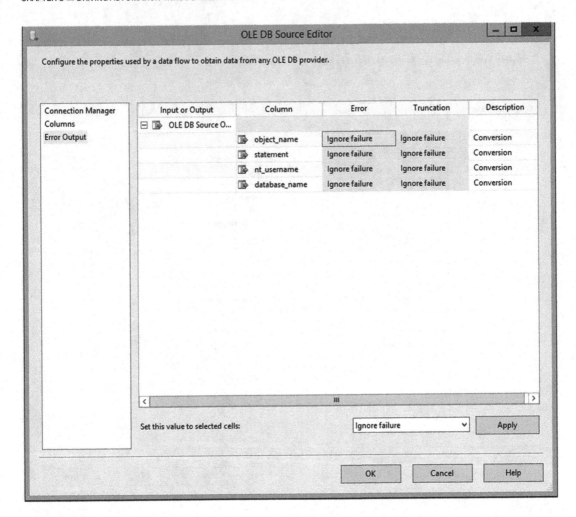

Figure 8-14. *Error Output page*

Now that our Data Source has been configured, we will drag a Derived Column component to the Data Flow design surface and connect a Success Data Flow Path from the Data Source.

We can now use the component's editor to create the collection_time and snapshot_id columns that must be inserted into our custom_snapshots.page_splits table. We will use the GETDATE() function, to generate the collection time, and a static value of -1, to pass to the snapshot_id column. This is illustrated in Figure 8-15.

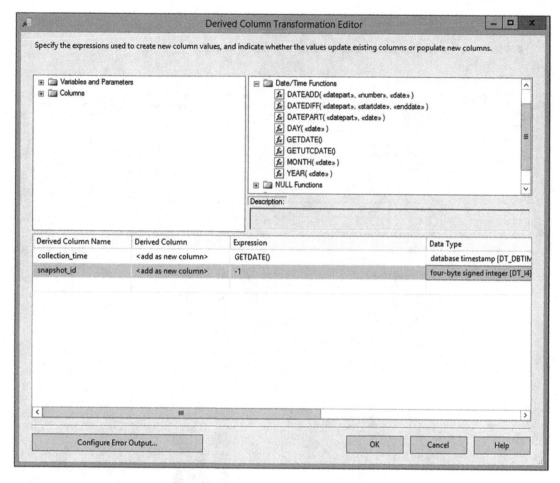

Figure 8-15. *Derived Column component editor*

We will now use the Destination Assistant to create a connection to the Master Data Warehouse. This will allow us to insert the data into our `custom_snapshots.page_splits` table.

As illustrated in Figure 8-16, after connecting a Success Data Flow Path from the Derived Column component to the OLE DB Destination, we will use the Connection Manager page of the OLE DB Destination Editor to configure the destination and insert the rows into the `custom_snapshots.page_splits` table. We will keep the default configuration of Table or View—Fast Load as the Data access mode, but we will change the batch size and commit size to 20,000 rows, as a performance optimization, for servers for which each collection has a large number of rows.

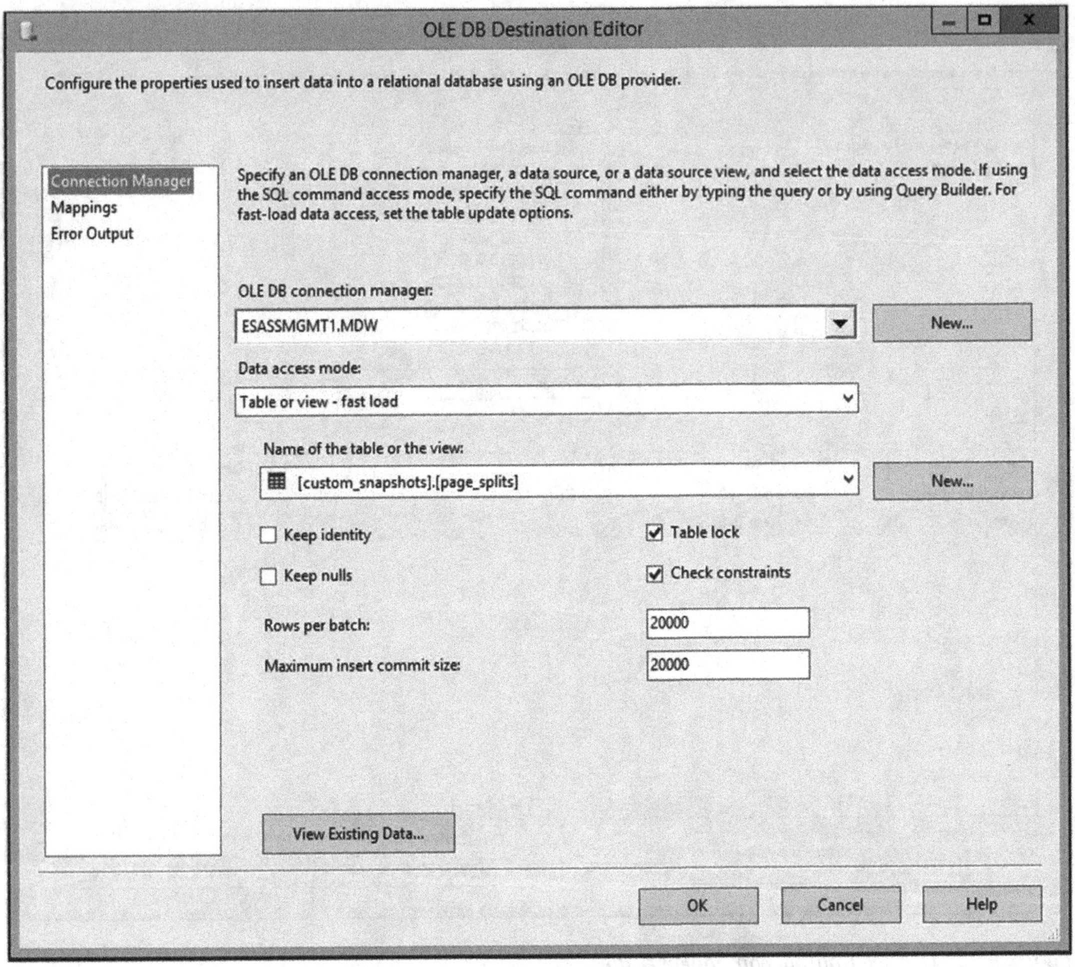

Figure 8-16. *Connection Manager page*

When we navigate to the Mappings page (Figure 8-17) of the dialog box, the columns that have been passed from the upstream component (the Derived Column component, in our case) will be mapped to output columns. These output columns should align with the columns of the destination table.

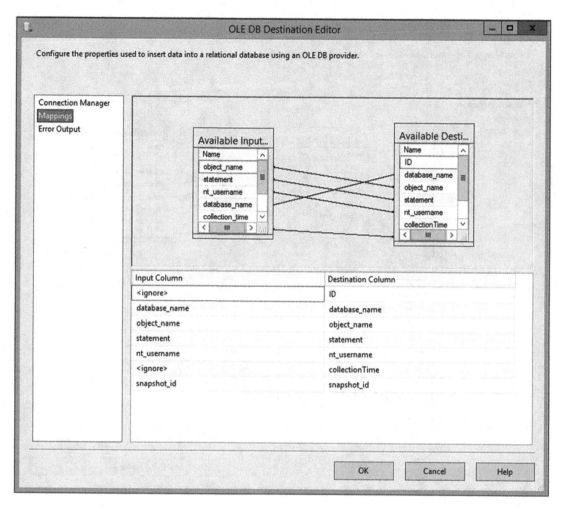

Figure 8-17. *Mappings page*

You will notice that the collection_time column has not automatically been mapped to the collectionTime column in the destination table. This is because the automatic matching is based on name, and the source column (created in the Derived Column component) has an underscore, which is missing from the column in the destination.

Therefore, we will have to map this column manually. We can achieve this by highlighting the row and using the drop-down box, to select a source column from a list of source columns that have not already been mapped to destination columns. This is demonstrated in Figure 8-18. The ID column in the destination table is also missing a mapping, but this is expected and correct, as the ID column has the IDENTITY property associated with it.

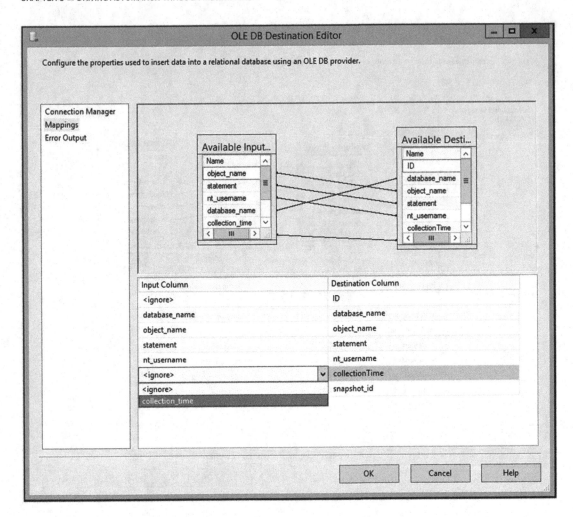

Figure 8-18. *Manually mapping a column*

Finally, on the Error Output page of the dialog box, which is illustrated in Figure 8-19, we will configure erroneous rows to be ignored, as not to fail the entire process.

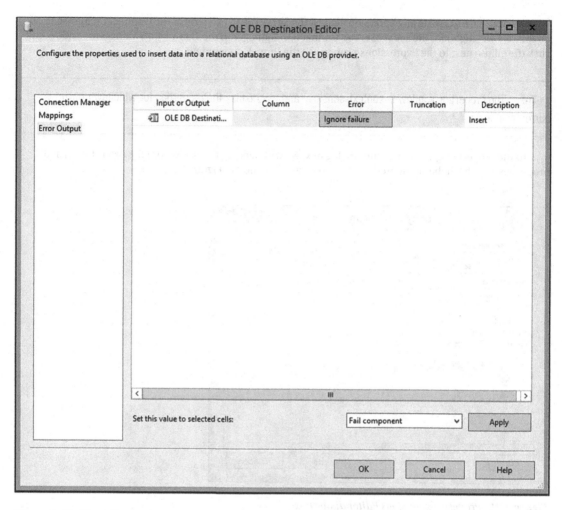

Figure 8-19. *Error Output page*

Now that our Data Flow is complete, we will have to parameterize the Server Name property of the ESASSMGMT1.Master Connection Manger. This will allow us to easily run the package against any server. We will also rename the connection, to SourceServer, as there will be no static connection to name it after. We can rename the connection manager by highlighting it in the Connection Managers pane of the design surface and choosing Rename from the context menu.

To parameterize the server name, we will first create a project parameter, called ServerName. We will do this by navigating to project.params in Solution Explorer and using the Add Parameter button, which will add a row to the parameters grid. We can now configure the parameter, with a name, data type, and initial value (which we will leave blank). We can also specify if the parameter contains sensitive information, if it must be passed, in order for the package to run, and, finally, we can optionally add a description. The project.params window is illustrated in Figure 8-20.

Name	Data type	Value	Sensitive	Required	Description
ServerName	String		False	True	Server Name of the Server that data is to be collected from

Figure 8-20. *project.params window*

We now have to create an expression against the ServerName property of the Connection Manager. To do this, we will highlight the SourceServer Connection Manager in the Connection Managers window and click the ellipse next to the Expressions property in the Properties window.

■ **Tip** The Properties window is context-sensitive and will display the properties for whichever object is currently in focus.

In the Property Expressions Editor dialog box, we will select ServerName from the drop-down list of properties, which can be configured on the object, as illustrated in Figure 8-21.

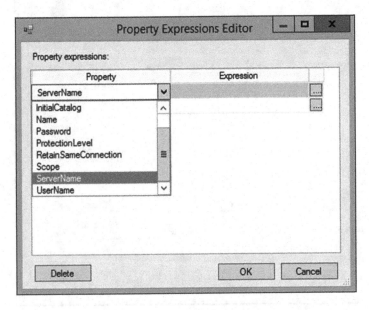

Figure 8-21. *Property Expressions Editor dialog box*

We can now use the ellipse next to Expression to invoke the Expression Builder dialog box. As illustrated in Figure 8-22, we can simply drag the ServerName parameter into the Expression window.

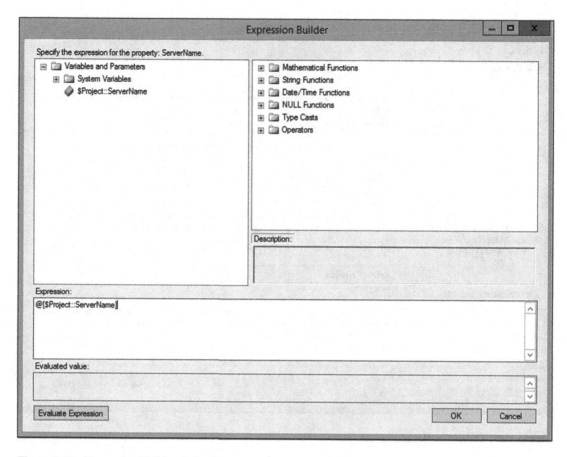

Figure 8-22. Expression Builder dialog box

■ **Tip** Because the ServerName property is dynamic, and we have not configured an initial value, we should configure the DelayValidation property of the Connection Manager to True. This will avoid the risk of validation errors when the package runs.

Deploying the Project

Now that our package is complete, we will deploy the project to the SSIS Catalog on ESASSMGMT1. Before deploying the project, you should ensure that an Integration Services catalog has been created on the Management Server. If it hasn't, you can create one by selecting Create Catalog from the context menu of Integration Services Catalogs in SQL Server Management Studio. This will cause the Create Catalog dialog box to be invoked, as shown in Figure 8-23. Here, we will use the check boxes, to ensure that CLR is enabled on the instance and that Integration Services stored procedures are enabled on instance startup. We will also specify a password, which will be used to encrypt the Database Encryption Key of the SSISDB database.

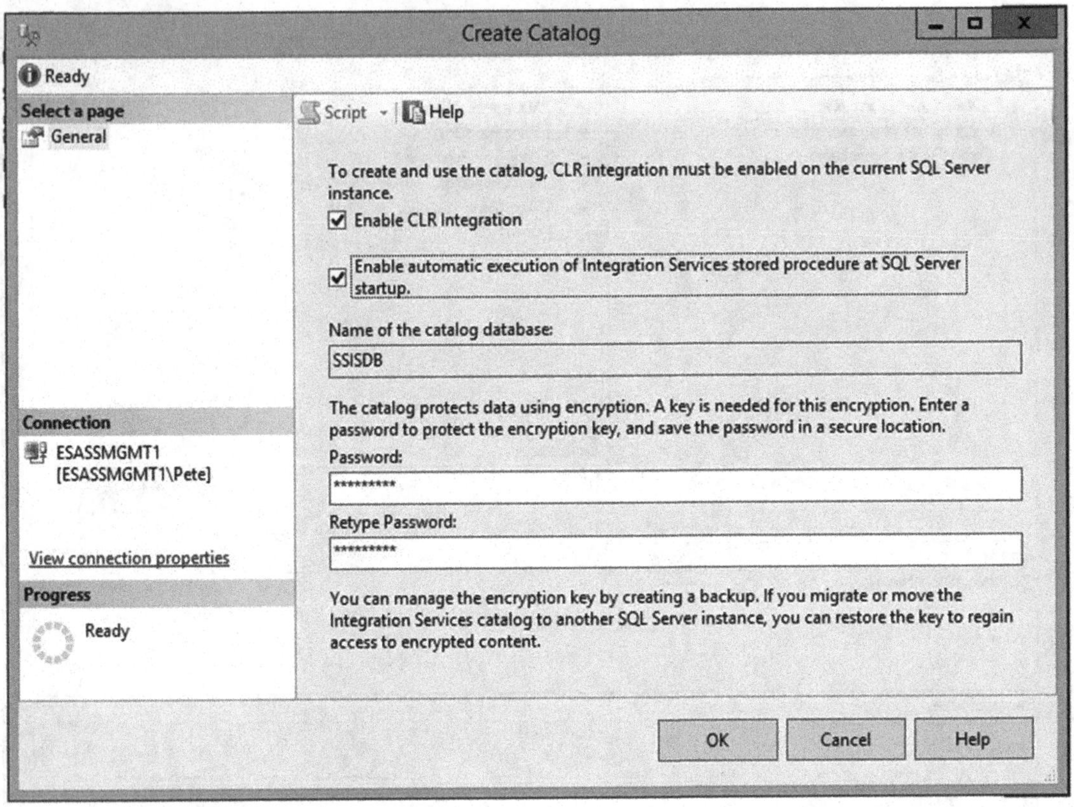

Figure 8-23. *Create Catalog dialog box*

There may be times when you have to script the configuration of the Integration Services catalog, such as when you are working with SQL Server on Windows Core, or as part of an automated deployment. You will also have to create the catalog programmatically, if the Integration Services Service is not installed. If you want to script the setup of the Integration Services catalog, you can use the PowerShell script in Listing 8-13.

Listing 8-13. Create SSIS Catalog

```
Import-Module sqlps


Invoke-Sqlcmd -ServerInstance "ESASSMGMT1" -Query "
    EXEC sp_configure 'show advanced options', 1
                GO
                RECONFIGURE
                EXEC sp_configure 'clr enabled', 1
                GO
                RECONFIGURE"

[Reflection.Assembly]::LoadWithPartialName("Microsoft.SqlServer.Management.
IntegrationServices")
```

```
$ISNamespace = "Microsoft.SqlServer.Management.IntegrationServices"

$sqlConnectionString = "Data Source=ESASSMGMT1;Initial Catalog=master;Integrated
Security=SSPI;"
$sqlConnection = New-Object System.Data.SqlClient.SqlConnection $sqlConnectionString

$integrationServices = New-Object $ISNamespace".IntegrationServices" $sqlConnection

$catalog = New-Object $ISNamespace".Catalog" ($integrationServices, "SSISDB", "Pa££w0rd")
$catalog.Create()
```

This key will be required if you ever migrate the catalog to a different instance of SQL Server. Therefore, it is important that you back up the key and, preferably, store it in an off-site location. The command in Listing 8-14 will back up the key to a file called SSISDBKey.key in a folder called c:\keys\.

■ **Tip**   Remember to change the file path to match your own configuration, before running the script.

Listing 8-14. Backup Database Encryption Key

```
USE SSISDB
GO

BACKUP MASTER KEY TO FILE = 'c:\keys\SSISDBKey.key'
ENCRYPTION BY PASSWORD = 'Pa$$w0rd' ;
```

If we were ever required to restore the encryption key, we could do so using the command in Listing 8-15.

Listing 8-15. Restore the Encryption Key

```
USE SSISDB
GO

RESTORE MASTER KEY FROM FILE = 'c:\keys\SSISDBKey.key'
DECRYPTION BY PASSWORD = 'Pa$$w0rd'
ENCRYPTION BY PASSWORD = 'Pa$$w0rd'
FORCE ;
```

■ **Caution**   The FORCE keyword, used in this example, will force the restore to continue, even if some keys that are encrypted by the Database Master Key cannot be decrypted. This can lead to data loss. Data loss, in regard to SSISDB, means that some projects may have to be redeployed.

The final step in preparing the Integration Service Catalog is to create a folder. We will create a folder named Chapter8, by drilling through Integration Services Catalogs in Object Explorer and then selecting Create Folder, from the context menu of the SSISDB catalog. This will invoke the Create Folder dialog box, shown in Figure 8-24.

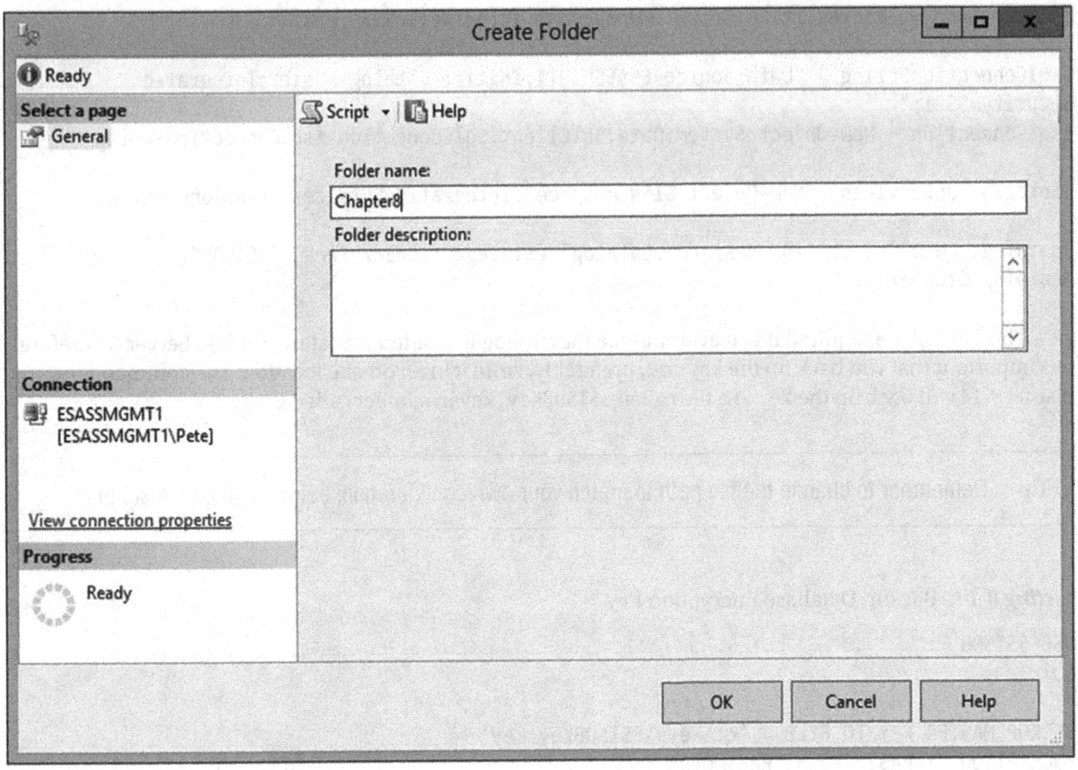

Figure 8-24. *Create Folder dialog box*

Alternatively, we could use the `catalog.create_folder` stored procedure to create the folder. The script in Listing 8-16 demonstrates this.

Listing 8-16. Create a Folder in the SSIS Catalog

```
USE SSISDB
GO

EXEC catalog.create_folder 'Chapter8' ;
```

To deploy the project to the SSIS Catalog of the management server, we will highlight the `PageSplitCustomCollector` project in Solution Explorer and select Deploy from the context menu. This will cause the Integration Service Deployment Wizard to be invoked. After passing through the Introduction page, the wizard will automatically populate the source details of the deployment and move you to the Select Destination page, which is illustrated in Figure 8-25. Here, we will add the details of the management server and the path to where we wish to deploy the package.

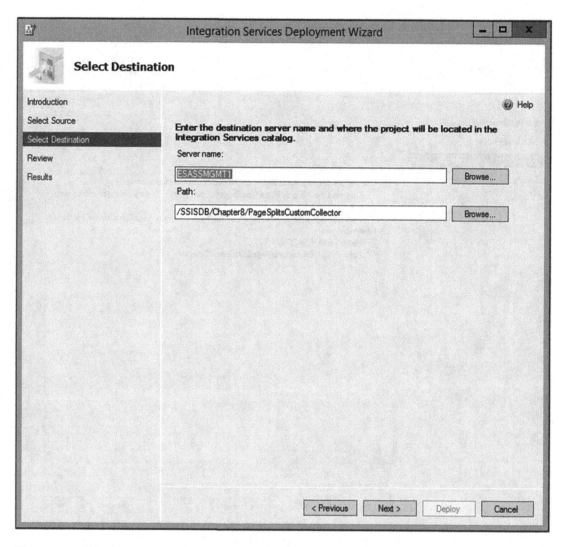

Figure 8-25. *Select Destination page*

On the Review page of the wizard, illustrated in Figure 8-26, you will have an opportunity to review the actions to be performed by the wizard, before the deployment is carried out.

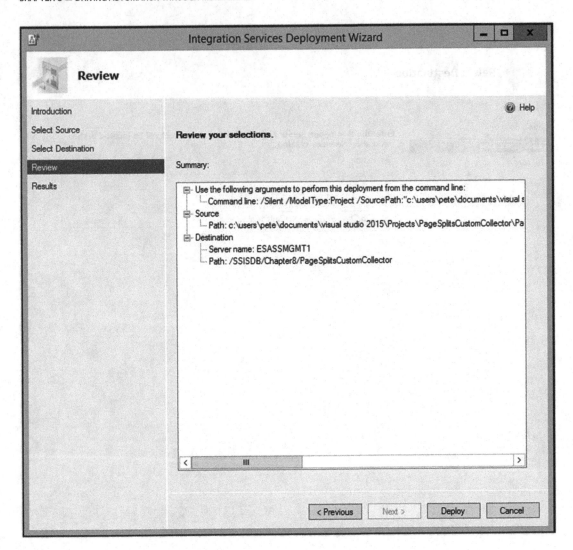

Figure 8-26. *Review page*

After checking for any deployment errors, on the Results page of the wizard, the project will become visible in the hierarchy of the SSIS Catalog. This can be viewed in SQL Server Management Studio, as shown in Figure 8-27.

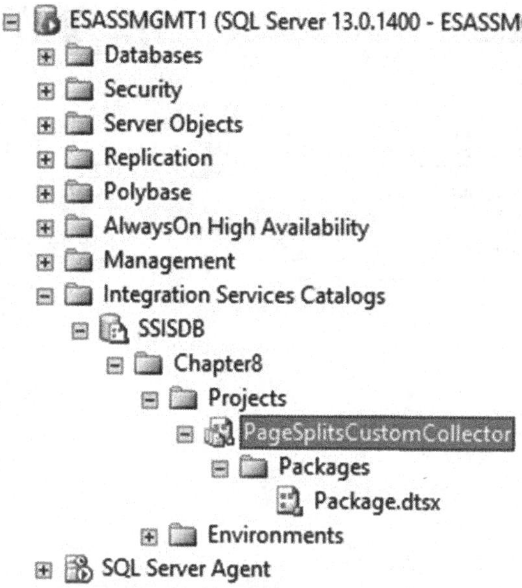

```
⊟ 🗗 ESASSMGMT1 (SQL Server 13.0.1400 - ESASSMGMT1\Pete)
   ⊞ 📁 Databases
   ⊞ 📁 Security
   ⊞ 📁 Server Objects
   ⊞ 📁 Replication
   ⊞ 📁 Polybase
   ⊞ 📁 AlwaysOn High Availability
   ⊞ 📁 Management
   ⊟ 📁 Integration Services Catalogs
      ⊟ 🗗 SSISDB
         ⊟ 📁 Chapter8
            ⊟ 📁 Projects
               ⊟ 🗗 PageSplitsCustomCollector
                  ⊟ 📁 Packages
                       🗗 Package.dtsx
         ⊞ 📁 Environments
   ⊞ 🗗 SQL Server Agent
```

Figure 8-27. *SSIS Catalog hierarchy*

Scheduling the Custom Data Collection

Once the project has been created and deployed, we are able to schedule the package to run, using SQL Server Agent. To create the Server Agent job, we will drill through SQL Server Agent in Object Explorer and select New Job from the context menu of Jobs. This will cause the New Job dialog box to be invoked. On the General page of this dialog box, displayed in Figure 8-28, we will specify a name for the job. We will call it collection_set_custom_page_splits_COLLECT_and_UPLOAD, which is close to the naming convention given to jobs by the Data Collector.

■ **Tip** Server Agent multiserver jobs are discussed in Chapter 3 of this book. A full discussion on Server Agent, however, including the creation and maintenance of local implementations, can be found in the book *Pro SQL Server Administration*, published by Apress. This book can be purchased at www.apress.com/9781484207116?gtmf=s.

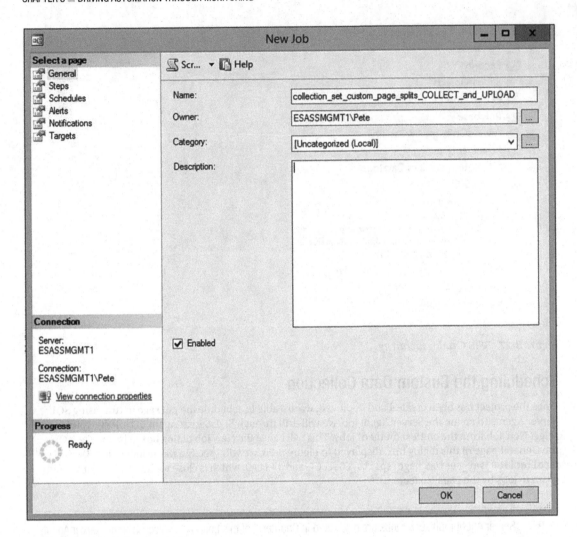

Figure 8-28. *New Job—General page*

On the Steps page of the New Job dialog box, we will use the New button to invoke the New Job Step dialog box. On the General page of the New Job Step dialog box, which is illustrated in Figure 8-29, we will configure the Job Step to run our Integration Services package. On the Package tab, we have specified the name of the Server\Instance that hosts the SSIS catalog and then selected our package from the hierarchy of the SSIS catalog.

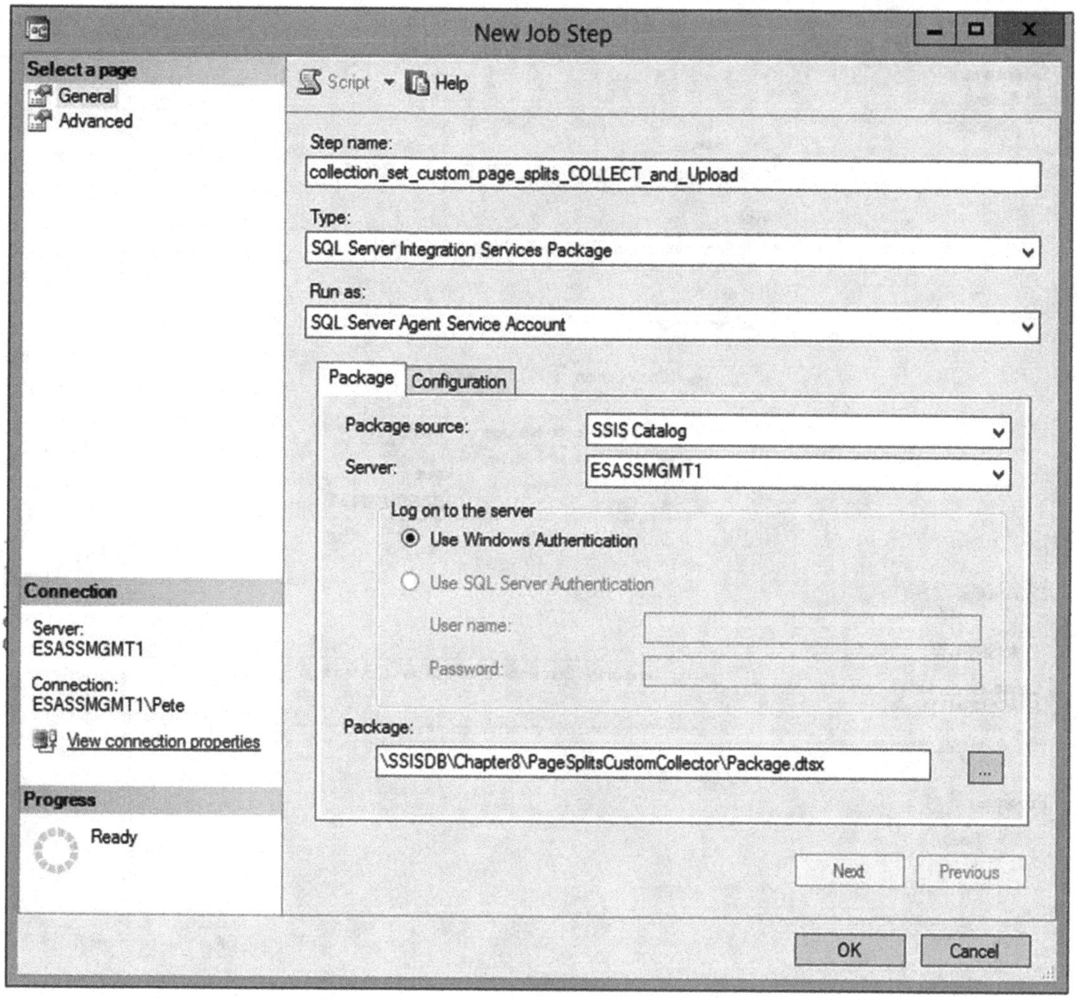

Figure 8-29. *New Job Step—General page (Package tab)*

On the Configuration tab, of the General page, which is displayed in Figure 8-30, we will add the name of the server we want to collect data against.

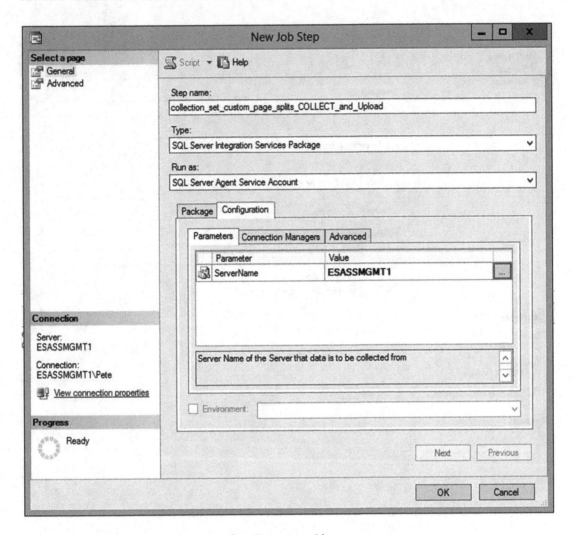

Figure 8-30. *New Job Step—General page (Configuration tab)*

On the Schedules page of the New Job dialog box, we will use the Pick button to select the 30-minute collection schedule. This is shown in Figure 8-31.

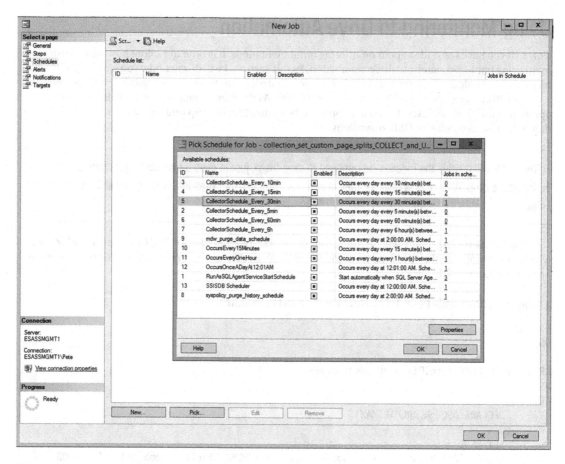

Figure 8-31. *Schedule page*

After the job has been created and scheduled, we can simply wait for it to run, before starting to investigate data in the custom_snapshots.page_splits table. The script in Listing 8-17 is an example of how we could use the collected data to look for the statements that have generated the most page splits.

Listing 8-17. Explore Page Splits Data

```
USE MDW
GO

SELECT
        [statement]
        ,COUNT(*) AS NumberOfPageSplits
FROM custom_snapshots.page_splits
GROUP BY [statement] ;
```

Using Monitoring to Drive Automation

Now that you have some idea about monitoring implementations, it is time to explore how we can use monitoring implementations to drive automation. In this section, I will discuss how you can keep a handle on rarely used indexes, by using the data that we captured earlier in this chapter regarding low-use indexes.

We will create a job, named DisableLowUseIndexes. As the name suggests, the job will disable (as opposed to drop) any indexes that do not appear to be in use. Cleaning up unused indexes is a good idea, as they will cause overhead for DML operations.

■ **Tip**   We will disable the indexes, as opposed to drop them, just in case a user suddenly complains of a performance drop. While this is unlikely, they may have a process that runs infrequently but still requires the index.

The SQL Server Agent Job will be configured to run a stored procedure called DisableLowUseIndexes, which will be stored in the core schema of the MDW database. The code to create the stored procedure can be found in Listing 8-18.

Listing 8-18. Create the DisableLowUseIndexes Stored Procedure

```
USE MDW
GO

CREATE PROCEDURE core.DisableLowUseIndexes
AS
BEGIN
        DECLARE @SQL NVARCHAR(MAX)

        SET @SQL = (
        SELECT 'ALTER INDEX ' + i.name + ' ON ' + SCHEMA_NAME(t.schema_id) + '.' + OBJECT_
        NAME(i.object_id) + ' DISABLE ;'[data()]
        FROM custom_snapshots.dm_db_index_usage_stats ius
        INNER JOIN sys.indexes i
                ON ius.object_id = i.object_id
                        AND ius.index_id = i.index_id
        INNER JOIN sys.tables t
                ON i.object_id = t.object_id
        WHERE i.type = 2
                AND i.is_disabled = 0
                FOR XML PATH('')
        )

        EXEC(@SQL)
END
```

We will now use T-SQL to create the job. We could, of course, use the dialog boxes provided in SQL Server Management Studio, but using T-SQL allows us to easily add the scripts to source control. See the script in Listing 8-19.

This script uses the sp_add_job system stored procedure to create the job. It then uses the sp_add_jobserver system stored procedure to register the job on the management server. The sp_add_jobstep system stored procedure is used to add the job step. Once this is complete, we can update the order of steps in the job, by using the sp_update_job system stored procedure. Finally, the script uses the sp_add_jobschedule system stored procedure, to create a schedule that will run the job once per week. We have chosen to run the job at 22:00 on a Sunday evening, as this is in line with our fictional maintenance window.

Listing 8-19. Create the SQL Server Agent Job

```
USE msdb
GO

EXEC  msdb.dbo.sp_add_job @job_name='DisableLowUseIndexes',
                @enabled=1,
                @category_name='[Uncategorized (Local)]',
                @owner_login_name='ESASSMGMT1\SQLServiceAccount' ;
GO

EXEC msdb.dbo.sp_add_jobserver @job_name='DisableLowUseIndexes',
                @server_name = 'ESASSMGMT1'
GO

EXEC msdb.dbo.sp_add_jobstep @job_name='DisableLowUseIndexes',
                @step_name='DisableLowUseIndexes',
                @step_id=1,
                @on_success_action=1,
                @on_fail_action=2,
                @retry_attempts=0,
                @retry_interval=0,
                @os_run_priority=0, @subsystem='TSQL',
                @command='EXEC custom_snapshots.DisableLowUseIndexes',
                @database_name='MDW',
                @flags=0 ;
GO

EXEC msdb.dbo.sp_update_job @job_name='DisableLowUseIndexes',
                @enabled=1,
                @start_step_id=1,
                @category_name='[Uncategorized (Local)]',
                @owner_login_name='ESASSMGMT1\SQLServiceAccount' ;
GO

EXEC msdb.dbo.sp_add_jobschedule @job_name='DisableLowUseIndexes',
                @name='DisableLowUseIndexes',
                @enabled=1,
                @freq_type=8,
                @freq_interval=1,
                @freq_subday_type=1,
                @freq_subday_interval=0,
                @freq_relative_interval=0,
                @freq_recurrence_factor=1,
                @active_start_date=20160516,
                @active_end_date=99991231,
                @active_start_time=220000,
                @active_end_time=235959 ;
GO
```

251

Summary

Data Collection provides a mechanism for DBAs to capture performance statistics and other pertinent information, from across the enterprise. Data Collection creates a data warehouse, which is used to store the data that is collected from the targets.

Data Collection provides a number of data collectors out of the box, which allow DBAs to run a suite of drill-through reports, which provide details of disk utilization, server activity, and query statistics.

Out-of-the-box data collection functionality is quite limited, however. The feature is highly extensible, and DBAs can create their own custom data collectors, empowering them to easily gather the information they require in their unique enterprise.

Data collection does have certain limitations. The most pertinent of these is its lack of support for XML. This means that if you want to collect data from sources such as Extended Events, you will have to implement your own custom solution.

SQL Server Integration Services is a great tool for building custom monitoring solutions. In fact, data collection uses SQL Server Integration Services under the covers, to collect data. When building custom solutions, it makes sense to reuse as much functionality of Data Collection as possible, to keep consistency and reduce the amount of code that you have to write from scratch.

CHAPTER 9

■ ■ ■

Automating Routine Maintenance and Break/Fix Scenarios

The more proactive a DBA team is, the better service that it can offer to its internal or external customers, and the more cost efficient it will be. Using the techniques that you have learned in this book, you will be able to automate virtually any repetitive task. This chapter will demonstrate how to put what you have learned into practice and give you some ideas for automating responses to operational scenarios.

■ **Tip** Automating operational routines is sometimes known as runbook automation.

Automating Routine Maintenance

In Chapter 4, you have already seen how to write some automated maintenance routines, such as intelligent index rebuilds, based on fragmentation, and, in Chapter 3, how to schedule these routines to run across your enterprise, using SQL Server Agent multiserver jobs. The following sections will demonstrate how to automate SQL Server patching activity and how to refresh a lower environment from production.

Automating Patching Activity

Imagine that you manage an enterprise that consists of 100 SQL Server instances. Fifty of these instances are running SQL Server 2014 RTM. You have a requirement to upgrade those 50 instances to SP1. Your company's maintenance window runs from 6 AM Saturday morning through 6 PM Sunday evening. You have two choices. You can either spend your entire weekend installing service packs, or you can run an automated process to patch the servers.

This section will assume that performing a dull, repetitive, time-consuming task is not the way that you enjoy spending your weekends and demonstrate how to create an appropriate automation routine.

We could choose either PowerShell or SQL Server Integration Services, as a tool for orchestrating our workflow. We will choose PowerShell, to keep our patching code consistent with our automated build, which we created in Chapter 7.

The first thing that our script will have to do is decipher which instances in our enterprise have to be upgraded. We will do this with the help of our inventory database, which we created in Chapter 6. To follow the demonstrations in this section, you can use the script in Listing 9-1 to insert some sample data into the Inventory database, which our process will use to determine which servers to patch.

© Peter A. Carter 2016
P. A. Carter, *Expert Scripting and Automation for SQL Server DBAs*, DOI 10.1007/978-1-4842-1943-0_9

■ **Caution**   If the servers or instances do not exist, the script will fail when attempting to apply the patch. Therefore, you may wish to modify the sample data, to reflect one or more server(s) and instance(s) that are available to you.

Listing 9-1.   Insert Sample Data into Inventory Database

```
USE Inventory
GO

DECLARE @ServerId        INT

INSERT INTO dbo.Server (ServerName, ClusterFlag, WindowsVersion, SQLVersion, ServerCores,
ServerRAM, VirtualFlag, Hypervisor, ApplicationOwner, ApplicationOwnerEMail)
VALUES ('ESPRODSQL14_001', 0, 'Windows Server 2012 SP1', 'SQL Server 2014 RTM', 4, 128, 0,
NULL, NULL, NULL) ;

SET @ServerID = @@IDENTITY

INSERT INTO dbo.Instance (InstanceName, ServerID, Port, IPAddress, SQLServiceAccountID,
AuthenticationMode, saAccountName, saAccountPassword, InstanceClassification, InstanceCores,
InstanceRAM, SQLServerAgentAccountID)
VALUES ('SQL14INSTANCE1', @ServerId, 50001, '10.2.2.5', 1, 1, 'sa', 'Pa$$w0rd', 1, 2, 64,
1),
        ('SQL14INSTANCE2', @ServerId, 50002, '10.2.2.6', 1, 1, 'sa', 'Pa$$w0rd', 1, 2, 64, 1)
```

We must also ensure that SQL Server 2014 SP1 is available on a shared location. Therefore, we will create a shared folder on ESASSMGMT1 called SQL 2014 SP1, based on the folder `c:\Software Updates\SQL 2014 SP1` and place the SP1 binaries in this location.

■ **Tip**   SQL Server 2014 SP1 can be downloaded from www.microsoft.com/en-us/download/details. aspx?id=46694.

Now that our management server has been prepared, we will begin to design our data flow. Spending time in drawing the data flow helps when you are developing the process. The data flow can also be used as documentation of the process, which assists new starters joining your team. It also provides a helpful reference, if you must alter or enhance the process in the future. Figure 9-1 depicts the workflow that our PowerShell script will use.

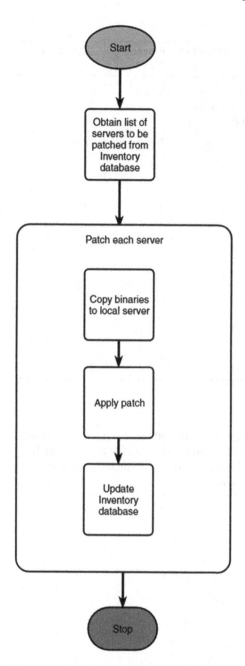

Figure 9-1. *Automated patching workflow*

More complex workflows may be modular. For example, you may have an orchestration script, written in PowerShell, which calls a series of other PowerShell script, with these child scripts actually performing the work. In this case, it is often useful for the process diagram to be supported by a spreadsheet, which registers the order of the scripts to be orchestrated, along with file names and parameters. An example of this can be found in Table 9-1.

Table 9-1. *Process Flow Documentation*

Task No	Process	File Name	Input Parameters	Output Parameters	Preceding Task	Subsequent Task
1	Obtain list of servers	N/A	None	Array of Server/ Instance names (NVARCHAR(128))	N/A	2
2	Loop around each server	N/A	Array of Server/ Instance names (NVARCHAR(128))	None	1	2.1
2.1	Copy binaries to local server	N/A	Management Server Name (NVARCHAR(128)), Target Server Name (NVARCHAR(128))	None	2	2.2
2.2	Apply patch	N/A	Target Server/ Instance name (NVARCHAR(128))	None	2.1	2.3
2.3	Update Inventory database	N/A	Management Server Name (NVARCHAR(128))	None	2.2	N/A

Creating a PowerShell Script

The script in Listing 9-2 demonstrates how to create a PowerShell script that will perform the tasks detailed within the preceding documentation. The script uses the setup executable of the patch. SQL Server patches are named after KB articles, and SQL Server 2014 SP1 is called SQLServer2014SP1-KB3058865-x64-ENU.exe. The arguments accepted by the executables are detailed in Table 9-2.

Table 9-2. setup *Parameters*

Parameter	Description
/action	Specifies the action that should be performed by setup. When installing an update (as opposed to the database engine), the acceptable values are • Patch—Indicating that you want the patch to be applied to one or more instance(s) • RemovePatch—Indicating that you want the patch to be removed from one or more instance(s) in which it has already been applied
/allinstances	Indicates that all instances on the server should be patched. This parameter should not be specified if either /instancename or /InstanceID has been specified.
/instancename	Specifies the name of the instance to which the patch should be applied. If specified, do not specify the /InstanceID parameter.
/InstanceID	Specifies the ID of the instance, to which the patch should be applied. If specified, do not use the /instancename parameter.
/quiet	Performs an unattended installation
/qs	Performs an unattended installation, with only the progress UI displayed
/UpdateEnabled	Specifies if setup should look for updates. Acceptable values are • True • False
/IAcceptSQLServerLicenseTerms	Indicates that you agree to the SQL Server license terms

■ **Tip** Before running the script, you should configure the file path and share to match your own configuration.

Listing 9-2. Automated Patching Routine

```
Import-Module sqlps

#Get a list of servers to patch

[array]$ServerInstances = invoke-sqlcmd -ServerInstance "ESASSMGMT1"  -Database "Inventory"
-Query "SELECT S.ServerName, I.InstanceName
FROM dbo.Server S
INNER JOIN dbo.Instance I
        ON S.ServerID = I.ServerID
WHERE S.SQLVersion = 'SQL Server 2014 RTM'"

foreach($ServerInstance in $ServerInstances)
{
   #Copy binaries to local server
```

```
    Copy-Item -Path "C:\Software Updates\SQLServer2014SP1-KB3058865-x64-ENU.exe" -Destination
"\\$ServerInstance.ServerName\c$\" -Force

    #Establish a session to target server

    $session = new-pssession -computername $ServerInstance.InstanceName

    #Run setup

    invoke-command -session $session {C:\SQLServer2014SP1-KB3058865-x64-ENU.exe /
iacceptsqlserverlicenseterms /instancename=$ServerInstance.InstanceName /UpdateEnabled=False
/quiet}

    #Update inventory database

    invoke-sqlcmd -ServerInstance "ESASSMGMT1" -Database "Inventory" -Query "UPDATE S
    SET SQLVersion = 'SQL Server 2014 SP1'
    FROM dbo.Server S
    INNER JOIN dbo.instance I
        ON S.ServerID = I.ServerID
    WHERE I.InstanceName = '$ServerInstance.InstanceName'"
}
```

■ **Tip** If you are patching a prepared instance of SQL Server, `/instancename` is not a valid parameter. You must use `/InstanceID` instead.

Automating Environment Refreshes

Environment refreshes are often required by development teams, to refresh data in a lower environment from production data. This data can then be used for purposes such as performance testing or to synchronize data structures between Production and UAT before testing a code deployment.

In some scenarios, this is a fairly straightforward process, which can be achieved through techniques such as a backup restore or DETACH...copy...ATTACH. In other environments, however, especially where there is a heightened need for security, the process can be a lot more complex.

For example, I once worked with a FTSE 100 company that was tightly controlled by regulators, and when developers required an environment refresh, there was no way that they could be given access to live data. Therefore, the process of refreshing the environment consisted of the following steps:

1. Backup the production database

2. Put the development server into SINGLE USER mode, so that developers could not access it

3. Restore the database onto the development server

4. Remove database users without a login

5. Obfuscate the data

6. Put instance back into MULTI USER mode

In this section, we will re-create this process for the AdventureWorks2016 database, which we will copy from ESPROD1 to ESPROD2. This process is depicted in the workflow that can be found in Figure 9-2.

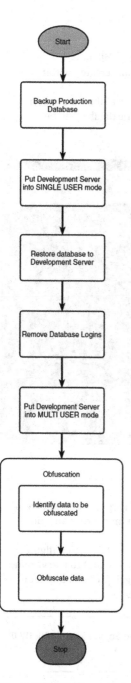

Figure 9-2. Environment refresh workflow

We will parameterize the process, so that it can be easily modified for any database. Again, we have the choice of orchestrating this workflow using either PowerShell or SSIS. This time, we will use SSIS.

Creating the SSIS Package

We will now use SSDT to create an SQL Server Integration Services Project, which we will name EnvironmentRefresh. We will give the same name to the package that is automatically created within the project.

Our first task will be to create three project parameters that will accept the name of the Production Server\Instance, the name of the Development Server\Instance, and the name of the database to be refreshed. This is illustrated in Figure 9-3.

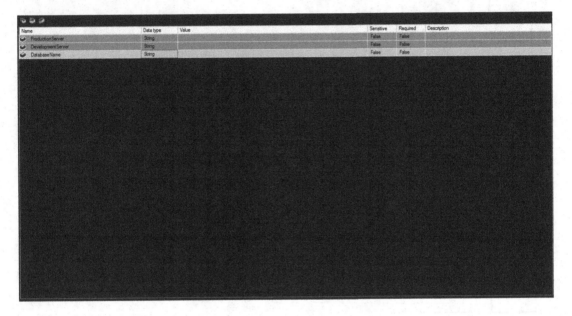

Figure 9-3. Creating project parameters

The next step will be to create two OLEDB Connection Managers, by right-clicking in the Connection Managers window and using the New OLEDB Connection dialog box. We should name one Connection Manager ProductionServer and the other DevelopmentServer.

Once the Connection Managers have been created, we can use the Expression Builder, to configure the ServerName property of each Connection Manager to be dynamic, based on the ProductionServer and DevelopmentServer project parameters that we created. Figure 9-4 illustrates using Expression Builder to configure the ServerName property of the ProductionServer Connection Manager.

■ **Tip** A full walk-through of using Expression Builder to create an expression of the ServerName property of a Connection Manager can be found in Chapter 8.

Expression Builder

Specify the expression for the property: ServerName.

- ⊟ 📁 Variables and Parameters
  - ⊞ 📁 System Variables
  - 🔷 $Project::DatabaseName
  - 🔷 $Project::DevelopmentServer
  - 🔷 $Project::ProductionServer

- ⊞ 📁 Mathematical Functions
- ⊞ 📁 String Functions
- ⊞ 📁 Date/Time Functions
- ⊞ 📁 NULL Functions
- ⊞ 📁 Type Casts
- ⊞ 📁 Operators

Description:

Expression:

@[$Project::ProductionServer]

Evaluated value:

[Evaluate Expression]   [OK]   [Cancel]

Figure 9-4. Expression Builder

■ **Tip**   Remember to configure the DelayValidation of the Connection Manager to true. Otherwise, the package will fail validation.

We must now create three package variables, which will hold the SQL statements that will be run to back up the database, restore the database, and obfuscate the database. We will enter the appropriate expressions to build the SQL statements within the variables, as illustrated in Figure 9-5. It is important to set the EvaluateAsExpression property of the variables to true. This can be configured in the Properties window, when the variable is in scope.

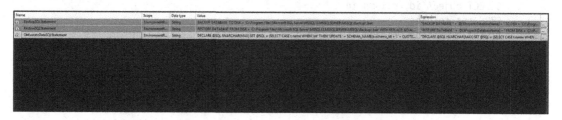

Figure 9-5. Creating package variables

■ **Tip**   In the expression scripts below, ensure that you change file paths to match your own configuration.

The expression stored in the BackupSQLStatement variable is detailed in Listing 9-3.

Listing 9-3. BackupSQLStatement Expression

```
"BACKUP DATABASE " + @[$Project::DatabaseName] + " TO DISK = 'C:\\Program Files\\Microsoft
SQL Server\\MSSQL13.MSSQLSERVER\\MSSQL\\Backup\\" + @[$Project::DatabaseName] + ".bak'"
```

The expression stored in the RestoreSQLStatement variable can be found in Listing 9-4.

Listing 9-4. RestoreSQLStatement Expression

```
"RESTORE DATABASE " + @[$Project::DatabaseName] + " FROM DISK = 'C:\\Program Files\\
Microsoft SQL Server\\MSSQL13.MSSQLSERVER\\MSSQL\\Backup\\" + @[$Project::DatabaseName] +
".bak' WITH REPLACE; GO ALTER DATABASE " + @[$Project::DatabaseName] + "SET SINGLE_USER WITH
ROLLBACK IMMEDIATE;"
```

The expression stored in the ObfuscateDataStatement variable can be found in Listing 9-5.

Listing 9-5. ObfuscateDataStatement Expression

```
"DECLARE @SQL NVARCHAR(MAX) ;
SET @SQL = (SELECT CASE t.name WHEN 'int' THEN 'UPDATE ' + SCHEMA_NAME(o.schema_id) + '.'
+ QUOTENAME(OBJECT_NAME(nkc.object_id)) + ' SET ' +  QUOTENAME(c.name) + ' = CHECKSUM(' +
c.name + '); '
WHEN 'money' THEN 'UPDATE ' + QUOTENAME(SCHEMA_NAME(o.schema_id)) + '.' + QUOTENAME(OBJECT_
NAME(nkc.object_id)) + ' SET ' +  QUOTENAME(c.name) + ' = CHECKSUM(' + c.name + '); '
WHEN 'nvarchar' THEN 'UPDATE ' + QUOTENAME(SCHEMA_NAME(o.schema_id)) + '.' +
QUOTENAME(OBJECT_NAME(nkc.object_id)) + ' SET ' + QUOTENAME(c.name) + ' = LEFT(RTRIM(CONVER
T(nvarchar(255), NEWID())), ' + CAST(c.max_length / 2 AS NVARCHAR(10)) + '); '
WHEN 'varchar' THEN 'UPDATE ' + QUOTENAME(SCHEMA_NAME(o.schema_id)) + '.' +
QUOTENAME(OBJECT_NAME(nkc.object_id)) + ' SET ' + QUOTENAME(c.name) + ' = LEFT(RTRIM(CONVER
T(nvarchar(255), NEWID())), ' + CAST(c.max_length AS NVARCHAR(10)) + '); '
WHEN 'text' THEN 'UPDATE ' + QUOTENAME(SCHEMA_NAME(o.schema_id)) + '.' + QUOTENAME(OBJECT_
NAME(nkc.object_id)) + ' SET ' +  QUOTENAME(c.name) + ' = LEFT(RTRIM(CONVERT(nvarchar(255),
NEWID())), ' + CAST(c.max_length AS NVARCHAR(10)) + '); '
WHEN 'ntext' THEN 'UPDATE ' + QUOTENAME(SCHEMA_NAME(o.schema_id)) + '.' + QUOTENAME(OBJECT_
NAME(nkc.object_id)) + ' SET ' +  QUOTENAME(c.name) + ' = LEFT(RTRIM(CONVERT(nvarchar(255),
NEWID())), ' + CAST(c.max_length AS NVARCHAR(10)) + '); '  END
FROM
(
        SELECT object_id, column_id
        FROM sys.columns
        EXCEPT --Exclude foreign key columns
        SELECT parent_object_id, parent_column_id
        FROM sys.foreign_key_columns
        EXCEPT --Exclude check constraints
```

```
        SELECT parent_object_id, parent_column_id
        FROM sys.check_constraints
) nkc
INNER JOIN sys.columns c
        ON nkc.object_id = c.object_id
        AND nkc.column_id = c.column_id
INNER JOIN sys.objects o
        ON nkc.object_id = o.object_id
INNER JOIN sys.types t
        ON c.user_type_id = t.user_type_id
        AND c.system_type_id = t.system_type_id
INNER JOIN sys.tables tab
        ON o.object_id = tab.object_id
WHERE is_computed = 0  --Exclude computed columns
        AND c.is_filestream = 0 --Exclude filestream columns
        AND c.is_identity = 0 --Exclude identity columns
        AND c.is_xml:document = 0 --Exclude XML columns
        AND c.default_object_id = 0 --Exclude columns with default constraints
        AND c.rule_object_id = 0 --Exclude columns associated with rules
        AND c.encryption_type IS NULL --Exclude columns with encryption
        AND o.type = 'U' --Filter on user tables
        AND t.is_user_defined = 0 --Exclude columns with custom data types
        AND tab.temporal_type = 0 --Exclude temporal history tables
        FOR XML PATH('')
) ;

EXEC(@SQL) ;

ALTER DATABASE " +  @[$Project::DatabaseName] + " SET MULTI_USER ;"
```

We will now create an Execute SQL task, which will be used to back up the production database. As you can see in Figure 9-6, we will use the Execute SQL Task Editor dialog box to configure the task to run against the production server. We will configure the SQL source type as a variable and then point the task to our BackupSQLStatement variable.

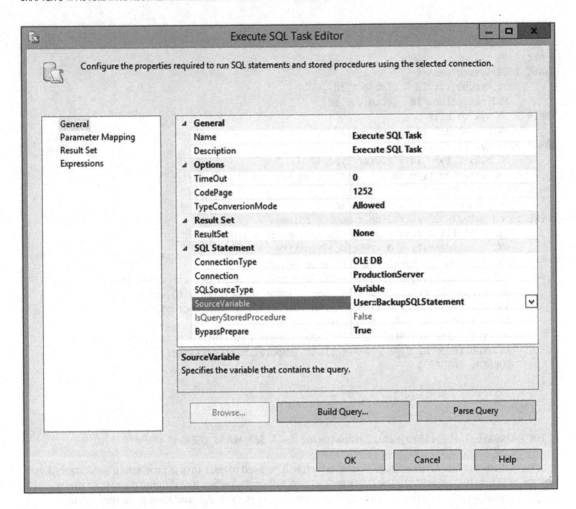

Figure 9-6. Configuring backup task

We will now add a second Execute SQL Task, which we will configure to restore the database onto the Development Server and place it into Single User mode. The Execute SQL Task Editor for this task is illustrated in Figure 9-7. Here, you will notice that we have configured the task to run against our Development Server. We have configured the SQL source as a variable and pointed the task to our RestoreSQLStatement variable.

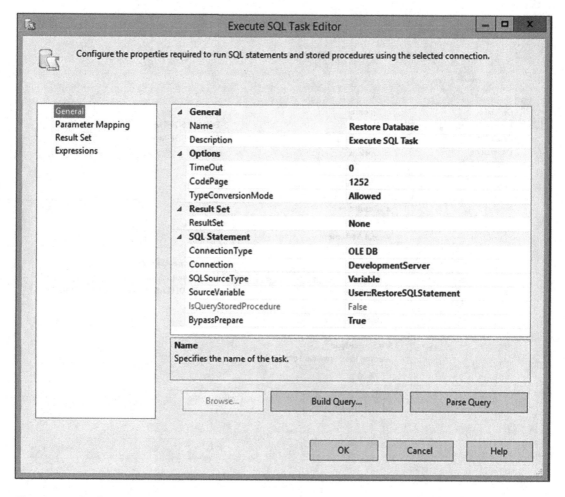

Figure 9-7. *Configuring restore task*

The next Execute SQL Task will be used to remove any existing database users without a login. Since SQL Server 2012, it is possible to create logins directly at the database level, as opposed to database users, which must map to logins at the Instance level. This feature is part of contained database functionality, which simplifies administration when using technologies such as AlwaysOn availability groups. In our scenario, however, database users without a login can cause an issue, because instead of being orphaned on the instance of the lower environment, unauthorized users could connect, if they have a database login and know the password. Therefore, we will remove all such logins.

Figure 9-8 illustrates how we will use the Execute SQL Task Editor dialog box to configure this process. You will note that we have configured the Connection property to run the query against the Development Server; we have configured the SQL source as direct input; and we have typed the query directly into the SQLStatement property. We have not used a variable, as this time, we will explore an alternative way of configuring the task to be dynamic.

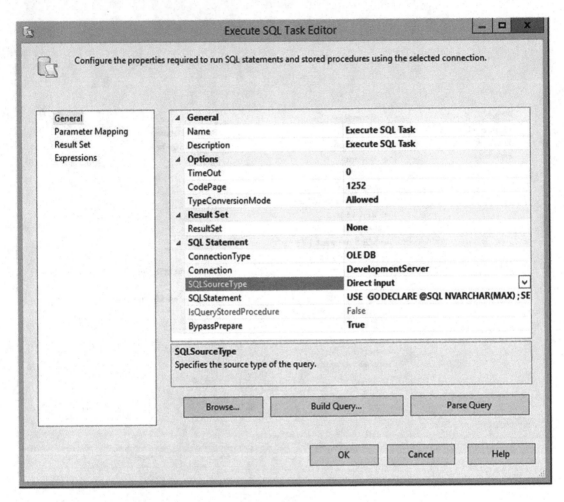

Figure 9-8. *Configuring remove database users without a login task*

The expression entered into the SQLSourceType property can be found in Listing 9-6.

Listing 9-6. Remove Database Users Without a Login

```
"USE " +  @[$Project::DatabaseName] + " GO
DECLARE @SQL NVARCHAR(MAX)

SET @SQL = (
SELECT 'DROP USER ' + QUOTENAME(name) + ' ; '
FROM sys.database_principals
WHERE type = 'S'
      AND authentication_type = 0
      AND principal_id > 4
FOR XML PATH('')
) ;

EXEC(@SQL)"
```

We will make this task dynamic by configuring an expression on the SQLStatement property of the task, as illustrated in Figure 9-9.

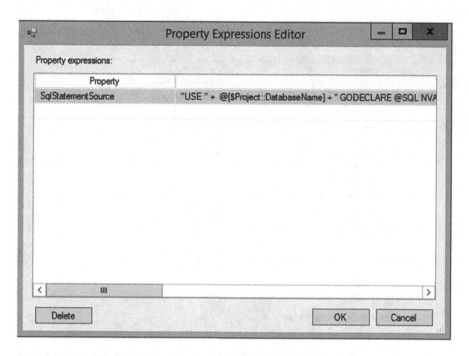

Figure 9-9. *Configuring expression on SQLStatement property*

■ **Tip** While the two approaches that we have discussed are functionally equivalent, I recommend using the variable approach. This is because your code will be much more transparent, easier to follow, and less prone to bugs.

The final Execute SQL task will be used to obfuscate the data and place it back in Multi User mode. As illustrated in Figure 9-10, we will use the Execute SQL Task Editor dialog box to configure the connection to be made to the Development Server and configure the SQL source as a variable. We will then point the task to the ObfuscateDataSQLStatement variable. The dynamic techniques that we have used to create the package mean that when we run the package (probably as a manual execution of an SQL Server Agent job), we can pass in any Production Server, Development Server, and database. The metadata-driven process will obfuscate textual data, integers, and money data in any database. If the need arises, you can also easily amend the script to obfuscate only certain data, such as a specific schema, within the database.

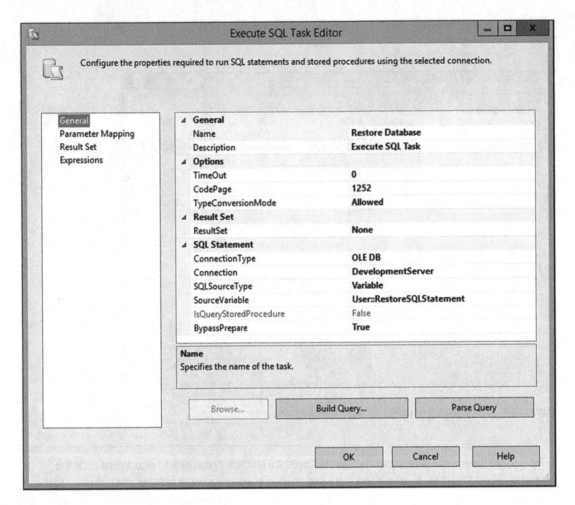

Figure 9-10. *Configuring obfuscation task*

All of the required tasks have now been created and configured. To clean up the package, join each task in sequence, using success precedence constraints. Because there are four Execute SQL Tasks, I also strongly recommend renaming them, to give them intuitive names. This is always a best practice, but even more important, when there are so many tasks of the same type, as by default, they will be named with a meaningless, sequential number. The final control flow is depicted in Figure 9-11.

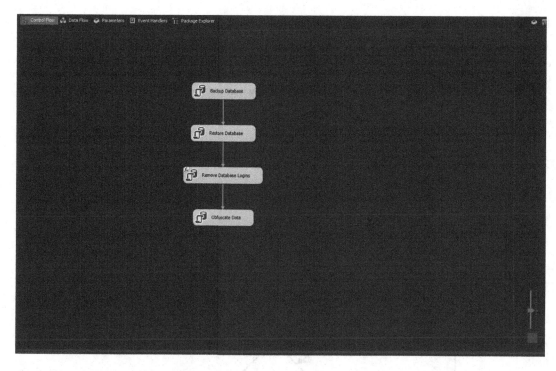

Figure 9-11. *Completed control flow*

Automating Break/Fix Scenarios

Automating responses to break/fix scenarios is the pinnacle of your automation efforts. When implemented well, it can significantly reduce the TCO (Total Cost of Ownership) of the SQL Server Enterprise.

If you attempt to design an entire break/fix automation solution up front, you are destined to fail. First, the cost and effort will be prohibitive. Second, each enterprise is not only unique but also changes over time. Therefore, break/fix automation should be implemented as CSI (Continuous Service Improvement).

The approach that I recommend is to use a simple formula to decide what break/fix scenarios that you should create automated responses to deal with. The formula I recommend is If issue occurs x times in n weeks and (time to fix X n) > estimated automation effort.

The values that you will plug into this formula are dependent on your environment. An example would be If issue occurs 5 times in 4 weeks and (time to fix X 20) > 4 hours. The formula is working out if you will recoup your automation effort within a three-month period. If you will, then it is almost certainly worth automating the response.

If your company uses a sophisticated ticketing system, such as ServiceNow or ITSM 365, you will be able to report on problems. A problem is a ticket that is repeatedly raised. For example, your ticketing system may be configured so that if a ticket is raised for the same issue five times in four weeks, it becomes a problem ticket. This allows effective root-cause analysis, but you will instantly see the synergy with our formula. Reporting on problem tickets against the DBA team's queue can be a great starting point when looking for candidate break/fix scenarios to automate.

The following sections will discuss how to design and implement an automated response to 9002 errors. 9002 errors occur if there is no space to write to the transaction log, and the log is unable to grow.

Designing a Response to 9002 Errors

As we did when I discussed automating routine maintenance, before creating a process to respond to 9002 errors, we will first create a process flow. This will assist with the coding effort and also act as ongoing documentation of the process.

Figure 9-12 displays the process flow that we will follow when writing our code.

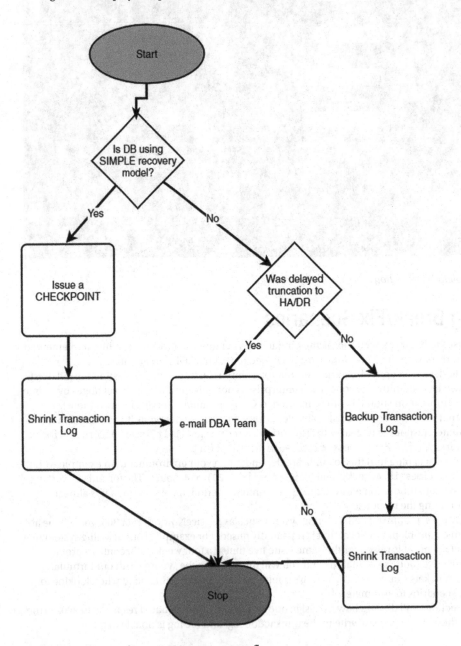

Figure 9-12. *Responding to 9002 errors process flow*

Automating a Response to 9002 Errors

We will use an SQL Server Agent alert to trigger our process, if a 9002 error occurs. To create a new alert, drill through SQL Server Agent in SQL Server Management Studio and select New Alert from the context menu of Alerts. This will cause the New Alert dialog box to be displayed. On the General page of the dialog box, illustrated in Figure 9-13, we will give the alert a name and configure it to be triggered by SQL Server error number 9002.

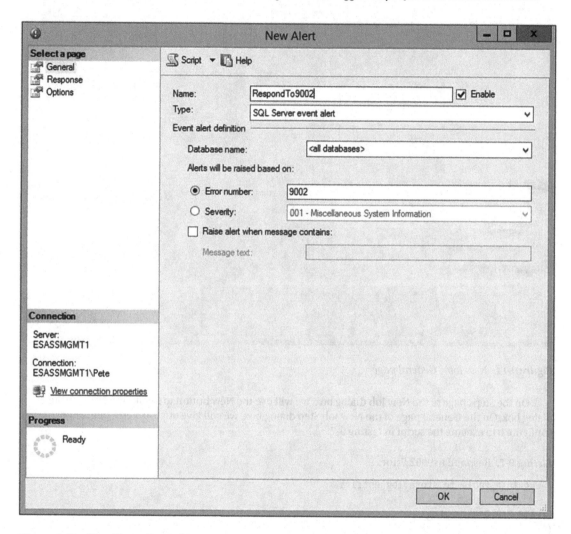

Figure 9-13. *New Alert—General page*

On the Response page of the dialog box, we will check the option to Execute Job and use the New Job button to invoke the New Job dialog box. On the General page of the New Job dialog box, we will define a name for our new Job, as illustrated in Figure 9-14.

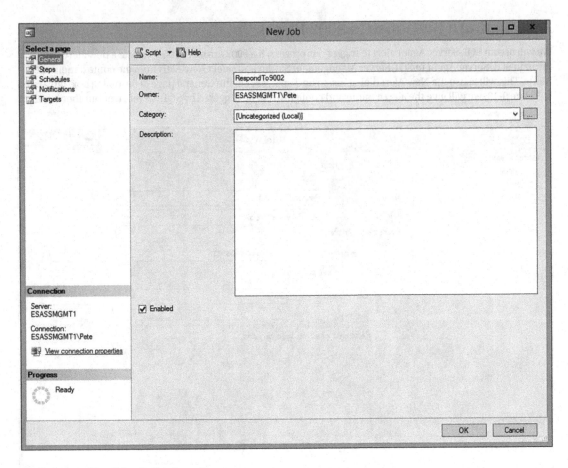

Figure 9-14. *New Job—General page*

On the Steps page of the New Job dialog box, we will use the New button to invoke the New Job Step dialog box. On the General page of the New Job Step dialog box, we will give our job step a name and configure it to execute the script in Listing 9-7.

Listing 9-7. Respond to 9002 Errors

```
--Create a table to store log entries

CREATE TABLE #ErrorLog
(
LogDate        DATETIME,
ProcessInfo    NVARCHAR(128),
Text           NVARCHAR(MAX)
) ;

--Populate table with log entries
```

```
INSERT INTO #ErrorLog
EXEC('xp_readerrorlog') ;

--Declare variables

DECLARE @SQL NVARCHAR(MAX) ;
DECLARE @DBName NVARCHAR(128) ;
DECLARE @LogName NVARCHAR(128) ;
DECLARE @Subject          NVARCHAR(MAX) ;

--Find database name where error occured

SET @DBName = (
                        SELECT TOP 1
                                    SUBSTRING(
                                        SUBSTRING(
                                            Text,
                                            35,
                                            LEN(Text)
                                        ),
                                        1,
                                            CHARINDEX(
                                                '''',
                                                SUBSTRING(Text,
                                                    35,
                                                    LEN(Text)
                                                )
                                            )-1
                                    )
                        FROM #ErrorLog
                        WHERE Text LIKE 'The transaction log for database%'
                        ORDER BY LogDate DESC
                        FOR XML PATH('')
) ;

--Find name of log file that is full

SET @LogName = (
                        SELECT name
                        FROM sys.master_files
                        WHERE type = 1
                                AND database_id = DB_ID(@DBName)
) ;

--Kill any active queries, to allow clean up to take place

SET @SQL = (
                        SELECT 'USE Master; KILL ' + CAST(s.session_id AS
NVARCHAR(4)) + ' ; '
        FROM sys.dm_exec_requests r
                INNER JOIN sys.dm_exec_sessions s
```

```
                            ON r.session_id = s.session_id
                    INNER JOIN sys.dm_tran_active_transactions at
                            ON r.transaction_id = at.transaction_id
        WHERE r.database_id = DB_ID(@DBName)
        ) ;

        EXEC(@SQL) ;

--IF recovery model is SIMPLE

IF (SELECT recovery_model FROM sys.databases WHERE name = @DBName) = 3
BEGIN
                --Issue a CHECKPOINT
                SET @SQL = (
                SELECT 'USE ' + @DBName + ' ; CHECKPOINT'
        ) ;

        EXEC(@SQL) ;

        --Shrink the transaction log

        SET @SQL = (
                                SELECT 'USE ' + @DBName + ' ; DBCC SHRINKFILE (' + @LogName
                                + ' , 1)'
        ) ;

        EXEC(@SQL) ;

        --e-mail the DBA Team

        SET @Subject = (SELECT '9002 Errors on ' + @DBName + ' on Server ' + @@SERVERNAME)

        EXEC msdb.dbo.sp_send_dbmail
    @profile_name = 'ESASS Administrator',
    @recipients = 'DBATeam@ESASS.com',
    @body = 'A CHECKPOINT has been issued and the Log has been shrunk',
    @subject = @Subject ;
END

--If database in full recovery model

IF (SELECT recovery_model FROM sys.databases WHERE name = @DBName) = 1
BEGIN
        --If reuse delay is not because of replication or mirroring/availability groups

        IF (SELECT log_reuse_wait FROM sys.databases WHERE name = @DBName) NOT IN (5,6)
        BEGIN
                --Backup transaction log
```

```
                    SET @SQL = (
                                            SELECT 'BACKUP LOG '
                                            + @DBName
                                            + ' TO  DISK = ''C:\Program Files\Microsoft SQL
Server\MSSQL13.MSSQLSERVER\MSSQL\Backup\'
                                            + @DBName
                                            + '.bak'' WITH NOFORMAT, NOINIT,  NAME = '''
                                            + @DBName
                                            + '-Full Database Backup'', SKIP ;'
                    ) ;

                    EXEC(@SQL) ;

                    --Shrink the transaction log

                    SET @SQL =  (
                                            SELECT 'USE ' + @DBName + ' ; DBCC SHRINKFILE (' + @
                                            LogName + ' , 1)'
                    ) ;

                    EXEC(@SQL) ;

                    --e-mail the DBA Team

                    SET @Subject = (SELECT '9002 Errors on ' + @DBName + ' on Server ' + @@
                    SERVERNAME) ;

                    EXEC msdb.dbo.sp_send_dbmail
                    @profile_name = 'ESASS Administrator',
                    @recipients = 'DBATeam@ESASS.com',
                    @body = 'A Log Backup has been issued and the Log has been shrunk',
                    @subject = @Subject ;
            END
            --If reuse delay is because of replication or mirroring/availability groups

        ELSE
        BEGIN
                --e-mail DBA Team
                SET @Subject = (SELECT '9002 Errors on ' + @DBName + ' on Server ' + @@
SERVERNAME) ;

                EXEC msdb.dbo.sp_send_dbmail
                @profile_name = 'ESASS Administrator',
                @recipients = 'DBATeam@ESASS.com',
                @body = 'DBA intervention required - 9002 errors due to HA/DR issues',
                @subject = @Subject ;
        END
END
```

■ **Tip** This script assumes that you have Database Mail configured. A full discussion of Database Mail is beyond the scope of this book. Further details can be found in the Apress book *Pro SQL Server Administration*, however. This book can be purchased at the following link: www.apress.com/9781484207116?gtmf=s.

This is illustrated in Figure 9-15.

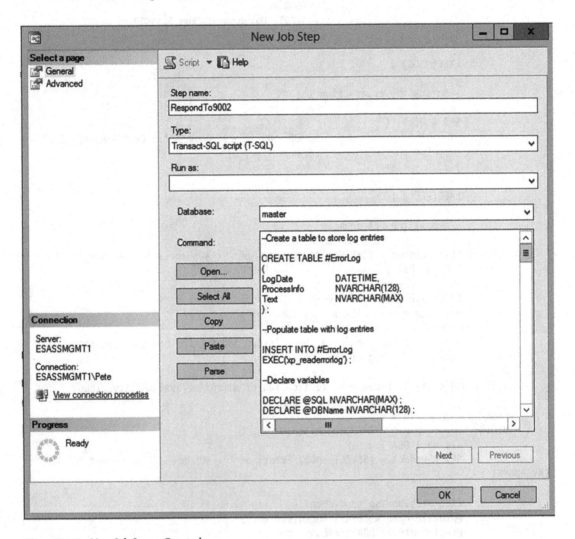

Figure 9-15. *New Job Step—General page*

After exiting the New Job Step dialog box and the New Job dialog box, our new job will automatically be selected in the Execute job drop-down list on the Response page of the New Alert dialog box, as shown in Figure 9-16.

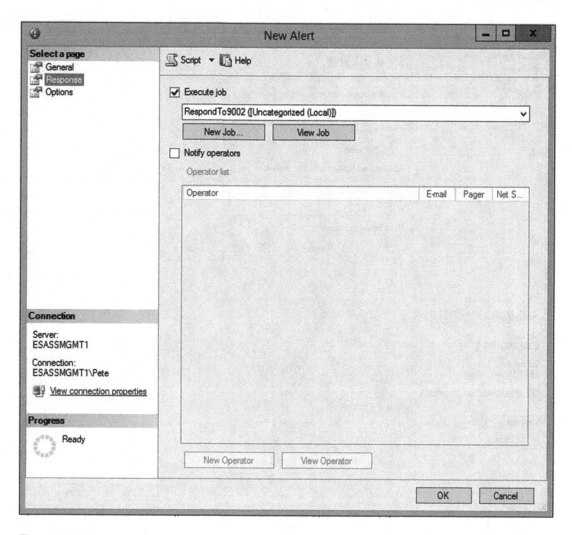

Figure 9-16. *Response page*

Figure 9-17 displays the Options page of the New Alert dialog box. While we do not have to configure anything on this page, in our scenario, you should be aware of the options that can be configured on this page.

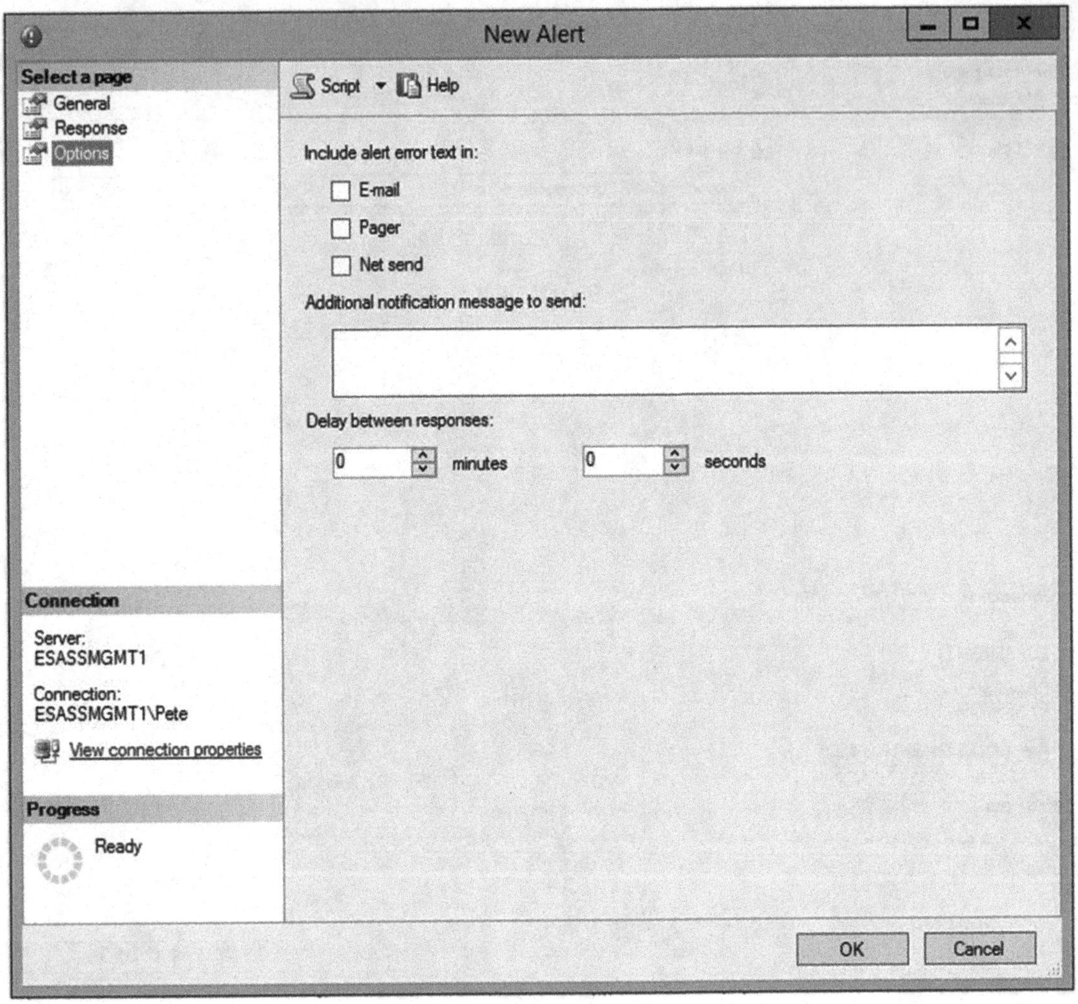

Figure 9-17. *Options page*

For me, the most interesting option is the ability to provide a delay between responses. Configuring this option can help you avoid the possibility of "false" responses being fired while a previous response is still in the process of resolving an issue. You are also able to use the Options page to specify if you want the error test that caused the Alert to fire to be included in any e-mail, pager, or NETSEND notifications that are sent. You can also add additional message text.

Summary

Automating routine maintenance tasks can save a DBA's valuable time and also improve the service to the business. Of course, it may not be possible to get to a position where 100% of maintenance is automated, because there are always exceptions. It is a good idea to aim for an 80/20 split of automated vs. exception. As well as automating tasks within the database engine, such as intelligent index rebuilds, as you have learned in previous chapters, it is also possible to automate tasks that have operating system elements, such as patching.

The more break/fix scenarios that you can automate, the better and more proactive your service to the business will become. It is not feasible to attempt to automate responses to all break/fix scenarios in one go, however. This is because problems will change and vary over time, and because such a large-scale effort would likely be cost-prohibitive. Instead, you should look to add automated break/fix scenarios as a continuous service improvement (CSI) program. It is helpful to use the problem management functionality of your tickets system, to help define candidate issues for automation.

Index

■ N, O

■ P, Q, R

Get the eBook for only $5!

Why limit yourself?

Now you can take the weightless companion with you wherever you go and access your content on your PC, phone, tablet, or reader.

Since you've purchased this print book, we're happy to offer you the eBook in all 3 formats for just $5.

Convenient and fully searchable, the PDF version enables you to easily find and copy code—or perform examples by quickly toggling between instructions and applications. The MOBI format is ideal for your Kindle, while the ePUB can be utilized on a variety of mobile devices.

To learn more, go to www.apress.com/companion or contact support@apress.com.

Printed in the United States
By Bookmasters